A Voyage

of

Heart & Song

For the redhead

You've got to have a dream
If you don't have a dream
How're ya gonna make a dream
come true?

- Oscar Hammerstein II
from *South Pacific*

FOREWORD

This account of my husband's and my sailing circumnavigation is true and correct to the best of my recollection – except for two things.

First, for privacy reasons, I have changed the names of boats and voyagers we met along the way, and in some cases, have combined characteristics of one or more persons, boats, or events. Any resemblance to actual individuals living or dead is strictly coincidental.

Second, this book contains no sex. Sex tends to occur often on a sailboat, whether at sea in the cockpit, or on the beach of a beautiful deserted bay, or at a marina dock with the portholes covered and music blaring, or on the sunny afterdeck of the boat at anchor. Maybe it's the sheer amount of free time. Maybe it's the minimal amount of clothing or the absence of mental stress. I don't know. What I do know is that I am ridiculously uncomfortable writing about sex. And I am particularly ridiculously uncomfortable writing about sex when one of the participants is me.

So you should assume that sex is happening, and happening a lot. But you will absolutely not be reading about it.

For the landlubbers, and you know who you are, a handy-dandy glossary of sailing terms has been included at the end of the book, along with a map of the circumnavigation route.

PROLOGUE
DALLAS, TEXAS

Q: My spouse and I want to sail around the world someday. What are the most important things we need?

A: A seaworthy boat and a sense of humor.

Q: Why on earth did you quit your jobs and go sailing?

A: Because none of us knows when we will run out of time to live our dreams.

The month I turned thirty-eight, I was diagnosed with breast cancer.

I went for a baseline mammogram, and it saved my life. The mammogram picked up a pattern of calcifications that signaled intraductal carcinoma.

I don't remember being devastated, or even crying. I didn't have time. I had barely rearranged my schedule to accommodate a biopsy when I had to rearrange it again for a three-day hospital stay and six-week recovery for a mastectomy and breast reconstruction. Family and friends rallied round. They seemed more upset about it than I could bring myself to be.

It must be a human thing when faced with the unthinkable to go straight into one-step-at-a-time mode. If you had asked me what my biggest concerns were the day before I went into the hospital, they were (1) to get everything in order so that my husband, Alan, would not be burdened with any paperwork, and (2) to hope that whatever happened, somebody would be kind enough to keep my hair clean.

Several moments are vivid in my memory, though. The first was the day of the mammogram itself. After a repeat test and then a sonogram, I was sitting in the clinic's inner waiting room to get my results. I would have been a fool not to suspect something was up after the additional attention. I knew with certainty I had cancer when I happened to glance up and see a nurse staring at me as she walked by, file clutched close to her chest. The look on her face said it all. It was part sympathy, part very human morbid curiosity as to who it was whose mammogram had been positive. It was part fascination, part disbelief that I was so young, part tragedy of what might lie ahead for me.

The look on her face told me everything I needed to know. The radiologist's pronouncement was a mere formality.

The second vivid memory was several days after the mastectomy, while I was still in the hospital. The surgeon had taken lymph nodes and sent them to the lab to find out if the cancer had spread, whether they had caught it in time. It took several days for the lab to conduct the tests, so for several days post-surgically my family and friends and I were all still in the dark about my future, or lack thereof.

Those days I spent stoned to the gills on morphine, so I have only the haziest recollections. I have impressions of seeing Alan asleep in my room, of sensing water on my neck as he washed my hair. I remember being awakened over and over again for a nurse to use a probe on the reconstructed area to make sure the graft hadn't gone bad.

But burned into my memory is the moment the surgeon came in with the lab report. We knew he was coming sometime that day. Alan and my mother and father were there. I had been drifting in and out of consciousness. The instant the surgeon walked in with my lab results, the haze cleared. Everything in the room came sharply into focus. For some reason, however, everyone began moving in slow motion. We all seemed to take several minutes to turn our faces toward him. He moved forward to my bed in exaggerated Bionic Man fashion, complete with metallic whakka-whakka soundtrack.

He smiled in what seemed like a two-minute effort and finally said in distorted Darth Vader audio slo-mo, "The nodes are clear. It hasn't spread. We got it all."

At that moment normal speed resumed. The surgeon's voice switched to a pleasant tenor as he explained further. Everyone stood up and started talking at once, animated, laughing. More people came in; friends arrived, and it was a party.

There were other memories, too, from the days and weeks afterwards. I remember standing in the shower and removing the bandages for the first time to see the fleshy blob that now formed the left side of my chest. The post-mastectomy breast reconstructive surgery used the "free-flap technique. The surgeon harvested muscle from my abdomen to form the new breast, and then replaced the abdominal muscle with mesh, much like a hernia repair.

I remember being outside, dressed and on my own two feet at last, still bent and shaky but going for a walk around the neighborhood – just because I could – exalted at the beauty of the day, loving the sun on my face. I remember being at my first post-surgery social event and watching male colleagues whip involuntary glances down at my chest.

The most vivid memory of the entire experience, though, was a conversation that happened a few days after I was home from the hospital. Cushioned and in a knees-up position that I had been told to maintain while waiting for my mid-section to heal, I lay stranded in the middle of our big bed. Until my abdomen regained functionality, I couldn't do much in the way of moving myself around.

Alan came in with my dinner on a tray. He set it down and helped me to sit up a little higher, a littler closer to the edge. He fluffed and patted and prepared a spot for my tray.

I sighed. "Is this it?"

"What – don't you want the soup?"

"No. I mean yes." I laughed. "No, I mean is this, to paraphrase the immortal Peggy Lee, 'all there is'?"

Alan was silent.

"Will we just go to work every day," I continued, "and then eventually die?"

"You left out watching TV."

"Very funny."

"And really good bowel movements. You didn't say a thing about bathroom time."

"Oh shut up. You know what I mean."

"Yes, I know what you mean. I just don't know the answer."

Kneeling down by the side of the bed, he took my hand in both of his. We stayed that way for a long time in silence. Cancer is so much harder on a spouse than on the person who is ill. We are busy – busy getting ready for the hospital, busy seeing doctors, busy being taken care of. And then we're medicated or sick or both, caught up in the physicality of it all. The spouse sits by, trying to be there, trying to be helpful if needed, trying to be strong, trying not to wonder if he'll be required to watch his wife die. And all without benefit of prescription painkillers.

Still kneeling, Alan squeezed my hand. He bent his head to kiss it a few times and finally looked up at me.

"Tell me what you want more than anything in the world."

"What do you mean?"

"If you could have anything in the whole world, what would it be?"

"Like what?"

"Like anything at all."

"I have no idea."

Another silence ensued. He roused himself and said, "C'mon. I'm serious. What's the first thing that pops into your mind?"

"Well," I hesitated.

"What?"

"Well, of course, spending all of my time with you."

"Besides that," he said. "What do you want for both of us?"

What I was thinking was silly. It was not possible. I wasn't even sure if I really wanted it – that is, if I really wanted it to actually happen as opposed to just fantasizing about it on a regular basis. I had mentioned it once in an offhand way to friends under the influence of extreme margarita, but otherwise I had never talked about it, never said it out loud. Of all the things that had flitted through my mind as possibilities when he asked his question, though, this was what had stuck.

"Well," I still hesitated. Oh, what the hell. I spit it out, almost as an apology. "I've always wanted to sail around the world."

His head jerked back slightly at the neck, but his face registered no reaction.

"Did you ever read Kon-Tiki?" I continued.

He nodded. He still hadn't blinked.

"I had the child's illustrated version of it, and I read it over and over. There was one picture with the raft being almost encircled by a spotted whale shark, I think, and I remember being scared and thrilled and really wanting to see the Pacific Ocean, really wanting to feel it, to cross it. What I'd really like to do, though, is sail all the way around. Cross all the oceans. See Australia. Sail the Med. Go through the Panama Canal. Ooooh." I continued rhapsodizing silently.

Looking up, I noticed he was still staring.

"What." I asked. He didn't reply.

Alan had actually sailed a whole lot more than I had. Before we got married, my sailing experience was limited to a Hobie-cat on Texas lakes and to crewing (*i.e.*, handing up the beer) on a friend's 40-footer on the west coast. But even before we chartered our first boat for the first of many Caribbean bareboat sailing vacations together, Alan had serious bluewater experience. When he got out of the Air Force after a four-year hitch to pay back his medical school education, he and a couple of buddies (a lawyer and a psychologist – and there has to be a joke in there somewhere) sailed a thirty-foot wooden boat across the Mediterranean Sea and the Atlantic Ocean, all the way from Crete to Antigua. Their boat had tiller steering, a hand-crank engine, a plastic sextant for navigation, and no indoor plumbing. Alan jokes that their Atlantic crossing took about a week longer than it took Columbus. I didn't fully appreciate the magnificence of their feat, however, until I sailed those same waters years later in a boat almost twice the size with hot water, GPS, and a microwave – and still barely beat Columbus's time.

I shifted my position slightly on the bed. He was still staring.

"What," I asked again, getting impatient.

He finally blinked. "I've always wanted to do that," he brought out. "Sail around the world someday. That's what I've always wanted to do myself."

A little chill shimmied through my shoulders. It could have been all the Vicodin I had on board, but I didn't think so. At that moment, looking into a face that was beginning to light up just a little, I knew that I did want to go sailing – not just continue to fantasize about it, but actually to do it, to go. I realized that what I wanted more than anything else before I died was to see the world – not just for two vacation weeks at a time – but to really see it, and to sail across all of the oceans on the way.

It is so trite to say that life is short. It is so trite, in fact, that the phrase has lost all meaning. How droll it is to note that on one's deathbed, one never says, "I wish I had spent more time at the office." And carpe diem, and eat dessert first, and blah de-blah blah blah. If I thought about it at all in the years before I got cancer, I just assumed that of course I would make time for my dreams. Of course I would do something a little out of the ordinary. Someday. My life was still ahead of me.

My life was still ahead of me. Lying on our bed, I read new meaning into that thought. My life was still ahead of me, but I understood now that it could end immediately and without notice of any kind.

Getting cancer was the luckiest thing that ever happened to me.

CHAPTER 1
FLORIDA TO THE VIRGIN ISLANDS
PART I

Q: *On passages, don't you worry about hitting one of those huge cargo ships while you're asleep?*

A: Yes. That's why one of the two of us is awake and on watch at all times when the boat is underway.

Q: *What sorts of things do you worry about on a boat?*

A: I worry about the following things:

- Sinking
- Drowning
- Sinking and drowning
- That our marine toilet will break
- Pirates

Pretty much in that order.

"You're going to sleep? What about the pump?" My tone was an unfortunate shade of whine.

We were pounding to windward in the Atlantic Ocean on the very first multiple-day passage of our circumnavigation, heading from Fort Lauderdale, Florida, to the Virgin Islands. It was wet-sauna hot. I had slept maybe three hours in the past thirty-six. We were single-reefed in twenty-five knots of wind, and the seas were at about five feet, steep and choppy – coming straight at us and punching like a middle-weight champion.

Bracing for hours and days against the buck and roll of our shiny new 54-foot sloop, my leg muscles were as rubbery as that Swiss woman's at the finish of the 1984 Olympic marathon. On a south-southwesterly course, we were tipped at a 45-degree heel that made moving around the boat require the skill sets of Tarzan, or possibly Cheetah. Colorful bruises marked the number of times I had missed my grip. Alan had a gash of unknown origin in his calf, which, when I finally noticed the trail of blood, I had clumsily wrapped in gauze and tape. Every thirty seconds or so, about a half-ton of green water thundered down the decks, and salty spray misted up onto my face and clammy t-shirt.

"Seriously, Alan, I don't know how to fix the water-pump, and it needs to be fixed."

Sweat dripped from my husband's jaw, and his face had gone that pasty pallor that said extreme fatigue.

"It'll have to wait."

Ignoring my "wait a minute," his head disappeared down the companionway ladder and moved past the cockpit porthole toward the aft cabin. Grrr.

What I really needed was a drink of water. On watch in the cockpit I was simply too lethargic to climb down into the galley to get one. Lethargy had indeed swallowed me whole. I thought about dehydration and sunstroke, and also about sinking and shark attacks after sinking, and various other ways to die.

The method du jour was rogue wave. At that particular moment, I was obsessing over the nautical chart for the corner of the Atlantic Ocean in which we were sailing. In the smallest font compatible with human eyesight, the letters spanning our current position said "Bermuda Triangle." Those words could not possibly have been on the chart when I was planning our route. I'm sure I would have noticed. Although law school drummed out what little predisposition I had to entertain the supernatural, I am quite sure I would not be in the middle of the Bermuda Triangle voluntarily.

Without regard to the paranormal, no one can dispute that the Bermuda Triangle has had more than its share of unexplained boat disappearances. Most mariners attribute the losses to a higher than normal incidence of rogue waves. Right now, however, that explanation was not the least bit more comforting than aliens or sea monsters. I glanced astern for the umpteenth time expecting to see a hundred-foot wall of water.

And at some point, now that the sandwiches were gone, somebody was going to have to do something about fixing some food.

"Alan?" Dang it. "Alan?"

No answer.

Sigh.

At that moment . . . at that moment, if there had been a taxi, I would have hailed it and gone home. I would have completely written off the last few years of planning and saving as a sunk cost, and I would have zoomed back to civilization without a backward glance. But there were no taxis out here, hundreds of miles off the coast of Florida, days from landfall in St. Thomas.

For that matter, there was no home, either. We had sold our house and cars in Dallas and used the proceeds to build the sailboat of our dreams. Alan had taken a leave of absence from his medical practice, and I had quit my job at an excellent Dallas law firm. We put a few boxes of our most cherished memorabilia and wedding gifts into storage in my mother's attic, and we sold most of our furniture to Alan's brother. Everything else was carted away by the Salvation Army. We were officially free. Unimpeded. We were world travelers, adventurers, explorers. We would discover remote islands rarely visited by outsiders, back-of-beyond villages accessible only by sea. We would, as an occasional change of pace, anchor off posh beachfront resorts and swim in for piña coladas by the pool. We would become self-sufficient, one with nature. We were going to circumnavigate the globe in a sailboat, just the two of us, and see everything there was to see along the way. In giddy anticipation, we U-hauled our few remaining worldly goods to Fort Lauderdale, Florida, to take possession of our boat.

Now only a few months later, various scenarios percolated in my head – scenarios that would allow me to abandon the venture completely without losing face. Broken leg? Not good enough. Hurricane destroying the boat? Overkill. Spinal meningitis? Hmm.

I regretted telling everyone I knew that I would circumnavigate. I regretted that big bon voyage party in Dallas before we left. I ached for my stuff. Although we had been underway less than a week, I had been living in minimalist fashion on the boat for months while hauling and provisioning and supplying and installing and sweating and testing and learning. I missed my piano and the bathtub. I even missed practicing law. At least, I missed yelling into the phone and having an assistant.

Maybe Alan would tire of being an unpaid laborer and insist that we go home. I could demur not too strenuously, then cave in and blame it all on him. I could hear the conversation with friends and family: "Yes, he just missed medicine too much. I know, but there was nothing I could do. He was so worried he would lose his skills, and he insisted on coming home. I was devastated."

But each daydreaming session – no matter how vivid and, in retrospect, neurotic it became – ended with the same thought: No way was I was going home so soon with my worthless tail between my legs. I would gut it out for a respectable time – say six months – then think of a way to slink back to work. Maybe Alan's brother would sell us back the furniture.

Actually, I should have seen it coming. From the time we arrived in Florida in January, nothing – not one thing – had happened according to plan. It had been five full months of head-banging frustration.

When the going gets tough, the universe is clearly setting you a test. The question is: Is it a test to see whether you're tough enough to persevere? Or is it a test to see whether you're bright enough to take the hint?

Our plan was excellent. The bare hull of our boat was to have been freighted by sea from the factory in Taiwan to meet us at a boatyard dock when we arrived in Fort Lauderdale. There the boat would be rigged and commissioned, and we would move aboard straightaway. She would be christened *Heartsong III*. I had already bought the champagne. My sister had designed a logo with two hearts pierced by a musical note, decals of which we would affix to each side of the bow. We reckoned it would take a couple of weeks of shopping to outfit her – oh, maybe a month – and then we would happily head to sea, fully prepared, fully stocked, fully competent, and perhaps a little smug (though only deservedly so).

That was five months ago. The hull had been delivered weeks late and, for reasons that will remain forever incomprehensible, to New Jersey rather than to Florida. The trucker who was then hired to haul it overland from

New Jersey to Fort Lauderdale proceeded to run into a bridge somewhere along the way. The bad news was that all the winches – the highest points on the hull at that early stage before installation of the mast and rigging – were sheared off at their little necks.

The good news, on which I forced myself to concentrate, was that the boat's fiberglass had been so solidly built at the Queen Long Marine factory that the platforms on which the winches rested had not sustained so much as a crack or a chip. Still, I seethed and fumed at the delay, worried about replacing the winches, about insurance claims, about hidden damage, above all about The Schedule.

Alan was no help. Moments after we heard the gut-wrenching news that our entire net worth had smashed into a bridge, he exclaimed: "Hey! Do you remember that scene in *The World According to Garp* where an airplane crashes into the new house that Robin Williams is looking at?"

"What? Vaguely." My teeth clenched as I wondered where the heck he could possibly be going with this.

"He bought the house on the spot because it was pre-disastered."

"Pre-disastered."

"Yeah. The boat is now pre-disastered. It's the best thing that could have happened. May the boat be free of evil spirits, be healed in the sight of the Lord." He smacked his forehead revival-tent style and launched into a sustained tirade – part medicine man, part TV evangelist.

It occurred to me, and not for the first time, that the most hazardous part of the entire trip might well be round-the-clock exposure to my husband's sense of humor.

But we persevered. The repairs and replacements proceeded. The boatyard workers began installing the mast and rigging and electronics and other equipment, and we worked alongside them. Each day ended with my going over the increasing amounts by which the workmen were over-shooting our budget, not only for money but also for time.

Aghast, Alan and I met with them and shouted and stomped our feet. We may as well have been Riverdancing. The denizens of the marine industry regarded us with amusement, when they regarded us at all, and proceeded at their own pace. We switched from shouting to pleading and got the same response. We moved straight to bribery with no appreciable change. It was our introduction to phenomena known to voyagers worldwide as "island time" (what's the hurry, mon?) and the "boat unit" (a thousand bucks, more or less). Everywhere in the world, we learned, boat work happens on island time, if it happens at all; and if any single project stays within two or three boat units of the original budget, it's an unprecedented bloody miracle.

You prospective voyagers who are reading this: you think you will be the exception, don't you. You think that your business savvy and force of personality, your sheer competence, will make for getting things done. Give up that idea now. Just give it up. Go ahead, give it on up . . . there you go. You'll thank me later. It is – pay attention, now – *not possible* to get things done in the world of marine outfitting, maintenance, and repair. The best result for which one can hope is partial success, on a sliding-scale basis, eventually.

In any event, The Schedule mandated departure from Fort Lauderdale in mid-April at the latest. By mid-May all we had done was to make a quick overnight shakedown trip to Grand Bahama and back. The first of June found us still testing equipment and buying spares. Hurricane season was imminent, and we were smack dab in the middle of the Florida hurricane zone. Our insurance company had given us a firm deadline by which to be south of said hurricane zone or forfeit the policy. That deadline, which had seemed laughably doable months earlier, was fast approaching.

With our eyes on the calendar, we curtailed preparations and spent a final few days battening everything down. On a bright June morning, we motored out through the Port Everglades harbor, set our sails, and – ready or not – plotted a course for the channel that would take us through the Bahama Islands and out into open ocean.

I'll just skip over the part where the auto-pilot failed, and we had to turn back to pick up a hydraulic pump, and also the part where Alan all of a sudden remembered he gets debilitatingly seasick the first couple of days at sea.

Rather, I will jump ahead two days and nights, to the point at which I was wondering what I possibly could have been thinking – in the middle of the Bermuda Triangle, half-prepared, incipiently dehydrated, and with no exit strategy. I looked aft yet again for the hundred-foot wall of a rogue wave that would surely be my doom.

A blur of freckles appeared at the companionway. Gripping the stainless steel handrails on either side of the hatch, Alan hauled himself up from the steps into the cockpit and collapsed onto the leeward bench cushion.

"It's too hot to sleep down there," he mumbled. "No air. Can't breathe. I'm sleeping up here."

Before I could voice my increasingly urgent desire for water, he was out like a light. He had slept even less than I had and was weakened by bouts of seasickness to boot. At least I had been spared that indignity.

But things were not going well. Even working night and day, we had not been able to learn and test every piece of equipment before our hurried departure. In strict adherence to Murphy's Law, the pieces we had bypassed all proceeded to malfunction. For two solid days, Alan had spent his off-watch time reading repair manuals. He had finally figured out how to adjust the float switch on the bilge alarm so it wouldn't go off every couple of hours and give me a heart attack. He had spent his last off-watch "rest" period trying to figure out where that awful smell was coming from. Fortunately, it was only a misdirected valve in the head. If it had been a loose or broken hose, it was not only disgusting, it could have sunk us.

Now the fresh water pump – which we had tested, dang it – was on the fritz. After wading through twenty pages of repair jargon written by someone who must have learned English from bathroom graffiti, Alan suspected an airlock. Fatigue and nausea, however, had halted the repair effort. Until the pump was working again, we couldn't retrieve any of the fresh water in our 200-gallon tanks. Fortunately, I had provisioned plenty of emergency spare drinking water in plastic gallon jugs. Assuming I could summon the energy to retrieve them, we wouldn't actually die. But we would certainly stink. I had now gone without washing my hair longer than I ever had in my adult life.

If this state of events were to continue much longer, in fact, I would have to bathe and wash my hair in salt water. There was certainly plenty of it. During my landlocked daydreams, I had envisioned using salt water for all purposes – yo ho. Counter to romantic ideas of the purity of the ocean, however, it turns out that salt water – the soup from which life sprang on earth – is teeming with very nasty bacteria. Said bacteria is contra-indicated when one has cuts and abrasions like the ones that decorated my body after a couple of tough days at sea. Moreover, upon reflection, I shuddered to think what my complexion would look like if I were to salt it down like an 18th Century

British Navy cask of meat. I kept looking at my face in the mirror and visualizing beef jerky.

My skin was already taking it on the chin, as it were. Through three coats of waterproof 30spf sunblock, the tropical sun reflecting off the water had blistered all unclothed segments a startling fuchsia. As far as I could tell, the sunblock was serving mainly to glue the sea salt permanently into my pores. The boat's canvas bimini top on a frame over the cockpit was good shelter, but the sides had to remain uncovered for visibility, and the rays angled in to burn what, even after weeks in the Florida heat, was still skin accustomed to going from house to garage to parking basement to pedestrian tunnel to office without the least necessity of ever seeing the actual sky. Despite the heat, I covered my unshaded parts with a beach towel, stiff with saltwater. What I needed was a jumpsuit with gloves and feet and a hood. And a hockey mask.

The ten-minute timer went off. I dutifully checked the horizon. No traffic, as usual in this godforsaken stretch of ocean. Wait. What was that hazy blob to port?

I lurched forward to get the binoculars. My stomach muscles – or muscle and mesh, I should say – had been tensed for some time to keep me stable as the boat moved. My abdomen chose that moment to give up the fight, and I sprawled backward onto the cockpit cushions. Ho-kay.

After pulling myself up hand over hand, sideways, I knelt on the windward-side cockpit cushion, put the binoculars to my eyes, and tried to focus on the blob. The horizon wobbled as a swell rolled under the bow. I did a better job of matching my motion to the boat's, and the blob came into focus. Without warning, a larger wave picked the boat up and set it down. Still clutching the binoculars with both hands, I ricocheted off the binnacle and down onto the wooden cockpit sole, where I lay like a bug on its back. Nothing broken – excellent. I pulled myself back up. This time, I was smart enough to hold the binoculars with one hand while hanging onto the large stainless steel dodger handrail with the other. I matched rhythms again, and . . ..

It was definitely a ship, a big freighter, the very first traffic we had seen since the Bahamas, and it was maybe ten miles away. I switched on the radar. I had taken a full Coast Guard course in radar operation during those weeks at the dock in Florida, and I was twitching with excitement to apply it. I was, in fact, a fully certified open-ocean sailing captain and merchant marine radar operator, and I was confident in my expertise.

This would be a piece of cake. All I had to do was to decipher the freighter's heading and speed relative to our own, and crunch the numbers. I would determine the "closest point of approach" or CPA, which is the margin of distance by which we would pass each other. In the unlikely event I determined that our courses would bring us too close for comfort, I would simply call the freighter's watchkeeper on the VHF radio, relay my calculation, and ask him to alter course – because as everyone knows, sailboats have the right of way on the high seas.

Five minutes later, I was shaking my husband's shoulders. "Alan wake up wake up wake up."

"What?" He sat up immediately, eyes open and alert. Say what you will about the inhumane schedules of medical internship and residency, they do prepare a person to wake up from a dead sleep instantly prepared to deal with crisis.

Alan took his bearings and calmly asked, "Problem?"

"I think that ship is going to hit us, and it won't answer the radio," I squeaked, hyperventilating. I moved to the helm and took the boat off auto-pilot. "Go look at the radar screen. Should I tack? Should I jibe? What should I do?" My voice stopped flirting with the fringes of hysteria and embraced it unreservedly: "WHICH WAY SHOULD I TURN? Hurry."

In the minutes since I first saw the ship, I had been glued to the radar screen. The electronic blip that represented the approaching ship had moved inexorably closer to our own blip at the center of the screen. While I watched the two blips converging, I kept getting a calculated CPA of zero. A CPA of "one" means that the two boats will never be closer than one mile apart. A CPA of "zero" means "look around because this is where you're going to die."

As a sailboat at sea under these circumstances, we clearly had the right of way. In marine parlance, we were the "stand-on vessel." The international navigational rules, which I had memorized in their entirety (down to the footnotes), required that we not deviate from course or change speed, so that the "give-way vessel" can take appropriate action to avoid a collision. One wouldn't want both vessels, each trying to get out of the other's way, accidentally turning into each other. So it is the responsibility of the give-way vessel to change course or speed, or both, to avoid collision. The only time the stand-on vessel is allowed to change course and speed under the international navigational rules is if it becomes clear that the give-way vessel doesn't intend to give way. While performing my radar calculations, I had dutifully maintained my course and speed, secure in my knowledge of the rules.

After 37,000 miles and six years at sea, I now know the real law of the sea is the Rule of Tonnage: He who has the tonnage makes the rules.

On that day of virgin encounter, however, I was still confident that at any moment the cargo ship would see us. I was confident he would make a big turn to give us plenty of sea room, confident that my radio call would be answered politely, possibly in a pleasant British accent, and all would be well. The freighter's blip was now converging with ours on the radar screen, and I was in a panic that I had waited too long to take action. He was less than a nautical mile away and doing about twenty knots. He was a speeding eighteen-wheeler to our mid-freeway armadillo. In fewer than three minutes, I would be roadkill.

I grabbed the radio mike again and squeaked: "Westbound container ship, westbound container ship, this is sailing vessel *Heartsong III*, sailing vessel *Heartsong III*. Do you copy?" No answer.

"Liza?" Alan said.

"What what what?" I squeaked again.

Alan's tone was perfectly even as he continued to look out to port. "Look at the profile of the ship."

I turned to resume my stare at the radar screen.

"No, not at the radar – look at the actual ship. There, on the actual water," he said.

"Oh." I looked up and to port and a little forward, and there it was – gargantuan even a mile away, moving fast, and yet somehow less scary in the flesh than the demonic blip I had been watching in frozen fascination. I could see the full side of the metal hulk as it motored from my left to my right, looming dead ahead, 12 stories high, rust-streaked and sprouting half a dozen huge cranes, kicking up a thirty-foot rolling wake from its grotesquely bulbous bow. No humans were discernible aboard. It looked like a vessel that might be used by a malevolent alien intelligence to invade our galaxy.

"Do you see how it's moving from port to starboard, from left to right, how it's starting to cross our forward path at nearly a right angle?" Alan continued, unperturbed.

"Yes . . .." I said, hyperventilating.

"Once it finishes crossing the path in front of us, it can't possibly hit us."

I watched it. The logic of his point hit home. "You're sure it'll cross well ahead of our position?"

"I'm sure."

"Positive?"

"Positive. If it were crossing too close, we wouldn't be able to see the profile so well. It would look more like the bow was aiming straight at us."

I watched it for a while longer, and pretty soon sure enough, the cargo ship's bow had nudged over the line we were sailing, so that we appeared to be aiming at its mid-section; then most of the ship was to starboard of our bow, then the whole big ugly brute had passed and was continuing towards the westward horizon. It had crossed – I glanced at the radar screen – with about three-quarters of a mile to spare. Crisis over. It occurred to me to exhale.

"Another tip?" he continued in a pleasant tone. "As long as the ship isn't on a head-on collision with us, like traveling down our reciprocal course or coming up directly behind us? As long as it's crossing our path ahead of us, like that guy, from one side to the other?

"Yes."

"Just aim at its stern. Keep our bow pointed at his stern. That way, he always crosses in front of us, and we have a little more control over the angle."

"Oh. Right. Sweetheart, I'm so sorry – sorry, sorry, sorry. Go back to sleep. Please go back to sleep. I'm so sorry."

He lay back down and was snoring in seconds. I glared the freighter completely out of sight, as if it might turn around and sneak back to finish me off. I then meditated on my cringe-worthy performance.

I had passed the exam for the United States Coast Guard charter captain license (informally called a "six-pack") at the top of my class. Upon review, however, it appeared that extensive book knowledge might not be enough to make me a good sailor.

To be fair, commercial ships at sea are a very real hazard for sailboats. The biggest cargo monsters are a quarter of a mile long – more than five football fields long, and one football field wide. The ships move at six to ten times the speed of our sailboat, and they don't have brakes. Once they are at speed, it takes at least a mile, usually more, for them to stop or to make a significant course change. The Titanic was a relatively nimble vessel in comparison with a supertanker, and it still lacked the maneuverability to dodge that iceberg.

If we were to find ourselves on a true collision course with a mammoth freighter that did not see us, or chose not to see us, our slow speed combined with the limited maneuverability of both vessels would give us very little chance. The classic sailor's yarn is an eyewitness account of a freighter making port with large bits of white canvas flapping from its bow.

The freighter's passing us in open water less than a mile away was too close for comfort. We came to learn that at least a mile's berth is the standard minimum in open ocean, often required by the ship's insurance company. And I had now found out how eager the big boys were to respond to a radio call. All I had gotten was crickets.

To give them the benefit of the doubt, perhaps the watchkeeper had to make a burdensome official log entry with each radio contact. Perhaps in this case, he had calculated the CPA, made the required minor adjustment in his course, and knew collision was averted. Perhaps he did not speak English (although it is the official language of the sea), or he simply chose not to waste time talking with some shrieking female on an inconsequential sailboat. On the other hand, perhaps he was asleep. Or drunk. Or, as we came to suspect later in various parts of the world, both.

The basic rule of thumb is that a collision occurs if a target decreases in distance while its bearing remains constant. It's not difficult with practice to make a quick-and-dirty assessment by eyeballing the situation. I learned to line the ship up with some landmark on my own boat – like a stanchion, or the edge of the liferaft – and monitor the ship's distance every thirty seconds on the radar screen. If his position relative to my landmark stayed the same while he continued to get closer, I knew I had a problem. Otherwise, no.

At that first traffic sighting, though, I was completely appalled at myself. It wasn't just that I had to admit my incompetence. No, the most difficult part to face was something else. I had panicked. There was a physical emergency, and I had panicked. Even worse, I had panicked in response to an emergency that didn't actually exist. Couldn't I at least wait for an actual emergency before I lost my cool? By what miracle did Alan sleep with me in charge?

I sat up with a jolt. He didn't. At least once an hour, he was up poking around and mumbling either that he couldn't sleep or that he needed to check on something. He needed to check on something all right. Me.

So I sat on in the cockpit staring out at the big Atlantic rollers. I had abandoned my professional career and spent a huge hunk of money to find out I was a wimp and a coward and a liability – overwhelmed already and fretting to go home. I also had filthy hair and was living in a space the size of my former walk-in closet. And I only had three pairs of shoes. Pulling myself back from the last two thoughts, I realized that in addition to everything else, I was also a spoiled, comfort-loving princess of a brat. Tears welled up and overflowed down my grimy sunburned salt-crusted cheeks. Great. Now I was a sniveling spoiled wimp of a cowardly incompetent princess of a comfort-loving liability.

If it hadn't been for what happened the next afternoon, my story would be a short one indeed.

CHAPTER 2
FLORIDA TO THE VIRGIN ISLANDS
PART II

Q: *What watch schedules do you keep?*

A: When we are underway, here is our watch
schedule:

Noon Watch	3 hrs	1200 to 1500	Liza
Afternoon Watch	2 hrs	1500 to 1700	Alan
Evening Watch	2 hrs	1700 to 1900	Liza
Midnight Watch	7 hrs	1900 to 0200	Alan
Dawn Watch	7 hrs	0200 to 0900	Liza
Morning Watch	3 hrs	0900 to 1200	Alan

Q: *Aren't seven-hour watches too long?*

A: No, at least not with an auto-pilot. We tried
the traditional four-on, four-off watch
schedule, and it kicked our butts. Less than
five hours of sleep per day over a week's
time is associated with psychotic episodes.

At this point, I should probably stop to mention that
on the boat, Alan has a clothes-optional policy. On our
overnight shakedown cruise to Grand Bahama the previous
month, we were no sooner out of binocular range of the
coast when he had started stripping.
    "What are you doing?"
    "Taking my clothes off."

"Um, why?"

Oh, I don't know . . . so they won't get dirty." He grinned and treated me to a full-frontal waggle.

I rolled my eyes and noted for the record that he was one heck of a good-looking guy. His reasoning made sense, though. I toyed briefly with the idea of joining him but an inner voice with a Southern accent forbade. Whatever else small-town Texas girls might do, they did not go around naked out of doors, regardless of laundry consequences.

Ten minutes into that first Florida-to-Caribbean passage, of course, he was again stripping down in the cockpit.

"What are you doing?"

"Taking my clothes off. It's hot."

"You said when we went to the Bahamas that you went naked to save on laundry."

"Oh, right. Even better. Yeah, that's the ticket. Laundry!" He grinned. Again with the waggle.

Hmm.

I know now what I suspected then, that what inspires him to go the full Monty whenever he can get away with it has nothing to do with any practical consideration whatsoever. It's the same feeling apparent on the face of every toddler running gleeful on the beach in his birthday suit. My husband is a nudist.

Even when the boat is at the dock he is apt to wear as little as possible, and the older and softer the garments the better. Our shore-going ritual usually includes a conversation similar to this.

Me: Ready to go ashore?

Him: Yep.

Me: Got your Tevas?

Him: Oh, I won't need shoes. We're just going to the landing.

Me: What if we decide to eat lunch ashore?

Him: Do we need shoes for that?

Me: Why yes we do. We're representing our country here.

Him *(turning on heel with sigh; returning in five seconds)*: Okay, got 'em. Let's go.

Me: Any holes in your shorts?

Him: Nope.

Me: Any holes in your shirt?

Him: Nope.

Me: Turn around, let me see.

Him: Oh, wait, there may be . . . yes, there is one. Or maybe two. They're really small though.

Me: I'm sorry, sweetheart. You know the rule.

Him: Civilization will fall if I go ashore in a shirt with holes in it?

Me: That's the one.

Him *(turning on heel; returning ten seconds later)*: Better?

Me: Looks good. Um . . . are you wearing underwear?

Him *(turning on heel)*.

Me *(sigh)*.

And that brings me to the point in that first passage, from Florida to the Virgin Islands via the Bermuda Triangle, when things started to turn around. Forty-eight hours after the cargo ship debacle, we were still thrashing to weather in 20-knot gusty winds and a steep choppy sea. It was even hotter than it had been two days before. Although I had managed to make some food and to drag a big jug of water up into the cockpit, we had eaten little and slept less. Part angst, part unfamiliar motion, part continuing efforts to de-bug our new equipment, part extreme muscle fatigue were responsible for the sleeplessness. Be that as it may, I was running on empty and still in a black mood, berating myself for being a bad sailor and sub-standard person generally.

It was early afternoon, and I was on watch again. Alan was dozing in the cockpit. Buck naked, he was sprawled in all his redheaded glory on the cockpit's leeward seat cushions in his usual pose – on his back with one arm behind his head, one leg draped over the cockpit coaming.

On one of my horizon scans aft, I noticed that a spare dock line was coming untied on the stern rail, so I put on the deck harness, hanked myself on to the safety line, and made my way laboriously, handhold by handhold, out of the cockpit to the aft deck. Holding on to the railing with one hand, I untied the line. Then looping my arm underneath the lifeline and bracing my feet against the stanchion base to secure myself from falling, I began rewinding it into a neat coil. I stood there in something of a daze, flying up and down with the stern as if I were strapped onto a carnival ride. I was a little giddy from lack of sleep, and at the apex of one wave, I may have emitted a small "whee."

All of a sudden I heard a shriek. It was a horrible screeching noise, a falsetto banshee wail of a noise. It was Alan. I turned my head forward toward the cockpit to see him gyrating, throwing himself across the cockpit, roaring, practically foaming at the mouth.

My reaction was oddly dispassionate. I stood there and watched. Experts say that lack of sleep over an extended period can lead to a psychotic breakdown. I figured I was watching him have one. Moreover, I could only assume I would be next. I carefully clove-hitched the spare line to the railing and made my way methodically, handhold by handhold, back to the cockpit to see if by chance our first-aid kit had any thorazine in it.

There on the cockpit sole was a flying fish, flopping and flapping against the teak grating. It looked like one of the very large ones that we had been admiring all day. Apparently, this one had gotten tired of merely skimming from wavetop to wavetop. It had flown a kamikaze mission up over our deck into our cockpit and had scored a direct hit onto my husband's flagrantly exposed lap. They were both pretty upset about it.

I couldn't help it. It was just . . . funny. I started laughing. Alan was inspecting the damage in gingerly fashion. I could see from where I stood that, notwithstanding the surprise *bris*, everything that should have been there still was. I giggled some more.

"It's not funny," he bit out.

"Yes it is." For the second time that week, tears were rolling down my cheeks. I snorted, and that set me off again. "You made me snort."

He looked at me. He looked down at his lap. He looked at the fish, still flopping around the cockpit looking for the exit. He gave a little harumph. And then he was laughing. And neither of us could stop. We chased that poor fish around the cockpit and returned it to the deep, where I envisioned it holding an audience spellbound. Together we held on to the dodger railing and howled until tears were rolling down Alan's face as well as mine, until my ribs ached, until Alan's haw-honking gasps finally diminished to the point where conversation was possible.

I was contrite for not being more solicitous about his injury. "Do you want me to go below and get you some pants to put on?"

He stood there, transferring his handhold to the binnacle as the boat continued its carnival-ride motion. I watched his gray-blue eyes in their deep-set triangular sockets look inward to assess his feelings. The thoughts flickered as he weighed the issue from both sides – the joys of nudity versus the merits of protective clothing. Freedom versus shelter. He wavered . . . but no. He stuck to his guns.

"No thanks," he said, not without dignity. "I'll just sleep on my stomach from now on."

The timer beeped. I turned to the horizon to check once more for traffic. But now I had a smile on my face.

* * *

It was that very night that I began my love affair with the sea.

Had I been asked, I would have said that I had loved the ocean for as long as I could remember. We had owned smaller boats and had bareboat-chartered in exotic places. I had rocked at anchor with friends and rum drinks and thought "this is the life" and "wouldn't it be wonderful to live on a sailboat." The exhilaration of a brisk few hours' reach between close-lying islands was nearly always capped, however, by a good night's sleep at the dock or in a protected anchorage or sometimes even in a hotel room.

I had been out of sight of land only once, and that for a few hours. With regard to the sea, I was a rank tourist, a mere acquaintance. Granted, my deep love of boats and of being on the water had made me dream of voyaging, had made me assume that I would love it. My relationship with the open ocean, the actual bluewater vastness of the ocean, however, was at best undefined. If anything, after the sustained physical and emotional discomfort of the first days of that first passage, the ocean and I were not exactly on speaking terms.

All that was about to change.

It's funny how a single event can precipitate a state of mind so compelling that it craves repetition, insists on it.

Or maybe it's not so funny; maybe any junkie would understand. From the night after the flying fish incident until we completed the circumnavigation almost six years later, the sole regret I entertained about my decision to go sailing was that we didn't have the money to sail forever. It happened in the space of ten minutes, just before dawn.

It had been a partly overcast, moonless night, the kind where you truly can't see your hand in front of your face without a flashlight. I was on watch, sitting in the cockpit. Alan was asleep belowdecks. The nearest land was more than a hundred miles distant, and I was alone with the ocean. Near daybreak, the sky became – well, I can't say it lightened exactly, but it did begin to de-blacken slightly to grayscale in the east. I glanced forward and caught the now just barely visible image of our genoa, the large forward sail, nodding rhythmically at the water. How beautiful, I thought, ghostly ivory against gunmetal gray, the shoosh of the hull cutting through the waves. I checked our course and speed, which were both fine. And then it happened.

In two heartbeats, everything went absolutely quiet, absolutely still. The breeze gave a little half-hearted gust, then extinguished itself completely. The waves hissed and flattened to horizontal swirls. The boat hesitated, as if it were confused. Startled by the sudden hush, I looked up and around. Across the face of the earth was a profound pause, a deep inhalation. It was as if an orchestra conductor, appearing at the world's podium, tapped her baton and suspended it in the air. The musicians came to attention, poised on the edges of their seats, instruments at the ready, expectant. The audience – me – held its breath in a long beat of anticipation.

And the symphony began. A single yellow beam shot over the horizon. Then another, and another. Shades of pink flooded across high cirrus clouds like watercolors saturating paper. Two seabirds, at first gray then magically snow-white, lifted yammering off the water. A wave, then another, slapped against the hull. The breeze puffed with a whistle in the rigging. The foresail billowed. The boat leapt forward. My soul leapt, too, and tears sprang into my eyes.

Thank you.

In the days and months to come, I knew there would be difficult passages. There would in fact be spine-emulsifying scary ones. There would be storms. We could expect to deal with power-hungry officials, with tropical diseases, with uncharted reefs, with pirates.

But there would be more 360-degree dawns. There would be perfect beauty. There would be time for introspection, clues to answers to questions I hadn't thought to ask. Landfall would be a window into lives far different from my own. Perspective was a distinct possibility and along with it, a remote but colorable chance of inner peace. Dare I even think it: Perhaps I would get another fleeting glimpse out of the corner of my eye at the face of God.

Later that day the wind reached an uncomfortable thirty knots true, and we were still on a hard beat against steep headseas. I moved to grind the winch yet again to take a second reef in the sails. Hey, my muscle strength was better. St. Thomas was less than a hundred miles away. In my immediate future were steel bands and umbrella drinks and endless white beaches, possibly even a hammock.

I looked out over the grey and silver sea, which looked right back, and I felt much better about the whole thing.

LETTER HOME
ST. THOMAS
U.S. VIRGIN ISLANDS

Hi y'all,

We're in St. Thomas, in the U.S. Virgin Islands after a more or less successful inaugural passage. We hardly hit a single thing or sank at all. Seriously, the passage was difficult but rewarding, and we have a few halfway decent tales to tell, preferably over large tankards of rum. Right now we're waiting for a tropical wave to pass through before we raise anchor. Next are three glorious weeks of gunkholing in the British Virgin Islands (BVI) and United States Virgin Islands (USVI). After that, we'll be heading south for the hurricane high-season, either to Grenada or to Isla Margarita, Venezuela, depending on the wind direction at the time.

In by far the biggest news of the day, speaking of already being homesick, we stumbled on a little boutique "gourmet" grocery store that has Ro-Tel, Velveeta, and the very rare, the highly coveted, authentic white corn restaurant-quality Doritos.

Gonna be some Tex-Mex tonight.

Love, Liza

CHAPTER 3
THE VIRGIN ISLANDS

Q: *Were you able to get all of your entry visas in advance? How does that work?*

A: No, we have to check in country by country, sometimes island by island within the same country. When we arrive, the law requires that we must first visit customs and immigration before we do anything or go anywhere else. Sometimes officials come out to us in a boat. Sometimes we tie up to a customs dock. Sometimes we land at the beach and spend a full day searching for someone who gives a darn. Although most countries give Americans an automatic 90-day visa upon arrival, some require us to get a visa in advance, from a consulate at the prior port of call.

Q: *How do you know what the rules are for any specific country?*

A: The laws are usually available in cruising guides or on the Internet. It's part of my job as Chief Logistical Officer and Goddess of Paperwork to research stuff like that in advance.

What is it about swimming in a flawless turquoise sea that inspires such a sense of well-being? One of the best parts of being at anchor in the Caribbean is hopping into the water whenever the mood strikes. As I float on my back in Cane Garden Bay, on the north side of Tortola in the British Virgin Islands, I feel positively sedated. The shoulder muscles that are always so tense loosen and get heavy. I breathe more deeply. My jaw unclenches. In the super-saturated saltwater I am bobbing like a cork. Does immersion in the sea bring back some subliminal memory of amniotic bliss? When one dives into the ocean, is it a dive back into the womb environment? I feel safe, supported, carefree.

At that moment, my next career move is self-evident. I will become a demotivational speaker. I will tour the country urging people to flout responsibility and enjoy their lives instead. I rehearsed my spiel: "Quit your job and go sailing! Decimate that career path! Alienate your family and friends! Obliterate your 401k!" Hmm, needs work.

My reverie is interrupted by the sight of a dorsal fin at about 50 yards, coming straight at me. I do a fair imitation of Bugs Bunny walking on water back to the boat's swim ladder, and then realize that it is not a shark but a dolphin. I name him Fred. Fred hangs around the rest of the day, but strongly prefers Alan's company to mine. I rename him Alejandro.

The Virgin Islands (both American and British) are a series of paradises an easy day-sail apart. They are Disney World for sailors. The beaches are palm-fringed and soft. The cumulus clouds look like cartoon sheep dipped in fluorescent white dye and clapped onto a felt-board in permanent symmetrical configuration. There are restaurants when you want them, and semi-deserted bays within a nice afternoon's reach. Although the snorkeling is second-rate, the schools of angelfish are beautiful when they do appear. The wind blows a steady fifteen knots from the southeast, and the marine weather forecast is so unchanging that we suspect they pre-record it twice a year. Swimming is as safe as it is anywhere. Theft is rare. The main body of the VI has a total of one navigational hazard – a huge reef clearly marked, onto which some poor charterer obligingly runs aground every season to enable the rest of us to feel smug.

I have heard complaints that these islands are too crowded, and I don't agree. A good chart, a little ingenuity, and an early start can conquer all. If I had a complaint, which I don't, it would be with the music. Steel bands are quintessentially Caribbean, and I adore them – at least the good ones. The sound of rolling mallets on steel drums floating across the water says "tropical island" in the most concise, light-hearted, and conclusive way possible.

Sadly, the sound of a steel band in the VI says not only "tropical island," but also "can't be bothered to rehearse." Sit long enough at a VI bar, and a local band will strike up one set's worth of America's Blandest Hits, which they will then proceed to repeat four or five more times in the course of the evening. It's "You Are the Sunshine of My Life," "Lady in Red," and "Misty" until you think you might scream. For a music lover, it is painful. But in the overall course of things it's a nit, so I'll give it a rest.

Except to say this: It was "Lady in Red" that wafted out to us from the bar at Pusser's Landing as we picked up a mooring in West End to check in with British Virgin Islands customs and immigration. The Virgin Islands are part American (St. Thomas, St. John, and St. Croix) and part British (all the rest). All but St. Croix are grouped in extremely convenient sailing proximity, but to go from an American island to a British one, or vice versa, one must present passports, clear the boat into customs, and, if applicable, purchase a cruising permit. Because for many years we have come to the British Virgin Islands for bareboat chartering – that is, chartering a sailboat on one's own without a professional captain or crew – we knew the ropes. The experience gained in those vacation trips saw us through many dozens of check-ins throughout the world.

A typical customs office in the tropics is a tiny un-airconditioned cubicle in which a man, or on rare occasion a woman, sits all day in a resplendent starched usually white full-dress uniform shirt, shorts, knee socks, shiny shoes, and often a hat. This official is locally well paid and highly respected. His or her own personality ranges from proud-but-reasonable to officious to insanely despotic.

There are many ways the hapless sailor can and does commit heinous breaches of etiquette. On one of our chartering vacations in the BVI years before, we saw what was possibly the worst offender ever to sail these waters. This tourist was German, and he was the bareboat skipper of a large yacht with what looked to be about a dozen family and friends aboard. Rather than gathering up all the passports and representing the yacht as its captain, he allowed about half the boat's occupants to accompany him into the tiny office. They were all in various states of bathing suits and un-dress, all talking loudly among themselves. He himself was in baggy cut-offs and a ball cap, with bare chest, bare feet, scraggly three-days' growth of a beard, and an attitude. Oh, and he was also wearing a watch, which he pointedly consulted from time to time with audible grunts of impatience. When I arrived to check in our own boat, the fun was in full swing.

I'll just back up here and go over the main points of a successful check-in, or "customs dance," as we came to call it. For the sailor, learning the steps to the customs dance is the key to voyaging equanimity. No matter the part of the world, no matter the language, the dance is understood by all. It virtually guarantees a smooth and successful entry into the country in question.

The customs dance is initiated by entering the customs office silently, pulling the door to with exaggerated care to refrain from disturbing. One then stands well back from the counter, meek and silent, as if one has wandered in by mistake and finds the various posters on the bulletin board to be just about as informative and interesting as the written word can be. One waits in that posture for the official to complete whatever business occupies him – whether it's reading a document or cleaning his fingernails. Only upon his acknowledgment does one approach, much as to a minor royal, and offer with down-turned eyes and possibly a sketch of a bow, one's ship's papers for his approval. Brief pleasantries often ensue at this point. After said pleasantries, one remains resolutely silent, speaking only when spoken to, addressing the official as "sir" or "ma'am" at least once but no more than twice, as to kiss up too blatantly engenders suspicion.

One final exercise in self-control remains. After the official's languid perusal of each of the ship's documents, during which one's attention is apt to wander off, the official will suddenly grab a stamping device and erupt into a frenzied attack on various sheets of paper with the same energy as I might wield Alan's shoe to kill a quick-moving spider. It is crucial at this juncture not to flinch. It is, one communicates, all in a day's work amongst professionals. Assuming that one's papers are more or less in order, one can, with a departing nod of thanks, be in and out of customs in, oh, fifteen minutes. The alternative? Hah.

The alternative is exactly what that German guy got in the BVI. There were three officials behind the counter, none of whom were occupied with a customer. When I walked in, the German guy was leaning, elbows on counter, wondering to the world at large what was taking so long. No official acknowledged him. The crowd of family and friends were milling, laughing, talking on cellphones. I considered backing out the door and returning later, but I figured I might as well give it a shot. I had donned my usual customs outfit of neat cotton slacks, collared shirt, and unscarred boat shoes with matching socks. My hair was in a subdued ponytail, and my papers were in an attache emblazoned with our boat logo. It took some effort to get this ensemble ashore clean and dry, and I hated for it to go to waste. So I stood back from the counter, removed my sunglasses, and initiated the dance.

After perhaps thirty seconds of staring into the middle distance, I noticed the official at the far end of the counter catching my eye. I approached, being careful not to touch the counter, and removed our papers from the attache. I handed them over as if bestowing the Order of the Garter, and the German guy went ballistic. He was here first, he had been waiting, and so on. I made no response, and my official stared him down and away. The captain threw up his hands and engaged in an animated Deutsche colloquy with one of his cohorts. My official performed the requisite languid perusal and frenzied stamping. When I left, the German guy had still not succeeded in even presenting his papers.

A couple of hours later, as Alan and I were having cocktails on a restaurant deck on the other side of the bay, we observed the German guy's yacht being scrupulously and systematically ripped apart and searched. I'm guessing his frustration had escalated into hostility, which of course was all the excuse the department needed to make him an example. When we left the bay after lunch the next day, the

German boat had been moved to the customs dock, and its occupants were huddled pitifully in the cockpit. Poor guy. The only requirements for an efficient check-in to a tropical island country are humility and a sense of the proper decorum. Of course, in some parts of the world there is an additional requirement – *i.e.*, the non-receipted fee, better known in Texas as a goddamned bribe. We got lessons about that later in the trip. In the Caribbean, however, life is simple, straightforward, and generally on the up-and-up. About the worst that will happen at a customs office, if one is polite and patient, is loss of dignity – not such a high price to pay for most sailors. In fact, on our boat its loss goes completely unremarked.

* * *

After a quick visit to one of the U.S. islands and then back into British waters, we checked back in to the BVI, this time at the port of entry on the island of Jost Van Dyke. There, I witnessed the following exchange that I will never forget. It was between an Australian sailor and a BVI customs officer I will call Thomas, and it took place at the customs house at Great Harbour. The Australian sailor had observed the opening niceties of the customs dance, and a rapport had been established.

SAILOR *(handing Thomas the passports and ship's papers)*: Pardon, mate – but when you have a chance, I have a question.

THOMAS *(drawling in heavenly Caribbean singsong)*: Yesss, mon, go ahead.

SAILOR: Is there a post office on the island?

THOMAS *(pausing distractedly for about 90 seconds while scrutinizing documents)*: Yesss.

SAILOR: Sorry to bother you – just hoping to get these letters in the post.

THOMAS *(shuffling papers for two full minutes, then erupting into usual frenzy of stamping)*: Hmmm? Yessss.

SAILOR: How do I find the post office, mate?

THOMAS: You must ask the Postmaster, mon.

SAILOR: Excellent. Where is he?

THOMAS: Who?

SAILOR: The Postmaster.

THOMAS *(handing sailor his cruising permit)*: That will be eighty-seven United States dollars, and thirty-six United States cents.

SAILOR *(handing him ninety dollars)*: Cheers.

THOMAS: Do you have the correct change?

SAILOR: No, sorry, mate.

THOMAS: Ah, one moment *(turns and disappears into a back office, where he stays for approximately three minutes)*.

SAILOR *(drumming fingers on counter, and finally, with raised voice)*: Pardon – no worries at all – please keep the change.

THOMAS *(returning to the counter)*: I'm sorry, mon, there is no change here today. If you come back tomorrow, possibly . . ..

SAILOR: No worries. Thanks very much. *(Turns to go, and remembers his letters.)* Right. Where is the Postmaster again?

THOMAS *(expansively)*: He's right here, mon.

SAILOR *(light dawning)*: Thomas, are you the Postmaster?

THOMAS: Yessss.

SAILOR *(laughing)*: And this is the post office.

THOMAS: Yessss.

SAILOR *(still laughing)*: Thank you. Here are our letters.

THOMAS *(looking at watch)*: Oh and what a shame. It is 3:02.

SAILOR: So?

THOMAS: The post office closes at 3 o'clock.

I promise you, I did not make this up. Luckily, the sailor was, as I say, Australian and true to his country's stereotype could appreciate a good joke. He and Thomas hit the bars together later that day, and all was made well. The last time we saw Thomas, he was napping on the beach next to a cooler.

He's a good man to know.

CHAPTER 4

ST. THOMAS TO GRENADA

Q: *I have heard that sailors get into ports more easily if they have the USCG "certificate of competence." Did you get that?*

A: I have never heard of anything called a "certificate of competence." Alan and I both hold a United States Coast Guard charter captain "six-pack" license. I'm sure it would serve as a certificate of competence. However, in the entire 37,000-mile circumnavigation, I have to say that we were never asked by any authority to document our competence in any way whatsoever.

After a few glorious weeks of island-hopping, we returned to Charlotte Amalie, St. Thomas, to wait for a reasonable weather window to head south. We were still laboring under the ridiculous belief that we could get around the world in the planned two to three years, so heading south was uppermost on our minds. Unfortunately, the mid-Caribbean was in the midst of a series of tropical waves.

Tropical waves, sometimes called easterly waves, or tropical easterly waves, are a type of atmospheric trough, an elongated area of relatively low pressure that moves from east to west across the tropics, causing areas of cloudiness and thunderstorms. Tropical waves are generally carried westward by the Caribbean's prevailing easterly winds. They can lead to the formation of tropical cyclones and make for uncomfortable sailing at best, and dangerous sailing at worst.

Choosing the right moment to dash down-island between summer tropical waves is a lot like trying to steal second base. Leave now? No! Pinned to the bag by 30-knot winds! Now? Local weather gurus behave like coaches signaling frenetically from the dugout: Go today, no wait, go tomorrow, okay the day after that for sure – no wait, after the next wave passes; well maybe the next one.

But for us, waiting for a weather window in off-season Charlotte Amalie turned out to be a joy. As charterers, we had been avoiding the island's urban afflictions on principle for a decade. Rebuilding after 1995 hurricane devastation, however, the city is spiffier, more upscale, and far less determinedly a tourist trap.

At least half the battle is finding the right anchorage. We favor West Gregerie Channel, particularly Ruyter Bay, far away from the main ferry and cruise ship routes. From here the dinghy dock at friendly Crown Bay Marina makes an excellent op-center.

Within five minutes' walk is a litany of voyagers' conveniences: three chandleries, a supermarket, laundromat, dive shop, etc. By readily available taxi (we patronized the "Love Cab"), one can reach excellent restaurants, nice shops, and other high-end amenities. There is no sales tax or duty. It was a welcome dose of civilization and a splurge of spare-parts buying.

The weather finally lifted, and a decent gap materialized between tropical waves. With hurricane high season upon us, we sprinted furiously southeast.

The trip down to Granada from St. Thomas took just under three days of easy, brisk sailing to weather at never less than a comfortable sixty-degree angle on the wind. We could have made it more quickly, but the whole of the final night we – or rather I – maneuvered in circles in an attempt to avoid thunderstorms. It was a Monty Python kind of night. Whenever I saw a storm cell ahead, I would tack at right angles (chanting "run away") only to see vertical lightning stab the water dead ahead, prompting another tack ("run away"), only to see a thunderhead forming in front of my eyes, prompting a jibe ("run away"), only to see . . . you get the picture. When Alan woke up, he was less than amused that in five hours of traveling at eight knots I had made maybe a mile and a half good toward our destination.

Say what you will, thunderstorms are tricky business. I used to love watching a really good one in Texas, but that was before I was living in the middle of the water at the bottom of an ungrounded 75-foot metal pole. We bought an expensive and complicated-looking lightning strike prevention contraption in Florida for the top of the mast, and from the amused looks on other sailor's faces when they see it, I'm guessing that a midnight ritual involving chicken bones might be equally effective.

Whenever I sight lightning on the horizon, I immediately rush below and put the laptop in the microwave. Don't laugh. Even a near miss would fry all things electrical on the boat. A fellow cruiser once told me with a completely straight face that the microwave RF-shield protects electronics from lightning damage. Someday I'll either find out that this microwave rigmarole is the cruising equivalent of snipe hunting, or else I'll accidentally nuke the computer.

* * *

"Where should we anchor?" I shouted over the wind. We had negotiated the entrance to a large protected bay on the south side of the island of Grenada and were motoring around taking depth soundings and eyeing the dozen or so boats that were already bobbing on their hooks. As usual, I was on the wheel, and Alan was at the bow. The wind, though light, was at its normal volume of loud. The distance between the cockpit and the bow is about thirty-five feet, long enough to require some oomph in the voice to be heard, even in a dead calm.

"What?" he yelled from the bow.

"Where. Should. We. Anchor?" I yelled from the cockpit.

"Oh," he roared, "how about . . ." and as he spoke he turned from facing me in the cockpit to facing forward into the wind, where the sound of his words was completely lost.

"What?" I yelled.

"How about . . ." again with the face-turn forward into the wind.

I sighed, backed down on the throttle, and engaged the autopilot to crawl straight ahead. I walked toward him along the deck to the bow.

"Sweetheart, when you turn forward like that, I can't hear anything you say because of the wind. Please face me until you finish the dang sentence, okay?"

"Oh, sorry, We need a better anchoring communications solution. I'll ask around."

I walked back to the cockpit and took *Heartsong* off auto-pilot. Alan faced me squarely and pointed vaguely ahead.

"Let's anchor between those two white boats," he enunciated clearly.

"Um, sweetheart," I answered, "they're all white."

"What?"

"All of the boats are white," I yelled. "Which two?"

"Oh, sorry. The ones that are . . ." and as he spoke he turned his face back into the wind.

Sigh.

LETTER HOME
SECRET HARBOUR
GRENADA, WEST INDIES

Hi y'all,

We're here at a nice sheltered anchorage on the Southern coast of Grenada, at the bottommost tip of the West Indies.

Grenada has some unique attractions. For example, on a cliff on the west side of the entrance to our anchorage is a structure that looks like a home for very wealthy hobbits. Round-doored and roofed with a living lawn, the place is built into the cliffside in such a way that I didn't notice it at all at first. I've been told that the interior is all exotic hardwoods and waterfalls. It comes with a beach house, a guard tower, and a 75-foot power yacht at the end of a concrete dock at the bottom of the cliff. The asking price is apparently US$10 million.

Now of the handful of people in this part of the world who can afford this, how many of them would want a tiny cliff house on a remote gravel road at least an hour away from any town, above a small beach with no access except via the sea, on an isolated coast of a Caribbean island?

Oh.

Yikes.

Maybe we should change anchorages.

Love, Liza

CHAPTER 5

GRENADA

Q: Do you ever see any other sailboats with people doing the same thing as you?

A: Absolutely. Many, many people from all over the world are out here voyaging. It is a sub-culture that I had no idea existed before I joined it. Maybe it's because we have the time, or maybe it's because we understand how profoundly we rely on each other for safety at sea, but nobody is more neighborly than the typical voyager. The neighborhood itself is constantly changing, of course, and one need only weigh anchor to find complete solitude elsewhere. But oh the celebration on pulling into a remote bay and finding a favorite friend one last saw months ago on a different continent.

It was our second week in Grenada, and I was spending the morning sitting in the cockpit doing nothing.

Nothing, as it turns out, is surprisingly difficult to do. It took me years of voyaging to get the hang of it. By the end of the trip I was spending a fair amount of time contemplating such profound matters as the anchor chain straining and slacking, or the slurp of wavelets against the stern. But Grenada was early days, and I was still a novice.

That particular morning the clang of the main outhaul against the boom was mesmerizing. The buzz of a dinghy outboard filtered into my thoughts. From the sound of the steady change in pitch, it was on a direct route to our boat. Maybe somebody had a lobster for sale. Although it looked like an easy swim to the reef to bag my own dinner, I wasn't sure I would ever have the nerve to stick my hand into a lobster hole.

We were anchored in the center of Grenada's southern coastline, a half hour's bone-rattling taxi ride south of the capital St. George's, in a large protected bay called Secret Harbour. The big semicircular bay has a different official name on the charts, but we who anchor there like to pretend we're keeping it to ourselves. The water was Caribbean blue and, even at our anchorage depth of fifty feet, crystal clear to the bottom.

One of the secrets of the harbor is that it is a relatively safe storm haven. Broken only by a narrow serpentine entrance (whose coordinates are another secret), the bay's barrier reef keeps the inner waters calm. Moreover, half of the bay lies south of the magical latitude line of Twelve Degrees North, which is most insurance companies' southernmost demarcation of the Caribbean hurricane zone. We were anchored about three feet on the correct side, safely underwritten. I hoped that the hurricanes themselves understood we were on base.

Surrounding Secret Harbour towards the interior is a movie backdrop of mountains, each peak slightly higher and darker than the one offset in front, with an occasional cumulus snagged on the highest one like a hiker's sweater stretching on a thornbush. The waterfront is thick with palm trees and prehistoric-looking ferns. Fountains of bougainvillea drip down every vertical surface. Slightly inland are wild orchards of nutmeg, cinnamon, and cocoa trees. By day, the air smells like hot spiced rum; by night, the open ocean. At two o'clock every afternoon it rains for precisely 20 minutes, and the sun shines uninterrupted otherwise. In short, there's simply not . . . a more congenial spot . . . for happ'ly ever-ahftering than . . .. Well, you get my drift. It's Camelot.

Grenada is large for an island nation in the southern Caribbean. It lies a hundred miles north of Venezuela, about an eight-hour flight or a nine-day sail southeast of Miami. Exports include spices and a dazzling batik cloth. Grenada would also like to export its white rum, despite the hint of WD-40 in its bouquet and the extreme questionability of the sanitation of its manufacturing process (think bats circling over open tubs). However, production has never been able to exceed local demand, especially during the tourist season.

Grenada's coastline is wide white beach punctuated by volcanic cliff. The interior is mountainous, covered thickly – in places impenetrably – by tropical rain forest. It was in the rain forests of Grenada that Alan and I first discovered the pleasures of eco-hiking. Basically, we learned, it involves packing out trash and cleaning up our blood after each laceration. I had one muddy cliff-slide after a hard rain that rivaled Kathleen Turner's in *Romancing the Stone*. At this point, there would be a close contest among our hiking injuries, our sailing injuries, and the Texas Chainsaw Massacre. Just kidding, of course. The Texas Chainsaw Massacre was a picnic compared to the body bruising, toe crushing, knuckle bashing, knee skinning, head conking, and muscle pulling that constitutes life on a boat in the tropics.

But back to Grenada. Between her beaches and her rain forests are pockets of congested, thriving, grimy, unabashedly flamboyant urban civilization. These are connected by a handful of deeply rutted roads over which flows a merry stream of rattletrap cars and vans at breakneck pace. If the number one pastime here is overthrowing the government, as so many historians have witticized, then a close second must be rebuilding car suspensions.

Now in mid-July in Secret Harbour, about 20 boats bobbed at anchor, another thirty or so out of sight in the bays on either side. Most of them were obviously blue-water voyaging yachts, complete with wind generators, solar panels, shade canopies, dinghies, spare fuel jerry-cans, and the other accoutrements of a life lived on the sea. At the rustic wooden docks of a small marina near the head of the bay were the local Moorings charter fleet and a handful of posh motor yachts with liveaboard professional crew, all of whom seem to be single and gorgeous and from all over the world, and engaged in endless boat-washing.

Riding the inflatable dinghy that was buzzing up to us that morning to interrupt my meditation, however, was not a professional crew contingent, but rather a suntanned couple who looked to be in their thirties or forties. I say "riding" the dinghy because they weren't sitting on the pontoons; they were standing up in the thing as it raced and bumped across the water. They looked like trick riders at a water sports rodeo. He stood behind her with one arm around her waist and one arm extended back to an outboard steering extension. She gripped the bow rope painter as if it were reins. She was carrying a clipboard in a two-gallon ziplock, her blond ponytail extending from the aft port of her ball cap. She wore a bathing suit top, khaki shorts, and trainers with socks. He was wearing stained baggy shorts with a couple of minor holes in them, a similarly unpresentable t-shirt of an indistinguishable shade of faded, and Teva sandals. In short, they were cruisers who looked a whole lot like us.

I moved to the rail as they shooshed up and stopped.

"Kate and John, *Sea Spirit*," she called. "Steel boat, brown mast – see her further in? – Dallas, Texas."

"Shut *up*. We're from Dallas."

"Shut *up*."

"Come aboard. Have you had breakfast?" I'm Liza, by the way, *Heartsong III*.

"Can't stay. We're signing people up for J'Ouvert."

"Zhyoo-what?"

"Zhyoo-VAY. Carnival." (She pronounced it Carni-VAHL.) "Starts at oh-six-hundred tomorrow morning in St. George's. Big parade. We're getting group vans at a discount. Leave at about oh-five-thirty. Wanna come?"

"Oh-five-thirty . . . in the morning?" I was dubious. We had trashed our alarms and pagers when we left Dallas – right after the pantyhose and stilettos burning ceremony.

"Well, yeah, but it's worth getting up a little earlier than usual, believe me."

A little earlier than usual? That would imply that other cruisers got up at a time that we would later know by the descriptive Australian term "sparrow fart."

I was saved from having to admit our slug status by Alan emerging into the cockpit from the forward head, where he does his own brand of meditation of a morning. Setting down his well-thumbed two-month-old *Newsweek*, he moved to the rail and gave me a hearty kiss on the neck. I made the introductions, and we all agreed to meet up at the Rum Squall Bar later to discuss this J'Ouvert nonsense over drinks at happy hour.

Happy hour among voyagers is a typical social event at anchor, conducted either ashore at some congenial watering hole within walking distance, or more usually on someone's boat. If on someone's boat, the standard operating procedure is for each couple to bring what they intend to drink, plus one appetizer-type food dish, plus whatever drinking and eating implements each requires. Juggling this BYOE (for Everything) in an inflatable dinghy while bouncing across a bay in a blow is a learned skill. But it is well worth it. Since nobody has to prepare anything special or go to any extra expense to have a party, parties are standard operating procedure.

Within hours of arriving at any bay, one may if one wishes, easily establish a quick connection with any neighbors who happen to be anchored within view. Voyaging may well be the last bastion of the frontier barn-raising ethic. When that anchor-dragging squall kicks up at midnight, the support system is firmly in place and on a first-name basis.

I don't mean to imply that socializing is required in the voyaging world. We often went for glorious weeks without seeing another living soul. It's just that, when desired, connections are easily and firmly made. The rapport is immediate.

Our introduction to this mutual-support phenomenon began in Florida, where we lived on the boat at a marina dock while preparing *Heartsong III* for sea. Living that lifestyle brought back warm, small-town, 1950s-type feelings: people sitting outside in the evenings; kids chasing lightning bugs; somebody cranking homemade ice cream; folks exchanging tools, casseroles, gossip, and the occasional bit of wisdom. Cruisers – at least the ones we know – appear above all else to value the concept of neighborliness. If someone were going to the store, he or she would ask if we had a list. The mere mention of a mechanical problem resulted in a relevant magazine article or the proper tool turning up on our deck the next morning.

We learned to live as much outdoors as in, along with everybody else. One morning in that Florida marina it occurred to me that I no longer thought it odd to traipse along the dock to the shoreside shower in my pajamas, bare feet, morning hair, and pre-caffeine disposition. The primary emphasis of this venture has always been the actual sailing of the boat. Just living the cruising lifestyle, however, has often been a big glass of Gatorade for this lawyer's parched urban soul.

To illustrate what I mean, consider this. What's the first question one asks at a party on land?

"So . . . what do you do for a living?"

Right? Imagine a world in which those words are never spoken.

I still don't know what half of the cruisers I met do or did for a living on land. I don't even know the last names of most. Nobody talks shop. Ever. The only reason that people know Alan is a doctor is because he kept saving lives. (More about that later.) The dot-commer/tech-geeks, too, were often conspicuous by the ready and efficient way they stepped in to solve fellow cruisers' laptop crashes. Other than that, we rarely knew whether we were drinking with a billionaire or a beach bum.

My first cruiser get-together in Grenada, then, was to be happy hour at the Rum Squall Bar, which we had been patronizing on a semi-regular basis since we arrived. The establishment was conveniently located next to the dinghy dock. We were a little early and took a seat dockside on the concrete deck in a molded plastic chair that had most of its back intact and may once have been white. After the usual ten-minute wait, the sole waitress emerged from beneath an overhang of thatch and corrugated tin. Carrying a brown plastic tray and wearing a long flowered skirt, t-shirt and flip-flops, she glided in our direction.

"Yessss?" She intoned mournfully.

"I'll have a glass of white wine, please."

"And I'll have a margarita." Alan added.

"I'm thinking we are just out of wine." She sighed. "I will look at the margarita machine. Perhaps it has been repaired."

She turned, being careful not to dislodge the weight of the world from her elegant shoulders. Alan and I looked at each other in alarm. We knew from experience that to let her get away without our order was to invite a thirsty half hour.

"No wait," I blurted. "We'll both have a gin and tonic. With lime, if you have it."

She paused to consider. "We are just out of tonic. For the lime, I don't know. It is possible we have the gin. I will look."

"No, no!" Alan stopped her and, catching my admonishing eye, changed his tone. "I mean, no . . . no, that's fine – no problem." He studied her face and made another stab at the correct answer. "How about," his eyebrows lifted in hope, "a beer?"

"OK." She shrugged. "But it is not cold."

"Uhhhh . . .." He looked at me helplessly.

"Well, why don't we just have our usual then, sweetheart," I chimed in. I turned to the waitress and said sweetly. "Rum and warm cola, please, and absolutely no ice. And the same for him."

Hah. I would at least short-circuit the three trips required to inform us (a) that she was out of Coke and would Pepsi do; (b) that the Pepsi was warm, did we still want it; and (c) that the ice was finished. I think I detected a gleam of amused acknowledgment as she turned to get our drinks. Humble even in victory, I picked up the menu with feigned interest.

I say "feigned" because, although the menu advertised snacks, hot dogs, fried calamari, and other goodies, we had never once been able to cajole anyone into making us any actual food. I'm not sure exactly what it says about us, but the Rum Squall was our favorite bar on the island.

Sometime later, our dinghy visitors Kate and John of *Sea Spirit* walked up, carrying large bags of take-out from the Chinese restaurant down the way. Clearly, this was not their first rodeo. We spent the remainder of the evening at the Rum Squall with them – better known, as it turned out, as Princess Katie and Captain John – and also with Layla and Eddie of *Lady B*, Vicki and Mack of *Enchantment*, Lily and Jasper of *Second Wind*, Dean of *Escape*, and a young Julia Roberts lookalike who went by the name of "Jaws." Kate, with whom everyone else was well acquainted, was tacitly acknowledged to be Activities Director for the Worldwide Cruising Community.

And she showed no mercy. Five o'clock the next morning saw Kate herding us and 12 other cruisers aboard a taxi-van with no doors and a maximum capacity of eight. We had been told to wear our oldest work shorts and t-shirts (Alan rejoiced). In celebration of J'Ouvert, people are expected to paint themselves up with whatever comes to hand, sometimes grease paint, often old motor oil. We hoped that as outsiders we would escape, but just in case, we came wearing sacrificial clothing.

At 0530 the taxi-van deposited us on the outskirts of St. George's, more or less awake and definitely excited. St. George's, the capital of Grenada, is known not only for its puzzling mobile apostrophe (placed before or after the "s," apparently at random) but also for its graceful British colonial architecture. The town is built like a football stadium, pastel-colored buildings packed around a horseshoe waterfront and clustered straight up the steep hills behind it. Brightly clothed ladies sell baskets of fresh nutmeg and other spices on the street corners. Cops in dress-whites stationed at podiums on the main streets downtown engage in traffic-control choreography that wouldn't be out of place in a hip-hop video.

But on this J'Ouvert morning, normal traffic was forbidden, and uniformed law enforcement was nowhere in sight. By dawn the road was jammed with Grenadians wearing thick streaks of paint on all visible skin, and not much else in the already muggy heat. Flatbed trucks began weaving their way among the crowds. The trucks carted sound systems that looked like the San Francisco skyline and would have served a heavy metal stadium concert. The speakers boomed out island music – hypnotic deafening pulsating break-neck calypso. My favorite song was "He Got Belly," a paean to – as well as I could tell – courage and success. Or maybe I was looking for a metaphor when the only aim was to celebrate fat happiness. Whatever.

The island calypso beat was unlike anything I had ever heard. It was like reggae on amphetamines, like an avalanche of samba, more hyperkinetic, even more joyful than salsa. It felt like a perpetual motion machine. The music thrummed and throbbed and drowned out all else but an irresistible urge to move, and move now.

Alan and I stood on the sidelines, hesitating – white middle-class Americans out of our element. In short order, two local women approached us with buckets, paint brushes, and smiles. A few swishes and slaps later we were no longer quite so white, but rather blue, grey, black, and red. The music started taking hold of my legs, then my arms and head, and finally my small-town Southern-girl butt. In no time at all it jumped to my pelvis, and I was officially astounded at myself.

The crowd swelled onto the main street just outside St. George's. Everyone was dancing in place, twirling and gyrating, bumping and grinding. Then as if on cue (and maybe I just missed it) people closed up into ranks, still moving with the music. All bodies facing in the direction of town, the mob condensed onto the street in a compact organized writhing mass that extended from curb to curb. Hands went to the hips of the reveler directly in front of each person. Occasionally an arm detoured to an adjacent waist. Then everyone started "chipping" – moving with small toe-pad steps to the beat, hips swiveling.

Then (again I must have missed the signal) it was forward march. This wasn't a street dance at all. It was a parade. Or actually it was more like a gigantic conga line, about 20 abreast and half a mile long. Alan and I had made the strategic error of allowing our enthusiasm to carry us into the middle of the road. Now we were surrounded. Alan shrugged, maneuvered me ahead of him, put his hands on my hips and started chipping forward with the crowd.

"Whatever you do, don't let go," I yelled back at him. "If anyone falls, they're toast."

"At least it's early in the morning," he hollered in my ear. "People are probably sober."

That seemed unlikely. Carnival had been going on since the night before – but I decided to let that point go unmade.

As I gyrated into and then instantly slid off the arm of the large woman next to me, I started appreciating the rationale for the motor oil. Then out of nowhere an amplified voice yelled, "reverse!"

This instruction precipitated a synchronized action worthy of the Borg. Everyone stopped stock still for a millisecond, then began hopping backwards in time to the beat. Thankfully the voice yelled, "reverse!" again seconds later, and we resumed our slow chipping forward progress. I was now less worried about someone being trampled than about mass anonymous pregnancies.

"Alan, is that still you behind me?"

"No, mon."

"Very funny."

We chipped and reversed until we could chip and reverse no more. As the parade entered town it fanned out a little, and we made our escape through the cracks. Collapsing at the first roadside food vendor we saw, we sipped icy bottled Cokes. Alan tried the mystery-meat-on-a-stick. I hit the CD vendor and bought up a bagful of calypso music.

Later that day, we returned to the south side of the island, where *Heartsong III* was bobbing gently at anchor, oblivious to all the excitement. We sat on the stern steps and stripped off our oil- and paint-stained clothes. Inside a nook above the stern steps are a fresh-water hot and cold shower nozzle, a bottle of soap, and a scrub brush. Half a tank of fresh water later, we finally pronounced each other fit to go below.

* * *

Our stay at anchor in Grenada was a busy and productive time. One of my priorities for the season was to learn our boat intimately from stem to stern. I had spent as much time as I cared to spend in on-the-job training while underway. Next on the circumnavigation agenda was the reputedly difficult week's passage from the ABC Islands to Panama, after which we would have the 3000-mile, multi-week Pacific Ocean crossing. Several months remained of hurricane season before we could strike out west to continue the route. The Schedule called for a thorough exploration of the southern coast of Granada, followed by energetic island-hopping elsewhere in the southern Caribbean as the weather allowed. I was entertaining a secret, revolutionary – nay, heretical – idea. I broached it to Alan.

"Say sweetie, what would you say if instead of sailing around the islands like we planned, we just stayed here in Secret Harbour for a little while?"

"Okay."

Huh? That was too easy. I felt the need to persuade.

"I mean, if we move around a lot, we'll spend half of every day just getting from place to place and finding a good spot to anchor and looking for places to get ashore and . . ."

"I was thinking the same thing."

"Whereas if we stay here we can start preparing for the big passages and not be always playing catch-up."

"You're right."

"Plus, I like this place a lot – as well as anyplace in the Caribbean we've ever been – so why not stay a while and soak it up?"

"Fine with me."

"I know it's not exactly on The Schedule to stay in one harbor, but this is a perfect place to sit out the rest of hurricane season before we move on. So what do you think?"

"Hello-o." Alan squared up in front of me, put both hands on my shoulders, and looked me in the eye. "I have an idea – let's hang out here for a month or so. What do you say?"

"Oooh, great idea."

So for the next few weeks, we each jubilantly set about our own priorities. I went through every single manual and organized a long-term weekly maintenance schedule for all aspects of the boat and her equipment. For example, the winches needed to be re-greased and serviced every six months; the fresh water tanks required a chlorine additive every other week; the liferaft needed re-certification every other year; all fourteen through-hulls needed to be exercised monthly. I found that there are virtually unlimited ways on a boat to indulge my anal-retentive organization fetish.

To wit: I refined our pre-passage checklist to reflect whether we were leaving on a day-sail, a simple overnighter, or a multi-night passage. I computerized our provisioning lists and set up a system for stowage and inventory control. We made a wish list of spare parts to obtain before we left for the remote regions of the South Pacific, where we might go weeks or months in areas with few if any stores or facilities. We tested our equipment. In the process, Alan took most of it apart and put it back together.

During that perfect Grenadian summer we learned how to varnish wood; how often we needed to clean the stainless steel to prevent rust; how best to haul each other safely and quickly up the mast to deal with a rigging problem. We practiced docking for fuel in relatively high winds without the aid of a bow-thruster. With the help of Dean, an intrepid Texan and professional captain of the immaculate wooden sailboat *Escape*, I learned how to throw a line twice as far as I thought I could ever throw it. Alan got his rescue diver certification. We re-packed our ditch bag and practiced abandon-ship procedures. Alan configured and installed dual fuel filters that, months later, saved us from harm in a narrow windless channel between reefs in Tahiti, when the engine died from water in the fuel. In short, we got ourselves and *Heartsong III* ready for the tough passages ahead. It felt better than I can say.

In the down-times, we jumped off the boat into the blue-green Grenadian sea and swam or snorkeled. We explored the island, went SCUBA diving, and sneaked onto the resort tennis courts. We took our dinghy and a picnic around to other bays and beaches. From time to time we had the other cruisers in the bay over for happy hour or went out to dinner. The makeup of the guest list changed daily, as people arrived and departed. One memorable night, a group of six long-term liveaboard boats chipped in for a room at the resort, where the women had a slumber party and – oh glorious! – took turns using the jacuzzi bathtub. Although I'm guessing there were one or two of the men who would have killed for a hot bath, they spent the night in martyrdom playing poker and eating chili elsewhere.

By far the majority of days, however, Alan and I were alone together. In the years since our wedding day, we had barely seen each other. At least it felt that way. We both worked long hours. At night it would be TV, take-out, and pass-out. Like most working couples, we spent a good portion of the weekend running errands on a divide-and-conquer basis. I estimate that in six months of 24/7 on the boat we spent more time talking and laughing than we had in Dallas the previous six years.

Most evenings we would take a glass of wine (in our new shatterproof acrylic wineglasses) out to the foredeck to watch the day end. The warm evening air glowed gold. The boat did its soothing rock-a-bye thing. Sitting with our backs up against the liferaft we watched the surf pour across the reef. The rich sounds – surf on reef, water against hull, rigging clanging a bit from time to time – were to new-age music what a ribeye is to lunch meat. Looking south we saw cliffs and ocean. Northward were the mountains and forest. Next to me was a face that looked different somehow. It wasn't wearing the overlay of distracted worry I was so accustomed to seeing.

The sun went behind the cliffs. Then it was too dark to see anything but the white foam of the surf. From time to time we inhaled the kind of sharp deep involuntary breath that one tends to take near the end of an hour with a really good massage therapist. Alan put his arm around me, and I snuggled closer.

"Do you miss TV at all?" he asked.

There was only one possible answer to his tone, a somewhat perjurious "Nope."

"Me neither."

He took my hand and starting rubbing the muscle at the base of my thumb.

I sighed. "You know, I could fall in love with you all over again."

"That's the plan."

A few days before we were to leave Grenada and sail the overnighter to explore the island of Tobago, we took a closer look by dinghy at the bay's barrier reef to see if it could be navigated safely for an exit in bad light. Then just before dawn on a day near the official end of hurricane season, we felt our way under engine power past the reef, with Alan on the bow with a spotlight. I was at the helm. When we passed the final buoy, I unfurled the mainsail and we came to course. From time to time I turned around to look at the cliffs of Grenada until finally I turned and they had disappeared.

The night before departure, Alan and I had sat on the deck and watched the sunset and vowed that someday we'd return to Secret Harbour. Somehow, I hope we never do.

CHAPTER 6
TOBAGO

Q: *What do you eat on board?*

A: In an astounding revelation, I have recently acknowledged that all over the world, people obtain and eat food. You could not have convinced me of this, however, during my Sam's Club provisioning frenzy before we left the States. That first few months, if we had lost the can opener, we would have starved.

Now, though, we shop at local markets and enjoy whatever we find there, whether it's callaloo, pamplemousse, or mystery packages with cooking instructions in Dutch. In remote areas, we bake our own bread and shop directly at local fishing boats. In urban areas, we stock up on staples and canned goods.

Trinidad & Tobago is an independent country at the southeastern extremity of the Caribbean Sea, just off the coast of Venezuela, and about a hundred miles south of Grenada. It is composed of two islands – the eponymous Trinidad and Tobago – about eighty miles apart. Large ferries ply between the two on a constant basis, but the ferries are about the only things that connect them.

With its offshore oil wells, Trinidad is a relatively wealthy industrial urban West Indian community with a healthy GDP and a sophisticated populace. In contrast, most of the people on primitive rain-forested Tobago have a subsistence lifestyle that depends mainly on fishing and a tiny amount of tourism. Tobago is well off the beaten track for North Americans, even for North American sailors, and once outside the capital town of Scarborough on the southernmost end of the island, the amenities are quite basic. Electricity, for example, is a luxury item.

Politically, Tobago often feels like a step-child, disrespected and under-represented in governmental decisions. Bustling Trinidad often feels, in contrast, as if she has an unemployed relative living on her couch. Nominally a unified country, Trinidad & Tobago always seem headed for the divorce court but somehow always accede to an uneasy reconciliation just before the papers are signed.

The political situation, however, was not our concern. In glorious solitude, we had slowly circumnavigated Tobago, deserted bay by deserted bay, one tiny fishing village at a time. Apart from hiking inland from time to time, our main activities, other than sailing, involved the hammock, which we suspended between the mast and the inner forestay. The tropical, almost equatorial, heat was easy enough to overcome by jumping in the turquoise water for a nice snorkel or a nap on tethered floats, wherever we happened to drop the anchor in the afternoons. And we had enough basic provisions to last for a while.

In the weeks before our departure from Florida, while the boatyard made what progress it made under Alan's superhumanly patient supervision, I had spent the majority of my days exploring Costco and Sam's Club. My goal was to stockpile a year's basic provisions. From fancy white albacore tuna in spring water to Tampax to bread flour to paper clips, I filled basket after basket. After all, who knew what absolute necessities of life would be unavailable outside America? I made pages of lists: moisturizer, canned peas, canned tomatoes, trash bags, brown rice, sunblock, Diet Coke, batteries of all sizes, salad dressing, bath soap, pasta sauce, printer toner, dried beans, spaghetti, juice concentrate, deodorant, spices, toothpaste, vitamins in most letters of the alphabet.

Buying the stuff and driving it back to the marina was only the beginning. Stage Two was transferring the carload from the parking lot to the dock to the deck to the cockpit down the companionway steps and into the main saloon. Stage Three was preparing the various items for stowage, which was Stage Four. One morning I pulled hundreds of zip-locks and trash bags from their cardboard packaging, then compressed and sealed them in small groups so they would take a minimum of space. Anything breakable (olive oil, salsa, Worcestershire sauce, tabasco) had to be bubble-wrapped. Each item was labeled and dated with waterproof marker before stowing it in a locker, where it might live underneath several layers of other goods.

I tried to organize items of the same type into the same locker, so that in case we lost track of our inventory list (I had zero expectation that Alan would bother checking things off) I could at least go to one spot on the boat to monitor a particular category of supplies. I contemplated weighty matters like whether cream of mushroom soup should be classified as soup or sauce; whether beans should be in with the canned vegetables; whether perhaps there should just be a whole separate locker for anything connected to Mexican food, rather than spreading salsa, tortillas, canned jalapenos, and enchilada sauce out all over the boat. Hmm. Hmm.

And where the heck was I going to put two hundred rolls of toilet paper? I flatly refused to take my chances on third-world toilet paper. After some reflection, I sealed each roll individually in a freezer-weight zip-lock before stuffing it in various nooks in deep stowage.

Twice a week or so I varied my program to drive to West Marine and buy them out of items such as waterproof flashlights, PFDs, foul weather gear, emergency signaling devices, varnishing supplies, courtesy flags, rustproof screws and washers and bolts and eyes, spare pumps and heat exchangers and solenoids and many other things that I had only the vaguest idea of why we needed them, except that they were on the lists that Alan and I had compiled from reading sailing books and how-to guides by the dozen for the past five years. At no time did I stop to reflect on how we self-proclaimed free spirits were proceeding to stockpile goods on an Armageddon scale.

I walked supermarket aisles in a daze, talking to myself: "Got that, got that, got that, got that . . . need that. Should I get some canned fruit cocktail? Will they have canned fruit cocktail in the South Pacific? In Australia?"

Mind you, I had never eaten canned fruit cocktail in my life – but maybe I would on the boat, you never knew. Maybe we would be down to fruit cocktail, and there would be nothing else. Hmm. Hmm. I shoveled six cans, my minimum provisioning unit, into the basket and moved forward eight inches, muttering, "Okay, dried fruit. How long does dried fruit keep?"

I remember the day I made it to the cleaning supplies aisle and almost broke down completely. I had failed to allocate space on the boat for cleaning supplies. Where on earth would I stow all that laundry detergent, bleach, liquid cleaners, foam cleaners? How could I protect the containers from leaking? After consulting several books on provisioning, I visited a pool supply store for large chlorine tablets, toxic to skin and lungs but far easier to store than liquid bleach.

Tobago, though, in the beautiful tropical southern Caribbean, was where I had the epiphany that food in some form would indeed be available planet-wide. We started shopping for dinner by hailing the local fishing fleet on their return to the island in the evenings. With less modern fishing gear than we carry in our aft lazarette, the Tobagans head out daily from their villages into the open ocean with handmade bamboo poles arched like spider legs over the sides of small wooden outboard boats. The sport-fishing industry would be horrified.

For about fifty cents a day, we would buy two healthy portions of cleaned, filleted, perfectly fresh wahoo, yellow-fin tuna, and various other scrumptious species whose names I do not know. I occasionally thought about dropping a line in the water, but I worried that I might catch something. We probably hold the all-time record for fewest fish caught during a sailing circumnavigation. But who needs to fish when the professionals deliver right to your boat?

Sunset after beautiful sunset in Tobago, a week passed. Then another, and another.

"Sweetheart," I climbed into the cockpit, where Alan was sitting in the shade rebuilding a spare winch.

"Yes?"

"If you feel like talking, I have a question."

"Shoot," he said, continuing to grease the inner assembly.

"I was thinking. The main part of hurricane season is almost over. We can start heading west to Panama in about six weeks."

"Right."

"We haven't seen Trinidad yet, or Venezuela – which we could easily do without crossing into the hurricane zone before the end of the season."

"True."

"How would you feel about making a move to Trinidad for a while? It's just an overnighter."

He leaned back against the cushion and looked over at the palm-fringed beige sand separated from us by fifty yards of cornelian blue water and backed by a slope of dense ferns and moss-covered trees, through which we had hacked a path for hiking and bird watching. Apart from the occasional sailboat seeking the same privacy as we were, we hadn't seen a soul other than local fishermen in a week.

"I'm pretty happy here."

"Me, too. But the thing is . . .." I hesitated.

"Yes?" he drawled again, meeting my eyes with a look that gave us both a smile. I moved over and stroked his bare shoulder while lifting my head to whisper in his ear.

"The thing is . . . I'm almost out of Diet Coke."

He guffawed. "How long can you hold out?"

"A day, maybe two."

It sounded like I was contemplating survival rations on a forced march.

He was still laughing. "I could hike to the road and catch the bus down to Scarborough again."

My hero had left before dawn a few days before for the ten-hour round trip on a bald-tired bus winding on unpaved roads through the mountains to score me some broccoli. He returned well after dark the proud owner of two scraggly heads, one of which turned out to house a cockroach the size of a hamster. We had been eating a lot of canned vegetables lately.

"Or," I said reasonably, "why go to all that trouble? We could weigh anchor and sail to Trinidad tonight. We have to go at some point – why not now?"

He sighed and then began to consider the upside. "Hmm. I understand they have electricity there."

"They do indeed. Also laundromats."

"We could spring for a marina slip and run the air conditioner."

"We could go out for pizza."

"I bet they deliver. Also, there'll be a lot of boats there. We could do a little information-gathering about the Panama Canal transit."

"And see if there's anything more about those piracy attacks off the mainland in Venezuela."

"OK." He set the winch aside. "Let's do it."

"Righty-ho. If we leave about midnight, we should arrive at the entrance channel with plenty of light. And that will put us into port well before dark."

"I'll get the check-list."

And without further ado, we prepared for an overnight passage.

Spontaneous departure decisions became our modus operandi for the duration of the trip. We never once left a port or bay because we affirmatively wanted to see the back of it. On the other hand, we never revisited The Schedule either. The impetus to move on would always spring from some provisioning or equipment necessity, or a weather condition, or sometimes because a nearby destination was a place we were itching to see. It sometimes arose strictly from the incipient change of a climate season that mandated our being in an entirely different part of the world, pronto. It's a good thing those external prods manifested themselves, too. Otherwise, we might never have made it past Grenada, much less Tobago, much less New Zealand. But I'm getting ahead of myself.

The overnight sail to Trinidad from Tobago was a glorious flying beam reach over smooth seas. We had to stand on the brakes to keep from arriving before dawn. And we knew we would not enter Trinidadian waters until then. We had started making a few hard-and-fast safety rules, most of which resulted from relatively cheap lessons in how to sail without actually sinking the boat or killing ourselves.

One lesson we learned from a near-tragedy was that we would never while underway – no matter how calm a day it might be – leave the cockpit without wearing an inflatable PFD vest and hanking said vest onto the safety lines that we always secured to the decks before departure. The worst nightmare that a sailor can contemplate is to wake up and realize that one's partner is no longer aboard. Where did he fall overboard? How long ago? It might have been five minutes; it might have been several hours. Retracing steps is almost certainly fruitless, although of course one would do it anyway, for hours and days. The current, the other hazards, sharks, an injury that causes immediate drowning – oh the list can go on and on and will torture one's soul. The only possible solution is prevention. Prevention means religious adherence to the procedure of always, always, always tethering oneself to the life lines while underway.

Another hard and fast rule was that we would never make landfall in the dark. Negotiating an unfamiliar port or anchorage is hard enough in the daylight. At night, it was impossible to tell whether a bright light was from a structure ashore or on the bow of a container ship leaving port and heading right at us. The Trinidad entrance waters were notorious for rock outcroppings, unmarked navigational hazards, and random currents. So our rule for entry by daylight was even more important here.

I got a little geek-thrill when we passed through the Dragon's Teeth referenced in the Hornblower novels. These very waters were the Caribbean grounds of 19th Century British Navy occupation, pirate holes, and sea battles. And also, as we neared Chaguaramas Bay, I hoped they would prove a reliable source of Diet Coke, and possibly even broccoli.

LETTER HOME
CrewsInn Marina
Chaguaramas Bay, Trinidad

Hi all,

What a place! We are in Trinidad, which is an island nation off the northeastern cost of Venezuela.

It won't surprise you to hear that Alan has been very busy. Apart from replacing chafed rigging lines, improving refrigeration and plumbing systems, and doing typical boat maintenance, the redhead rushes off in the dinghy to a medical emergency every couple of days. He has officially saved at least one life. There are two other doctors and an ER nurse among the sailors here, and we joke about setting up a call schedule.

Surprisingly, lawyers are less in demand.

Love, Liza

CHAPTER 7
TRINIDAD

Q: Do you ever get to meet local residents in the places you visit?

A: Yes! One of my favorite parts of this adventure is meeting folks and learning about their lives. People have been uniformly welcoming, helpful, and friendly. In return we share what we know. At a minimum, we try to be good guests.

As we were having lunch on the boat in Trinidad a week or so after our arrival there, the radio spluttered into life: "Mayday, Mayday, Mayday. This is Sadie on *Whisper*, at anchor in Chaguaramas Bay. I need a doctor. Someone fell off my mast. Please respond, over."

We broke into our emergency routine. I moved to the radio to respond to the Mayday call. Alan grabbed our large padded first-aid kit and his medical bag, threw them into the dinghy, and jumped in after them. In less than 20 seconds, he had started the outboard and was zipping across the bay.

Alan had been a family doctor in the Air Force for four years, and after completing his residency, became an anesthesiologist in private practice afterwards. Many people think anesthesiology involves putting patients to sleep. That's only part of it. The primary responsibilities are keeping patients alive during the controlled chaos of surgery and restoring them to consciousness afterwards. Accordingly, an anesthesiologist is a specialist in crisis management, emergency care, life support, human chemical response, and CPR. Alan loves medicine. He is a doctor down to the core of his being. This would be his third house call, or rather boat call, since our arrival in Trinidad.

Trinidad, we discovered, is a thriving, upwardly mobile island country with over a million people, about 40% of African descent, 40% from India, and 20% "other." The markets are fascinatingly ethnic, while the malls and supermarkets are familiarly American. In addition to its broad industrial base, Trinidad has developed a maritime reputation as a cost-effective venue for expert boat repair and maintenance.

And that is the basis of the real story here. In and around Chaguaramas Bay at any one time are about 3,000 sailboats from all over the world, some in the water, some "on the hard." This transient nautical city without a country has its own informal governing body, monthly news magazine, regular social and cultural events, and yes, a suburban gossip mill. (Of course, the guys call it "exchange of information" or "having a beer.")

There are some remarkable people here. Anchored near to us, for example, is an American woman who singlehandedly sailed her blind, dying husband through the Panama Canal because it was his lifelong dream. It was not unusual at all to meet people in their 80s who hopped nimbly from dinghy to dock, and hoisted sails and hauled anchors by hand. One female septuagenarian dynamo was a longtime singlehanded voyager, and we won't discuss the tender age of her current boyfriend/crew. My favorite, though, was the guy from North Carolina. He went out for a daysail one afternoon, decided to turn south for a while, and just kept going. That was eight years ago. He says his car is still in a parking lot on the North Carolina coast.

There were a number of circumnavigators in Trinidad while we were there, some who had done it single-handed. There were many families who sailed with and home-schooled their children. Many people were out sailing after a life-threatening wake-up call. Many, many people were seeing the world on a budget that wouldn't feed a small cat.

Within the context of this huge gathering of international sailors, we were humbled at our ordinariness. Even with 2,500 open-water miles under our belts, I felt like a cream-puff rookie in this crowd.

Every morning at 0800, Alan and I would take our coffee over to *Heartsong*'s nav station to listen to the Net, a moderated two-way radio forum for sailors' announcements, requests, barter, arrivals, departures, "health and welfare" checks, and whining. If you missed the Net, you were behind for the whole day – kind of like in the early 1990s if you went to work on Friday morning having missed Seinfeld the night before.

The Trinidad Net took place on VHF radio, as do similar voyager nets around the world. VHF radio is a short-distance radio based on line of sight. Its maximum range is about 20 miles or so. By law, every boat in the United States must have a VHF radio, and as a practical and safety matter, virtually every other boat in the world has one as well. Although nets and informal conversation take place on other channels, Channel 16 is the official hailing frequency worldwide.

It was over Channel 16 that the Mayday medical call from Sadie on *Whisper* had come.

When Alan arrived at *Whisper*, he found a man unconscious on his back, arched unnaturally over a closed hatch on the foredeck. The man's skin was pale blue, and he was in respiratory distress. The captain, Sadie, was trying to do CPR. Alan took over and cleared the airway. The man still wore a bosun's chair – a seat made of straps for hauling a person up the mast – and it was clear what had happened. He was a local resident working on Sadie's boat. She had been hauling him up the mast in a bosun's chair to examine the rigging. The chair was connected to the hauling line by a shackle, or clasp. The shackle had come undone. He hadn't tied a safety knot to double-attach himself to the hauling line. When the shackle separated, he plunged fifty feet from near the top of the mast down to the foredeck – the equivalent of falling off a four-story building onto his back.

Alan got on the radio and asked for a wide board or door to be sent out and when listening cruisers brought it, as we knew they would, Alan immobilized the local worker onto it with sheetlines and duct tape. With the help of several others in the anchorage, the man was taken ashore to a waiting ambulance. Alan went with him to the hospital. A few hours later the marina office called me on the radio to say I had a telephone call in the office. It was Alan, calling from the hospital's phone.

"Hi sweetheart, sorry that took so long."

"No problem. Is the guy OK?"

"He'll be fine. It's a good hospital. They've taken him into surgery, and there's nothing more I can do here.

"OK, see you in a bit."

"Uh, that's actually why I'm calling. I don't have any money to get home."

I laughed. He hadn't taken his wallet. I made a mental note to hide some American dollars in the first-aid kit.

"I'll grab a taxi and bring you some. Be there in a flash."

"Um, could you bring me some shoes?"

I made a mental note to throw in a pair of flip-flops as well.

The man turned out to have a serious head injury and a broken pelvis. It's a miracle he didn't have a broken neck. A few weeks later, he came hobbling on crutches down our dock with a big grin on his face and a bottle of excellent Chilean Chardonnay for Alan. It was the first of many such offerings all over the world – from fruit to rum to kava to coconut milk to live chickens, crabs, fish, and lobster; from home-cooked meals and coffee ceremonies to guided tours, boat work, and – among other voyagers – cakes and cookies and services in kind. Alan made it clear he would never accept any money, but we loved the gifts and the good will.

Whenever we would first arrive in a non-industrialized country, particularly in the more remote areas accessible only by sea, we would casually make it known during the customs clearance process that Alan was a medical doctor. We carried several large lockers full of non-narcotic medications and medical supplies, heavy on the antibiotics and tropical remedies. Valuable bookshelf space was devoted to medical tomes. In the Marquesas Islands, the redhead gave out antibiotic cream to mothers of children whose leg surfaces were all but covered by staph infections. We sat on well-swept earth floors while he offered prenatal advice through an interpreter. In Malaysia, he treated malaria and dengue fever; in Fiji broken ribs and internal injuries when a tourist was hit by a local speedboat. In Thailand, he saved the life of a small child with meningitis and of a teen-age victim of a motorcycle accident. He treated pink-eye and burns, seasickness and strained backs, broken limbs and rheumatism and cardiac arrest.

The most unusual "clinic" happened on a small island in an Islamic archipelago in the Indian Ocean several years after we left Trinidad. But more about that later.

Of course, every time Alan got a call in a matter of life and death, the lawyer in me cringed for fear of a potential lawsuit. But we had no problems at all. In fact, people from countries other than the United States appear to be amused by our litigious nature and its corollary, the ever-present fear of being sued. The word "amused" may be understatement. In truth they find it ridiculous and tend to laugh long and heartily at our expense. People all over the world never seem to tire of rehashing the bizarre American lawsuits that make the international news, such as the huge award against McDonald's for hot coffee in the lap. As an American, and particularly as an American lawyer, I shrug it off. Throughout the trip, the attitude toward us as traveling Americans was overwhelmingly warm and friendly, even for the most part in Southeast Asia and the Middle East. More about that later as well. For now, I will just mention that when we did get to know someone well enough to inspire his or her confidence — and it happened regularly as we lingered in some places for weeks and months — we found a rare opportunity to hold a mirror to our own country and culture, to discover how we are viewed from the outside by our counterpart individuals.

On a related note, we were cognizant of our position as ambassadors on the ground. Indeed, on remote islands we sometimes found ourselves in the position of being the only Americans a person had ever met. On passage to a new country, we would always learn the basic dozen or so polite words of the language. We would consult our research on not only entry requirements and other legal matters, but also on cultural recommendations. For example, we read on the overnighter from Malaysia to

Phuket that in Thailand it is considered rude to sit with the soles of the feet facing another person or to touch another's head. Believe it or not, those issues came up on a regular basis during the two months we were in Phuket, as we sat on the floor in people's homes and kidded around with workers every day at the marina. Other examples are many. In Greece, the classic American "OK" hand sign is quite rude; they use a thumbs-up to express the same thought. In New Zealand the word "fanny" is obscene, and we had to train ourselves to say "bum bag" instead of "fanny pack."

In the Kingdom of Tonga, it is inappropriate to say "no" outright. In the smaller non-touristed towns of central Turkey, Alan had to be careful not to make eye contact with young women. In Australia, our American cruiser friend Randy actually had to change his name. Whenever he said "Hi, I'm Randy," the Aussie crowd invariably melted down in fits of laughter.

On the subject of international relations, we took all questions and asked many of our own. We learned that the people we tended to meet would, as a matter of course, distinguish the actions of government from the beliefs and preferences of the people they govern. In other words, as individual travelers we neither benefitted from nor were held responsible for two hundred years of American foreign policy.

I received the great gift of learning to mature as a citizen. I learned to view my own country with new eyes, much as a post-adolescent might come to view and appreciate a parent as a fellow adult – fallible, sometimes transcendently right and sometimes dead wrong, but loved and respected nonetheless. For all of its faults, America is amazing — inclusive and tolerant like no other, generous and innovative and vital. And when I say "for all of its faults," I say it with the understanding that my definition of "fault" is another American's definition of "strength." May it ever be so.

Beyond all else, we are wealthy — wealthy beyond belief. There is poverty and ignorance in America, and it is shamefully inexcusable, but the poor and ignorant in much of the rest of the world die from it, early and in large numbers. I have little patience these days with my fellow citizens who wail about economic downturns and diminishing opportunity. Compared to what? Sometimes we sound like kids worried there aren't quite as many presents under the tree this year as last. Most everywhere else, people are lotto-winning lucky just to have the tree. Six months in any other industrialized country in the world will convince you that America is to be cherished and appreciated and nourished for the wonder that it is. Six months in the third world will have you kissing the ground at the happenstance of your birthplace.

End of rant.

LETTER HOME
ST. VINCENT & THE GRENADINES

Hi all,

We are spending a few weeks gunkholing in the Grenadines. Right now, we are anchored at the Tobago Cays, a shallow sandy-bottomed spot in the middle of steep drop-offs, with no land whatsoever in sight. It's like being anchored in the middle of the ocean. The only people for miles are the ones on boats, and all that is between us and Africa are the Atlantic and an underwater coral barrier reef.

We snorkeled today until Alan's sun-exposed back was more colorful than the fish. Vendors in small motorboats come each day from the closest inhabited island to sell lobster, fish, and produce. In a desperate bid for salad, I bought four tomatoes at US$1 each. I won't even tell you what they wanted for the lettuce. We spent some time in Bequia as well, at a sheltered anchorage crowded with boats from all over the world, from mega-yachts to rustbuckets that look like the smallest gust of wind will topple them over and sink them to the bottom.

Bequia (pronounced by the locals as BEK-way) is a populous and charming island with miles of beaches, simple open-air restaurants, and a laid-back Caribbean atmosphere. This is the island, you may recall, where the American yachtie couple were accused of gunning down a local water taxi driver and held in jail in St. Vincent for about a year without trial, then released for lack of evidence. We were a little nervous about staying here, but we had no problems and would recommend the island as a cruising destination.

Mustique, in contrast, was like one big expensive resort – manicured beaches and gardens, country club homes, and little shops that carry Tommy Hilfiger and DKNY. We didn't run into Mick Jagger or Princess Margaret, but their vacation homes are very nice.

Love, Liza

CHAPTER 8
VENEZUELA TO PANAMA

Q: *I have asked around amongst my boatie friends, and they don't know either: What is "gunkholing"? I see that word often in American magazines, but it is not used here in Australia.*

A: I've never heard an actual definition of this word, so I'm basically making this one up: Gunkholing is sailing in fine weather a very short distance among multiple lovely anchorages in a relatively small geographic area. Liberal ingestion of tasty alcoholic beverages and good food is implied. Much recreation and enjoyment of sun, sea, and sand is similarly assumed, and boat work is strictly forbidden.

Looking at the water, I could see eight distinct shades of turquoise. No, nine. We were at anchor in the reef-encircled bay of an island smaller than a typical Wal-Mart, about 85 nautical miles north of Venezuela and at least 20 miles from anything else. The island is Isla Sur, and it is in the Las Aves island group.

I saw white-caps on the reef and a thick copse of mangroves above a tiny beach – no other boats, no other people. The cumulus clouds were not white; they were pastel green – a trick of light, I suppose, reflecting the clear, shallow Caribbean below. I had never seen green clouds before. The color reminded me of sherbet. It is astonishingly tranquil.

This isolation was welcome after Trinidad's Carnival frenzy and a week on the hard doing pre-passage boat maintenance and repainting *Heartsong*'s hull with anti-fouling paint. We had done a lot of sailing the prior month as well – from Chaguaramas to the abandoned leper colony at Chacachacare, north to gunkhole St. Vincent and the Grenadines, back to Trinidad, then westward to the Venezuelan resort island of Margarita, on to the Venezuelan marine park of Los Roques, and finally to the very remote Las Aves – about 600 miles all told.

I was happy to be at anchor for a few days. All I could hear were rhythmic surf, screeching sea birds, and a familiar baritone cursing mildly in the vicinity of the forward bilge pump.

A splash told me that Alan had either completed the pump maintenance or abandoned it entirely, and had proceeded with a swim. I settled into my book.

"Hey!" the redhead called from the stern.

"Hey what. I'm busy," I responded from the cockpit.

"No, you should see this."

"Okeydoke." I carefully dog-eared my book, stepped across the coaming, and padded quickly to the aft deck on my toes. Ouch, hot hot hot. I was again happy that we had declined to have teak decks. Even the white fiberglass was plenty warm in the direct tropical sun.

Alan had hoisted himself from the water onto the stern steps via the stainless steel swim ladder, an ingenious device that telescoped up to fit into the steps when we were underway. He was holding an immense conch shell.

"Look what I found." He was gleeful. "The bottom is full of 'em. And they are inhabited. We can have conch stew for a week."

"Do you know how to get the conch out of the shell?" I asked with some trepidation, not least because I was not sure I wanted to eat conch stew at all, much less for a week.

"How hard can it be?"

Half an hour later, he grumbled his way belowdecks to consult various cruising books and how-tos. I contemplated accidentally knocking the poor thing back into the water, but I wasn't quick enough. Alan re-emerged with a collection of knives, rags, and household tools. But no amount of strategy, guile, or brute force would separate that overgrown snail from its shell. Casualties included one screwdriver (dropped overboard), two scratches in the stern paint (from a skidding conch shell), a large gouge in the teak steps (from a misdirected hammer blow), and Alan's pride. He admitted defeat.

We stood on the aft deck and gave the conch its freedom in the manner a Roman emperor might have done for a particularly valiant gladiator. We salute you, intrepid conch. I did a couple of verses of "I fought the conch and the . . . conch won."

Afterwards, I slid into the ocean and floated on my back for a serene half hour. The clouds were still green.

* * *

A few days later, it was time to haul anchor and continue heading west. We hit Bonaire (an underwater Disney World) and Aruba (a salsa-dancing Vegas-by-the-Sea); and then set sail for the multi-day passage from Aruba to the Panama Canal, the transit of which would be one of the Big Events of the circumnavigation.

The passage from Aruba to Panama was a busy one. I am pleased and somewhat embarrassed to say that by this time, I had honed my radio voice until it was sort of a cross between an airline pilot drawl and Jessica Rabbit. My success in getting the big boys to answer me had improved dramatically. I loved my conversations with freighter watchkeepers, especially on night watch when there was time to chat. They would, in exotic accents, tell me about the ship and its cargo; about their homes that they missed; about their sense of the majesty and loneliness of the ocean; about dreams of owning their own boat and setting off to sea. I would in my turn answer what was always their first question: What is it like to live in America? And I could take to the bank what question would arise when I said I was from Dallas: Did I know J.R.?

But wow there was a lot of traffic on this leg of the trip. The underwater shelf jutting from the northern coasts of Venezuela and Colombia is a natural condition that sometimes creates giant seas. Vessels in the southern Caribbean thus tend to pass north of those waters on passage east and west. The preferred route is a compromise between giving that alley a decent berth while still navigating as directly as possible to the Canal. So vessels going to and coming from Panama are compressed into a relatively small sea area, especially as one gets closer to Panamanian waters.

During the daytime, I would glance up from my book, eyeball each of the closest supertankers' courses, give one or more a quick radio call, make an adjustment if necessary, and go back to my book. At night, it was actually easier, believe it or not. The navigational light configurations, which I had obsessively memorized while in Florida, made it quicker to determine the direction of each vessel. Red lights are displayed on the port side of a ship. So if I look directly ahead and see a red sidelight, I know I am seeing the ship's port side, and the ship is therefore moving across my bow from right to left. If I see a green light directly ahead, I am seeing the starboard sidelight, and the ship is heading left to right. And so on.

At one point on the passage, I counted ten of those commercial behemoths within line-of-sight, at various points of the compass. I felt like a Pomeranian being walked with a pack of Great Danes.

The log tells me that our route from Aruba was 697.6 sea miles, which took us 92 hours, or just under four days. Our average speed was 7.6 knots. Our high speed of 10.2 knots occurred on a broad reach, with 20 knots of apparent wind and four- to six-foot seas. In short, it was for the most part a fast, fun ride.

For about eight daylight hours during the passage, however, we experienced an ocean phenomenon that in the entire 37,000-mile trip we were never to see again. The waves came directly from our stern and were at least 25 feet high – a classic following sea, but on steroids. The ocean could not have entertained me more had it been tap-dancing.

From my perch on the cockpit coaming (safely hanked onto the lifelines) facing aft, I watched each approaching wave like a rat mesmerized by a cobra. On about a 90-second cycle, each roller would build from eye level to the Great Wall of China. Its crest would tease white and boiling – surely this wave would be the one . . . that . . . would break . . . and swamp us . . . but no. By some miracle, each wave would roll beneath our stern and lift the boat to a cartoon height on a cartoon pillar of water. From that mountain I would scan the horizon for traffic. Then I would turn my rat focus aft to the approach of the next cobra. And so went my entire watch. In the troughs, I would look up and see nothing but cauldrons and cliffs of blue water to the sides, and blue sky above.

* * *

The morning of a blustery Wednesday in March, we reached the breakwater of the Panama Canal Zone. Entering, we called the harbor master on Channel 16, and he cleared us to proceed to anchorage area "F." We obediently dropped the hook there and set about our usual post-passage task checklist and clean-up.

I looked around. It was a crowded nautical parking lot, thick with sailboats, motoryachts, freighters, and container ships of all sizes and states of repair, all waiting for transit. I mentally pinched myself. This was the Panama Canal!

While rolling up the safety lines and wiping the corrosive salt off the stanchions, I began daydreaming. This is the point of no return. Inner squeal. Once we transit the Canal, we will stop for a few days on the Pacific side of Panama to do some final provisioning and pick up our mail. Then we'll depart across the Pacific Ocean for the Galapagos Islands and then on to French Polynesia. Inner squeal.

I helped Alan lift the dinghy from the deck and heave it across the lifelines into the water alongside. Our inflatable dinghy is our only means of transportation when at anchor. If the boat is our house, then the dinghy is our car. We usually keep it in the water when at anchor, and we often drag it along behind the boat on daysails. However, we have heard too many stories of storms and high seas sinking a towed dinghy in open water, so during passages we always haul it aboard, deflate it, and lash it to the deck. One of the first items on our post-passage checklist is to put the dinghy back in the water, so we can have transportation immediately if we need it.

After tossing the dinghy into the water, Alan went below to change into clean, shore-going clothes to check in with customs. I moved to tie the dinghy to the stern handrails. Next on the checklist would be for me to open the aft lazarette and pull out the air pump to reinflate the dinghy. Instead, I stood and stared and resumed my Pacific daydream.

Alan emerged from the companionway and stepped out onto the deck in long khaki shorts, a collared polo short with our *Heartsong* logo, new Teva sandals, and clean shiny hair. He was possibly even wearing deodorant, he looked that good. He had our boat papers in a waterproof bag and was ready to go ashore to make obeisance to the local authorities.

He strolled aft. "Uh . . . where's the dinghy?"

I looked up. Whether I had absent-mindedly failed to tie a proper bowline, or whether some diabolical force had intervened (okay, it was probably the former), the dink had slipped its tether and made a break for freedom. The current being strong here in the direction of the Canal, the poor thing had already tottered along for ten or fifteen yards on its pathetically deflated little pontoons that I had not yet gotten around to pumping up.

With a sigh, Alan tossed the boat papers back into the cockpit and started climbing over the lifelines to jump in.

"No, wait!" I yelled.

"What?" He looked over at me, hopeful that perhaps I had an alternative solution to a swim in this very murky water.

"You've got clean clothes on."

"Oh, right." He stripped off the shorts and shirt and stood on alternate feet to take off the Tevas. He dived into the water, swam to the dink, and hoisted himself inside. I stood there, hands clasped to chest, thinking "my hero."

It was only then that both of us realized that the dinghy had not yet been re-equipped with oars, lines, air pump, or anything else. My poor redhead was sitting in an empty dink, partially submerged and now at least fifty yards away, with no means whatsoever of getting it back to the boat.

Moreover, he was not only stranded and sinking, he was also – due to his preference for going commando – stark naked and moving at a steady 1.5 knots towards the entrance to the Panama Canal.

I did the only thing I could think of to do. I sat down on the stern steps and started laughing my fool head off.

From across the water, Alan glared at me for a while before he saw the humor and launched a grin. He continued to float helplessly towards the Canal entrance. By that time, of course, an audience had formed on the decks of the surrounding boats and ships. They began applauding appreciatively.

Alan stood and took a bow.

The crowd went wild.

I stopped giggling long enough to hail our next-door neighbor, a large, very posh French motoryacht, whose captain fired up his dinghy, swooshed over to Alan, and tossed him a line, which Alan secured to the dinghy's bow. Being a good citizen of the high seas, the captain was happy to help. Being French, however, he didn't deliver Alan back to our boat until he had towed him on a victory lap (pun intended) through the cheering anchorage.

Alan sat tall and practiced his royal wave.

* * *

Late that night we were awakened by shouting on a neighboring sailboat. We dressed quickly and ran out on deck, expecting that someone (maybe us) had dragged anchor, or that there had been a collision.

Instead, it was a shouting match, which then turned into a fist-fight – between the (presumably) husband and wife on a 48-foot sailboat about 20 yards away. Since the wife was about twice the husband's size, we weren't concerned for anyone's safety, and we stood there horrified and, I will admit it, somewhat enthralled. It was a Three Stooges fight, each of them throwing punches and missing, falling down while trying to dodge a fist, raring back and screaming with anger. At one point, she actually put her hand on his forehead and held him off while he flailed out of range of her torso. I had started thinking we should just slink back down to our cabin and put in earplugs when she picked up a dinghy oar, took a full swing, and bashed him in the head.

"Hey!" Alan roared. "You stop that, or I'll call the port authority."

I picked up our spotlight and shone it full on them.

They reacted like vampires caught in a sunrise – hand over eyes, hissing. And then they turned and went belowdecks. We switched off the spotlight and looked at each other, eyes wide and eyebrows raised. Wow.

The next morning, there they were in their dinghy, rapping on our hull near the stern steps.

Alan climbed over the coaming, walked aft, and said "Can I help you?" in that specific tone of voice that really means "go away."

The man squinted up. He was thin and pale, with a sparse gray-blonde goatee and mustache.

"I'm George, and this is my wife Tammy. Our boat is *Stunner*. I wonder if you could do us a favor?" he asked.

His wife smiled engagingly. She looked to be about five-ten and 280. Her graying hair was up in a bun on top of her head, and she had on a long flowery skirt and tank top.

"Would you crew for us through the Canal?" he continued. "We have an appointment to transit in the morning. My brothers were supposed to crew, but they haven't gotten here yet, and we don't want to lose our slot. We have one guy, but we need one more."

No apology. No explanation. No nothing. Every fiber of my being was sending telepathic messages to Alan: Say no, say no, say no.

"Sure, of course – glad to do it."

Sigh.

Okay – great, thanks. Please be on board at 6:30. We're meeting our pilot at 7:00. He says we can probably get through in a day, but there's a chance we might have to spend the night on the lake, so . . ..

"No problem. I'll come prepared."

With a "thanks again," they motored off.

"Prepared for what?" I said when they were out of hearing range. "Refereeing? Self-defense? Why on earth would you say yes?"

"For the experience. It will be good to go through the Canal with somebody else before we do it ourselves. Anyway, they were probably just having a bad night. It'll be fine."

"Experience," I muttered darkly as I set about polishing stainless. "Hmmph."

It was actually standard practice to "crew one before you do one." Going through the Panama Canal in a small sailboat, as opposed to a cruise ship, mega-yacht, or tanker, is difficult. It takes a combination of nautical skill and knowledge of the hazards. It requires at least four people on board, plus a local pilot.

The year we went through the Canal there had been a fair few accidents and some significant damage to sailboats. Some of those incidents may have been connected to the Canal's transition from not-for-profit status to a Panamanian profit-oriented enterprise. Canal pilots and advisors admit to a work "slowdown" in their effort to secure, among other things, overtime wages for a portion of the Canal's grueling round-the-clock schedule. The overall Canal work force and wage scale had been reduced by failing to replace retirees and by requiring remaining workers to work longer hours for the same pay.

But even in a good year, it's best practices to learn the ropes beforehand. Both Alan and I did a stint as crew prior to our own transit. I signed on as a line handler on a friend's 43-footer. As fate would have it, we were involved in a significant accident in one of the locks. In the final moments before lockdown in the Miraflores locks, a visibly indifferent Canal worker failed to secure a crucial stern line ashore. As a result, wind and lock turbulence forced the stern to pivot rapidly to port. In a sickening crash, the boat collided stern-to with the rough and jagged lock wall. Line tension then forced the Canal worker to release his line into the water. Almost instantly, it fouled the boat's propeller and rendered the engine useless to move the boat clear.

Grabbing snorkel gear, my friend, who was the captain of the vessel, went over the side. The water began to churn as a large commercial vessel entered the lock chamber astern. I grabbed a free line and rigged a safety harness to protect him from being swept away by the current. At substantial risk to himself, the captain was able to cut the line, free the propeller, and return safely aboard before lockdown was complete. We maneuvered the boat out of danger. Only by luck and decisive action did the incident end without anyone being injured.

On Alan's initial crewing venture, he got back to *Heartsong III* two days after he departed.

"How did it go on *Stunner*?" I asked.

"Those poor people are going to sink that boat someday," he shook his head.

"Why do you say that?"

"Their boat is a mess, and they squabble constantly. Have I mentioned how much I appreciate you?"

"Yeah, whatever. But I don't see how being messy is going to sink them."

I was a little defensive on that score. Alan is meticulous with regard to equipment maintenance and detail-cleaning. If he is ever your anesthesiologist, you will appreciate those character traits. I, however, have had to up my game substantially to meet even his minimum standards. He still tells the tale of how when I was in law school in Austin and renting a small apartment there while he stayed in Dallas to work, he had to drive down twice a month to do a heaping sink's worth of dishes and take out the trash, or else the landlord might have a code compliance problem.

On a boat, adjustments must be made. The space is way too small and the environment is way too demanding not to have a concerted approach on the major issues. On the particular topic of cleaning and maintenance, I didn't even try to argue the superiority of my innate slobbery. Lawyers know when they don't have a leg to stand on. I took one look at his work area and one look at mine, and realized that the best I could hope for was an early settlement. From the get-go, I knew I would have to step it up in the neat-and-clean department, or he would be miserable the whole trip. Generally speaking and in the main, without prejudice to actual data (mileage may vary), I had succeeded in that effort.

"They can't find anything, and when they do find it, it has to be cleaned or repaired before they can use it. And they would rather stand there and yell at each other than get anything done. I slept on deck to get away from it. Hoo boy. What a nightmare. And then we lost the front crank shaft pulley and had to be towed."

"Well, thank you for doing that." I nodded as if I had a clue what a front crank shaft pulley was. "Are you ready for me to request a transit time?"

"Not yet. We should go through as crew a couple of more times, just to be sure we know what we're doing.

"Okay. Let's keep good notes. I'll write it all up as a how-to for a sailing mag. Maybe it will help somebody else."

CHAPTER 9

THE PANAMA CANAL

(excerpted from my article "Toward Safer Transit of
the Panama Canal,"
published in *Ocean Navigator* Magazine)

The Panama Canal is approximately 45 miles long. That's a l-o-o-o-n-g way in a sailboat. To transit from the Caribbean Sea to the Pacific Ocean, each boat is raised 85 vertical feet in the three Gatun Locks. The boat then crosses Gatun Lake for 21 miles to enter the Pedro Miguel Lock. At Pedro Miguel, the yacht descends 31 feet to traverse the mile-wide Miraflores Lake. Beyond the lake at the Miraflores Locks, the boat is lowered in two stages to the Pacific. All told there are six locks, three up and three down.

Most ocean-going sailing vessels make the trip in one 10- to 13-hour day. In our case, the canal pilot boarded our boat in the Cristobal anchorage just before 0500 hours. By 1600, we were moored at the Balboa Yacht Club on the other side. Because of late departure or slow speed in Gatun Lake, some boats must stop for the night in the lake's Gamboa anchorage and resume transit the next day.

There are three methods of transiting the Panama Canal: (1) center chamber, (2) alongside a tug, and (3) alongside the lock wall. The voyager is asked to designate methods, in order of preference, when he or she initially applies for transit.

Method number three is for large vessels only. Serious damage to hull or rigging is virtually certain for small yachts tied alongside the rough, uneven concrete walls. As a result, only the first two methods are viable for boats such as ours.

Lying alongside a tug, which is itself secured to the lock wall, is arguably the easiest method of all. That method, however, is "subject to availability" and only rarely available to sailing vessels under 65 feet. It cannot be chosen to the exclusion of other methods. Therefore, as emphasized in the rules, each small boat must be prepared to transit via center chamber.

In the center chamber method, the crew members station themselves two forward and two on the port and starboard aft-most corners of the vessel. Each crew member tosses a very long line — forward port and starboard, and aft port and starboard — to workers on either side of the lock chamber. The workers secure the lines on bollards at the top of the lock walls, and the boat is suspended in the center of the chamber, which is about 100 feet across. The yacht's crew is then responsible for maintaining the vessel in the center of the chamber by keeping equal tension on all four lines. The lines are sometimes parallel to the water and sometimes almost perpendicular to it, depending on the lock and the circumstances.

As the chamber fills or empties, the forces on those lines are intense and capricious. If anything goes wrong, only the skilled use of cleats and winches, sometimes in combination with engine maneuvering, can counteract the pressure. Moreover, those measures succeed only if there is enough time to react.

Although it is possible to transit alone via center chamber, recent Canal economics dictate that a small sailing vessel be rafted with one or two others in each lock. That is, the boats pull up alongside each other, and each boat ties itself to the one next to it. In a three-vessel raft, the outermost boats are responsible for line-handling. The center boat, usually chosen as the one with the most powerful engine, is in charge of maneuvering under power.

In situations where only two yachts are rafted together, each will have line-handling responsibilities, and each will handle some of the power maneuvering. In both scenarios, the boats are inter-dependent for safe passage. In almost all cases, a yacht or raft will share the lock chamber by being in front or behind a large commercial vessel, such as a cruise liner, tanker, or container ship.

Whether transiting alone or rafted, several issues are crucial to success: proper lines, good line-handlers, a reliable engine, strong deck cleats, adequate fenders, good communication among captains before and during the transit, and an understanding of the role of the pilot aboard each vessel.

More than any other consideration, having proper lines can make or break a transit. Under Canal rules, each boat must have four nylon lines at least 125 feet long. Each line should be of one piece and not spliced or knotted together. The landward ends must have a very large loop, spliced or knotted, for the lock bollards ashore.

As to line diameter there is no firm rule. The Canal Commission recommends 7/8-inch line for all small vessels. Recommendations by others range from 3/4-inch line for the smallest yachts to 1-inch line for 65-footers. For our 55-foot, 26-ton vessel, the 7/8-inch line was exactly right.

One need not be fully equipped before arrival in Panama. The Panama Canal Yacht Club (PCYC) rents proper line by the day. Spools of 600 feet of line are available wholesale in Panama City and Colon's Free Zone. Alternatively, four lengths may usually be bought from previous passage-makers. The morning PCYC net on VHF channel 72 at 0730 local time is a valuable resource for locating line and other equipment.

We did what many people do and went in on a spool with another voyager, and then divided it into two lengths of 300-foot line. During the transit, we cleated the centers of each length, one forward and one aft, so that the required 125 feet of line was available port and starboard. And at completion of the transit, we and our spool-partners each had 300 feet of good spare anchor rode.

What is amazing to me is how many voyagers try to fudge the line requirement. The Canal officials don't really check the length or quality of each boat's lines prior to transit. In our first week in Colon, a yacht was damaged when a chafed, knotted line broke under the extreme pressure of the backwash from the propeller of the container ship in the same lock. The boat had been slated for the center raft slot, and its owner had gambled that lock lines would not be needed. When re-scheduled at the last minute to transit alone, the boat was unprepared.

Canal line requirements are not overstated. Each vessel really needs the minimum length required. I witnessed an otherwise superbly equipped yacht suffer a near miss at a lock accident when one of its lines was only about 15 feet short.

Under the rules, each boat must have four line-handlers in addition to the boat's captain and the Canal-supplied pilot. In other words, the minimum number of people on a boat in the Canal is six, including the pilot. If volunteer crew is not available, one may hire line-handlers at the yacht clubs on either side of the Canal. The going rate was $50-$75 per day when we went through. On a two-day transit, voyagers must be prepared to put everyone up for the night except the pilot, who disembarks upon anchoring. In addition, all hands must be fed and watered at the appropriate times.

The evening before transit, line-handlers should be rounded up and schooled. Some voyagers ask that line-handlers spend the night before transit aboard, as passages often begin in the pre-dawn hours. In any event, first-timers should be instructed in what to expect.

The basic tenets of line-handling bear mentioning. Always keep one's line at least partially secured around a cleat, even if the line is slack. The goal is to keep the boat or raft in the very center of the lock chamber. If unable to cleat off a line because of line pressure, stand on the line outboard of the cleat and get help immediately. Wear gloves; bring rain gear and a good pocketknife. Strength is not as important in a line-handler as concentration and willingness to work consistently throughout the day.

The day before transit, the scheduling office is able to tell each voyager his or her schedule and mode of transit. Do not hesitate to make several calls to confirm and double-check. Important questions to ask at that time are (1) when one's pilot will come aboard; (2) the time one is scheduled in the first lock; (3) whether transit will be alone or rafted; and (4) if rafted, the names of the other boats and one's assigned position in the raft. This information will give the voyager an idea whether transit will likely take one day or two. More importantly, it will also allow him or her to contact the other boats in the raft.

Getting to know the other voyagers in your raft can make the difference between a successful trip and a day best forgotten. The evening before our transit, we headed to the PCYC bar with the other crews scheduled to transit with us.

The first order of business was agreeing on the proper way to raft. The outer boats would approach and offer bow and stern lines to the central boat. They would then accept spring lines from the central boat after bow and stern were secured. Great care would be exercised to stagger the masts so that when the boats rolled in a swell, the spreaders and masts would not make contact. We confirmed that each boat had solid cleats and adequate lines and fenders. We agreed that the central boat's captain would command the raft. Most importantly, we established a rapport that enabled excellent communication on the day.

As it happened, one of the boats in our raft was re-scheduled at the last minute for later in the day. The two remaining yachts rafted up before dawn on a moonless night in a narrow channel with a good chop and the occasional tugboat wake. Our preparation, combined with the flexibility of good communication, paid off in spades.

Before leaving the subject of communication, a word or two about language is in order. Cruising is an international pastime. Most voyagers, including myself, value it in part for its diversity. Diversity of language can be a problem, however, when good verbal communication is critical to safety.

The Canal Commission states formally that the language of the Canal is English. In practice, however, the primary spoken language is Spanish. About half of the pilots we met understood very little English indeed, and most spoke to each other in Spanish solamente. One raft on which I served as line-handler was comprised of an American boat, a French boat, and a Venezuelan boat with two German line-handlers. Faced with multiple language barriers, the captains had so much difficulty rafting that the raft missed its lock time. During the process, as the boats rolled from a large wake, an outer boat sustained damage to its spreader and radar antenna from the central boat's mast. International cruising relations were set back a decade.

For these reasons, it behooves the English-speaking voyager to learn a few critical words and phrases in Spanish, and preferably in another of the primary cruising languages, before transit. Suggestions include the following: line, slacken, tighten, forward, aft, port, starboard, bow, stern, amidship, spring, raft, cleat, secure, release, engine, reverse, neutral, slower, faster, right rudder, left rudder, please, thank you, and "heads up."

In the Canal, a boat's engine gets a hearty workout. Under the rules, each boat must be able to sustain a speed of five knots under all conditions, or else must contract with a tug to be towed. Before transit, a voyager should check out the engine carefully and should be certain that the boat has enough fuel for a full day's motoring.

Some of the most harrowing experiences in the Canal come from engine failure at a pivotal moment. For example, the center boat of a raft on which my husband was line-handling lost its engine in the final lock of its transit from Caribbean to Pacific. That chamber, the second of the Miraflores Locks, is extremely turbulent because of the co-mingling of Pacific and fresh water. The turbulence in this case was exacerbated by the wash of a freighter briskly entering the same chamber astern. As the raft's lines were being secured to the wall, the center boat was forced to shift rapidly between forward and reverse to avoid being pushed into the forward lock doors or sucked back into the freighter. Unbeknownst to anyone, the propeller shaft coupling came apart.

When locking was complete and the forward doors opened, the captain of the center boat powered up. He immediately knew something was amiss with the engine, but was puzzled because the raft appeared to be making way at a good clip. In the nick of time, he realized that what was propelling the raft forward was not his engine but the bow wash from the freighter astern. The freighter was approaching fast, and he had no power to maneuver.

Good communication brought the outer boats' engines to the rescue. Only after separating from the raft at the end of the day, however, did the center boat's captain comprehend the full extent of his engine failure. Fortunately, he and his crew had the superb seamanship to set sail in a crowded shipping channel at dusk and to sail onto their anchor after dark in a 20-knot wind.

In another incident, a boat's front crank shaft pulley came off completely as it left the Gatun Locks. The boat sailed across Gatun Lake, then rafted with another boat that towed it to Gamboa anchorage. The crew jury-rigged a garden hose from the deck wash-down pump to the engine, forcing cool water through the heat exchanger. The pulley was bolted on temporarily to run the fresh-water pump. Their only immediate consequence was an extra day of transit. Without knowledgeable crew, they might have also been out a substantial tug fee.

Under the Canal rules, each boat that is underway must maintain its engine running while in the Canal, even if under sail between locks. No boat should attempt transit with an engine known to be infirm.

After proper lines and a healthy engine, the next most important equipment for transit is a sufficient number of strong deck cleats. The rules of the Canal nominally require ship-sized bollards and enclosed chocks for transit. Those rules are waived for smaller yachts, though a notation appears on one's paper work that one's cleats are "substandard."

Ideally, cleats should be through-bolted with backing plates. One voyager, in the usual transit post-mortem, told of his trials in the last lock. One minute, he was looking down at his cleat; the next minute it was gone. It happened so quickly that nobody saw it rip out of the deck and catapult off the boat. The pressure on nearly vertical lines had taken its toll. Every voyager should have a back-up plan, such as employing the windlass and other winches, in the event one or more cleats prove ineffective on the day.

Fenders to protect one's hull during Canal transit are free and easy to obtain in Panama. A good supply of old tires is usually present at or near the yacht clubs on either side. Like most cruisers, we wrapped our tires in garbage bags and duct tape to protect the hull from oil and rubber marks. For further protection, we secured some old carpeting and lashed it to the lifelines beneath the tires.

Most voyagers do not think to protect the bow and stern. I did only because I had witnessed the stern-to accident discussed herein. A couple of tires hung over the stern transom and across the anchors are a prudent precaution.

One of the questions a voyager is asked during the paper-work phase of transit is the value of his or her boat. Only boats valued at more than one million dollars or longer than 65 feet overall will be assigned an experienced Canal pilot. All others receive a pilot in training, called an advisor.

Advisors vary in experience, dedication, seamanship, and communication skills. Technically, the advisor is in charge of the transit. He keeps the yacht on schedule and coordinates with all other boats and ships nearby. The captain who disobeys his or her advisor is subject to a fine or, in extreme cases, denial of transit. The advisor has the power to turn the boat around and go home.

On the other hand, an advisor is not responsible to the boat owner for any damage or injury that may occur.

Before transit, each voyager is required to sign a very broad release absolving the Canal Commission and all of its employees from any liability whatsoever in the event of an accident that results in damage under $1 million. Virtually all small vessels, therefore, would have no recourse against a negligent advisor.

For that reason, the relationship between captain and advisor is a tricky one. The advisor has all the official authority and no responsibility. The captain has all the responsibility but no official authority. For our transit, we were fortunate enough to have an excellent advisor. Others with whom we transited as line-handlers were not so lucky.

For example, one boat suffered serious damage because of an advisor's direct command. A three-boat raft on which my husband was line-handling left the Gatun Locks, still making about four knots of speed. The advisor on the starboard outside boat decided the time was right to separate the raft. With no warning and no coordination with the raft, the advisor ordered the crew at the bow of his boat to release the bow lines. They did. All other lines were still in place as the raft's speed forced the starboard boat's bow to turn outward. Unfortunately, the boat's helm was over to starboard as well. Even more unfortunately, one of the raft's spring lines had been secured inside the starboard boat's stanchions and lifelines. The raft, in increasing chaos, continued to make substantial headway.

As the starboard boat began peeling off in earnest, the spring line began popping stanchions one by one out of the deck, right down the line. A fast-thinking line-handler on the center boat grabbed a knife and cut the spring. Then as the starboard boat pivoted violently, in danger of ramming the central boat with its stern, the line-handler cut the stern line as well.

This accident, like most, was caused by a combination of mistakes and misfortunes. The precipitating factor was, however, an advisor's ill-considered command.

Multiple transits have taught some hard lessons. In matters related directly to safe boat-handling, captain and crew must not abdicate their usual responsibilities in reliance solely on the Canal advisor. Crew should be instructed before transit to look to the captain for orders or confirmation before acting. The captain, in turn, must maintain excellent communication with the advisor. He or she must also carefully balance his or her own judgment with the advisor's instructions.

The captain's task is to follow an advisor's directions while maintaining control over the details of execution. With the benefit of hindsight, we can analyze the scenario above. The advisor merely wanted the raft to separate as quickly as possible. The captain should have tactfully stepped in and coordinated slowing of the raft and the order in which lines would be released. The crews should have looked solely to their captains for a command to release the lines. Thus both the advisor's wish and safe boat-handling could have been accommodated.

In all cases, establishing a good working relationship with and showing respect for one's advisor is paramount. He has been through the Canal many times and is an invaluable resource. In matters related directly to locking and to traffic management in the channels, his expertise is indispensable, and his directions must be obeyed.

Transiting the Panama Canal in a small boat is a genuine adventure. We were fortunate enough to complete the transit with no damage to our boat or our spirits. Part we owe strictly to luck of the draw; the rest we owe to the lessons learned from voyagers who went before. May all blue-water cruisers experience the exhilaration of a successful transit of this undisputed wonder of the voyaging world.

LETTER HOME
BALBOA YACHT CLUB
PANAMA CITY, PANAMA

Hi y'all,

We had a successful transit of the Panama Canal last week, thanks primarily to Alan's meticulous preparation and leadership. Thank you to our voyaging buddies who crewed for us. You did a great job. Unlike many sailboats that have gone through this year, we had zero damage and completed the transit in one day. The champagne flowed.

In more good news, we have been told that our boat, the Hylas 54, has won a very nice award, Cruising World Magazine's Cruising Boat of the Year. Our heartiest congratulations to Hylas Yachts and to Queen Long Marine in Taiwan.

To those of you complaining that naked-Alan stories are getting a little old: I'm sorry, but it's not my fault that he never does anything funny with his clothes on.

Love, Liza

CHAPTER 10
THE BOAT AND HER EQUIPMENT

Q: What were the biggest challenges for you during the circumnavigation?

A: Going through the Panama Canal, crossing the Pacific Ocean, getting Alan to wear underwear, and finding spare parts in undeveloped countries.

Q: Why do you carry around all that extra equipment to maintain – like the genset, refrigerator, watermaker, microwave, washer-dryer, and so on?

A: Sadly, in between sailing and exploring, one must cook, clean, and do laundry. I did not go to sea to become a frontier housewife.

I have always heard that the islands of the South Pacific are a limitless collection of gorgeous deserted anchorages, virgin reefs, powder beaches. Sitting on a mooring at the Balboa Yacht Club, however, just past the Bridge of the Americas that marks the Pacific side of the Panama Canal, I felt I would probably never get to see any of that. Our global positioning system (GPS) unit had malfunctioned.

The GPS is an electronic device that coordinates with a series of geo-synchronous satellites to pinpoint one's position within about thirty feet or better, virtually anywhere on the planet. It continuously spits out one's latitude and longitude, which one can then transfer to a nautical chart to plot an almost exact position, even in the middle of the ocean. As it had on land, GPS had completely taken over the world of marine navigation by the time of our trip. Even better, about halfway through the trip, the U.S. government rescinded the military restrictive filters governing GPS, and its accuracy had shot up to amazing. With GPS and the chart-plotting system we finally sprang for in Australia, our navigation system pinpointed our location literally to within a foot or two. At a marina, the screen would show our little boat icon snuggled inside its actual slip.

We did carry a sextant, which is a centuries-old device for plotting latitude by "shooting" positions of the sun or stars. The one time I tried to use it, I managed to pinpoint our position to within, oh, about a hundred miles of where the GPS told me we actually were. So no, that wasn't going to work very well – not that it stopped us from carrying our notes from the celestial navigation course all the way around the globe.

Luckily, we had several handheld GPS units as backups. Unluckily, we had only the one built-in unit that would interface with our auto-pilot and other nav instruments. And that was the unit that had malfunctioned. We traced the problem to the demise of a small antenna, which we then duly ordered (along with another unit and two antennas as spares) from a Panamanian electronics shop. The shop had to import it from the States. That was ten days ago. And we were still waiting. Sitting on a mooring at the Balboa Yacht Club. Waiting.

I broached the subject of our delay to Alan as he was reading the GPS manual for the umpteenth time.

"I listened to the Vagabond Net this morning," I said. The Vagabond Net was a single sideband radio net that a couple dozen of us had formed as a safety check-in and information exchange for the Pacific crossing. The frequency was open for business twice a day.

"Anything interesting?"

"Yeah, *Andiamo* arrived in the Galapagos. *Sea Spirit* has left the Galapagos for the Marquesas already."

"Very good."

"I can't believe we're so far behind."

"Mmm."

I shook my head and paced for a while and then turned back to him.

"Let's just go," I blurted.

"We can't go."

"No seriously, let's just go."

"We can't go," he said reasonably. "The GPS antenna isn't here yet. Then it may be a day or two before the guys can deliver it. And then it may take me a while to figure out the installation and interface."

"That's why we should just go."

He looked up from the manual. "Are you really suggesting that we cross the largest body of water on our route without the single most important feature of our navigation system?"

Well, when he put it like that.

"No." Sigh. "No, I'm not. You're right. Of course not. We're just getting so far behind."

"Behind what?"

"I mean we're getting really far behind. Everybody. Everybody else is going to get there ahead of us."

"Everybody else is going to get to the South Pacific ahead of us."

"Right."

"And what. Grab the good beaches? Take all the parking spots? Use up the good weather?

"Okay, okay."

"Eat all the pineapples? Flatten out the waves? Dive the good spots and scare all the fish into the Atlantic?"

"I said okay."

In a reprehensible Fu Manchu accent, he intoned: "She arrives safely who prepares patiently, Grasshopper."

"Oh shut up."

* * *

I have not said much so far about *Heartsong III* herself or about our equipment. Those of you who aren't interested in that aspect of a sea story should probably skip the rest of this chapter.

Heartsong III is hull #1 of the Hylas 54 performance offshore semi-custom cruising series from Hylas Yachts, built by the Huang family of Queen Long Marine, in Kaohsiung, Taiwan. The design is by German Frers, who also designs the Swan yachts and led the design team for the Italian IACC racing boat, Prada, which won the international America's Cup Challenger Series in New Zealand in 2000 before losing the finals to New Zealand (more about that later).

The boat is a center-cockpit sloop. According to the builder's specifications, her overall length is 55.5 feet, and length at the water line is 45.93 feet. Displacement is 47,184 pounds in light condition. Maximum beam is 16.1 feet, and the draft is 7.5 feet. The hull is made of fiberglass and twaron, a kevlar-like bulletproof material, which stood us in good stead later on in pirate waters.

Heartsong III is rigged for short-handed sailing. That is, either Alan or I could and did handle her alone for extended periods of time, sometimes days. In addition to the in-mast furling main and roller-furling Genoa, we carried only an asymmetrical gennaker, a storm jib, and an emergency trysail. That's not much of a sail suite for a circumnavigation, but our plan was to start with that and find out what else we needed along the way. It turned out that those sails were so flexible in their configurations that we never needed to supplement the suite.

We did not have electric winches. We listened to good advice that warned of fouling the sheets because of too much juice cranking the winches. So our winches were all manual. In Australia, however, we bought an electric "arm" that attached to the winches and did the heavy-duty grinding for me when I got tired. I blessed it many times in the Red Sea.

Heartsong III's hull is awl-gripped dark blue with gold cove stripe and red boot stripe. The deck is white fiberglass and twaron, with gel-coat and non-skid, varnished teak handholds and an oil-sealed toerail. Each major portlight is fitted with Lexan storm shutters. At the stern, teak steps serve as a dive platform, with storage and a fresh-water shower underneath. Over the cockpit is a hard dodger, bimini, and roll-down clear enclosure panels that in a 40-knot gale with pelting rain made my life worth living.

On our circumnavigation, *Heartsong III* sailed over 37,000 blue-water miles. Her best noon-to-noon day of 215 nautical miles was logged between Tonga and New Zealand, on reaches between 60 and 100 degrees, in 20-30 knots of wind with beam seas of two to three meters. Highest speed sustained for ten minutes or longer was 12.1 knots through the water. That speed was achieved under single-reefed, poled-out Genoa flying alone, with 35-knot winds directly astern and three-meter quartering seas.

Highest speed sustained for one hour or longer was 10.5 knots through the water and over ground, under single-reefed jib and main in 25-30 knots of wind abaft the beam, with confused seas of two to three meters. Average cruising speed under sail in five years of widely varying conditions was about 7.5 knots.

That, my friends, is one fast voyaging sailboat.

Belowdecks on *Heartsong III* are three private staterooms (one king, one queen, one double) and two heads with separate shower stalls. The double berth folds back to a stainless steel work bench. In the main saloon is an eight-seat dinette and settee, which pulls out to become a wide pilot berth. The L-shaped navigation station is fitted out with computer desk, adjustable captain's chair, and office storage. There are handholds throughout the boat's interior at convenient intervals. Because *Heartsong III* had such great headroom, the handholds on the ceiling were too tall for me to reach. We purchased rubber anchor snubbers and secured them to the ceiling handholds. They hung down about 18 inches and gave us – especially me – the jungle vines by which we Tarzan-ed across the main saloon while underway in rough conditions.

The interior is primarily teak, with royal blue microfiber upholstery. The sole is teak and holly. All portable pieces of the sole have stainless steel lock-down devices to prevent dislodging in the event of a roll.

The "alley" galley's pantry can accommodate approximately 90 days' provisioning, with an additional year's provisioning in deep stowage elsewhere on the boat. I had to fight for that pantry in the initial design (what?! – a pantry on a sailboat?), but it was awesome for provisioning, and it made me the object of considerable envy among female voyagers. One could actually see what food and supplies were on the shelves in there, as opposed to looking down into deep locker stowage from above.

We traveled to Taiwan several times during the process of the boat's design and construction – in part because it was just fun to travel to Taiwan, but in part to give input and to try to influence the boat design as much as we could towards our own preferences. Although the Hylas 54 would be a production boat, *Heartsong III* was Hull #1 of the series, and nothing was in stone yet. We pitched the idea of a retractable rudder. Blessedly, that idea got shot down, because later in the South Pacific we became aware of a boat that lost its retractable rudder, in part because of that retraction system.

However, we declined to compromise on some features. For example, we dug in our heels and insisted on watertight bulkheads. We also were able to add a liveaboard perspective to the rock-em-sock-em yacht racing mentality of boat building.

We knew the boat would be fast (hello, Frers hull design). We knew that Hylas was as committed as we were to its being safe. What I wanted to make sure of was that it was also – assuming safety and speed – as comfortable and user-friendly as it was humanly possible for a bluewater sailboat to be designed to be.

Our first point of contention was the design of the head. Conventional wisdom says a sailboat's head should be as tiny as possible, usually with a combination shower and toilet cubicle, and a minuscule sink off to the side. We introduced the radical idea that at least one of the heads – mine! – should be as big as the space would possibly allow. After all, voyagers spend only about 30% of nights underway. And women spend more time in the head. And what was so wrong with wanting a proper bathroom?

The boat builders hemmed and hawed and scratched their heads and argued that a minimum-sized head was backed by hundreds of years of seafaring history.

"Um," I responded, "that would be because all of those seafarers were men, who probably stank to high heaven and didn't care."

Well, why did I want to waste space, and what did I need all that room for anyway?

"Is there a problem removing the walk-through between the aft head and the nav station, and using that space to enlarge the aft head instead?"

I really didn't want anyone walking through from the main cabin straight into my bathroom in any event. There was a perfectly good mini-head, the size of which the boatbuilders roundly approved, accessible from the main cabin for guests.

It emerged that no, there was no real reason why that empty walkway space couldn't be used for the aft head. They had just never done it that way before.

"Aha! Let's do it. You'll love it! Future female boat buyers will bless your names!"

So on one trip to Taiwan, I stood in the space where the head would be, blue-taped where everything should go, and they built the head and shower space around me, on the spot. It was a thing of beauty.

I did the same thing with the nav station. Traditionally, the nav station is a bench with paper chart storage, with a large flat desktop for reading said paper charts, and the electrical and instrument panels alongside. I wanted a laptop docking station in there, with a lockable hinged cover to secure the laptop, and the whole nav station in an L-shape with a chair that I could wedge myself into while underway to work on the computer. With the laptop in that position, we could supplement paper charts with electronic ones as appropriate, and we could take advantage of modern route guidance.

The marine builders got it exactly right, except, hilariously, they apparently thought – since I was female, presumably, and to be fair I had definitely played the girl-card on the aft head design – that the hinged docking station top was meant to be a vanity. Because when the boat was delivered to us, we found that they had put a mirror on the inside of the hinged laptop station lid. Whenever we lifted the lid the first few months, we were puzzled anew. But that nav station was the perfect command center while underway and a nice little office at anchor.

One thing is for certain. The marine builders in Taiwan are artists of the highest caliber. The hull mold was flawless. The joinery (teak work) was superb, every grain perfectly aligned, every join perfectly made, every bit of the wood varnished to soft satin perfection. They freehanded the bulkhead arcs, and they were exact. They built and rebuilt the cockpit coamings until they were the perfect height – high enough to keep green water out, low enough to be streamlined and comfortable. The spaces for eventual electronics and mechanical installations were ideal. The engine and engine room were works of art.

We got exactly the boat we wanted. She was fast and beautiful and blissfully comfortable. More importantly, she was seaworthy and forgiving when we made a mistake, even a big mistake.

She saved our butts over and over again.

In addition to all of the sailing equipment, we had the maximum number of creature comforts that the space and weight allowance would let us have. We had a non-venting washer-dryer, which worked like a charm while not underway. We had air-conditioning, which we ran sparingly, but oh how fabulous it was to close up the aft stateroom in the tropics and run the air on occasion. We had a microwave, and we had a generator to supply power for all those things. We had a reverse-osmosis watermaker that supplied all the fresh water two people would ever need. We had a refrigerator, a deep refrigerated receptacle beneath our galley countertops that held a whole lot of pre-prepared food cooked up for a passage. We even had a small freezer – never cold enough while underway for ice or ice cream, but cold enough to lengthen the life of fresh meat.

Why are those creature comforts so important?

The topic of how many creature comforts to carry on a cruising boat is one of heated debate amongst voyagers and in the sailing magazines. My response to minimalists is this: Either we spend time and energy maintaining and repairing mechanical conveniences, or we spend time and energy compensating for their absence.

For example, without the domestic mechanical conveniences listed above, a voyager in remote areas must haul fresh water by hand in jerry jugs from village to dinghy to boat (repeat ad infinitum); do laundry in buckets; cook over a hot stove in the tropics instead of quickly nuking dinner; deal with skin problems from salt water showering; do without perishable food or go to time-consuming lengths either to preserve it or to make it daily in small quantities from scratch; and on and on and on.

The ability to make fresh water on board is particularly important to health and happiness. So many times I have heard a voyager talk about "fresh, clear water" available ashore. The color or clearness of fresh water coming out of the local spigot has absolutely nothing to do with whether it will kill you or not. You simply can't tell by looking. We know of several cruisers who have contracted giardia lamblia, a dangerous tropical parasite, from drinking fresh water obtained ashore on remote islands. On one boat, the wife became so ill from "crystal clear" water obtained in the Marquesas Islands that the couple was forced to go home, and worse, to sell the boat to pay medical bills.

The best possible solution is to install a watermaker. In my view, a watermaker is second only to a GPS in importance of equipment onboard a long-distance cruising boat. Human beings can sail for long periods of time without food or fuel, but we simply can't survive without safe, fresh water. In the space you would need to store jugs of drinking water while on passage, you can install a watermaker that makes about six gallons per hour, on 12-volt power that can be generated with solar panels. Moreover, there are good hand-held models that can be installed in a bracket to make them portable in the event you must deploy your liferaft. The watermaker essentially distills water so that there is zero chance of bacteria surviving. It prevents the necessity of ever having to rely on local fresh water for any purpose.

In any event, all crew members need to be on the same page with regard to the hierarchy of importance of creature comforts. We have known more than a few couples who have experienced the following scenario: Man wants to have wonderful, rugged, primitive, self-sufficient life on water and see world, be captain, cross oceans, hooya!

Woman gamely gives up career and 21st Century American electronics and domestic conveniences to share the joy.

Man is very happy as Captain of Ship – yo ho! – but, oddly, he doesn't seem that interested in hand-washing clothes and sheets and towels in bucket, hanging them on lifelines to dry, hand-washing dishes, de-mildewing possessions on a regular basis, canning meat and preserves, picking bugs out of flour, cooking over hot propane stove in pitching storm while seasick in the tropics, etc.

Woman misses hot showers, grows weary of doing all domestic chores as if she lives in the 18th Century when appliances are readily available in this Year of Our Lord Twenty-Whatever; doesn't get to explore or enjoy because she's too busy being a domestic servant; takes first plane out from next civilized port; uses her half of cruising kitty to buy condo in Boca Raton.

Man gets divorce papers by email.

Sound familiar?

In my view, there are four keys to a happy partnership afloat: communication, kindness, competence, and compromise, mixed with a healthy dose of mutual respect. Also important for a significant voyage is a rigorous pre-departure negotiation and agreement with regard to route, safety, size and type of boat, sharing of domestic duties, division of authority, and equipment lists. Creature comforts are a significant part of this pre-negotiated status quo. But my position is clear. As I have said often and will continue to say, I did not go to sea to become a frontier housewife.

With regard to the relationship of a seagoing couple, there is an even more important concept that must be considered: The "One Captain Rule." It is an indelible truth that on a boat, there can be only one captain. Basic safety and seamanship require that only one set of instructions be carried out, immediately and consistently and without backchat, even if those instructions do not necessarily represent the very best possible decision in the universe of possible decisions at sea at the moment, and even if someone thinks he or she has a better idea. The boat and crew are far safer working toward the same goal, even a less than perfect goal, than they are if they are working at cross-purposes.

Accordingly, everyone who is not the captain must bite his or her tongue and do as he or she is told, unless and until faced with conclusive evidence of a captain's irrefutable incompetence. No good ever comes of doing otherwise. This is why mutiny at sea has historically been punishable by keelhauling and/or death.

Alan and I analyzed the One Captain Rule at length. For better or for worse, we decided from the get-go that whoever was on watch would be captain for all purposes. That is, we modified the One Captain Rule to be the One Captain at a Time Rule. For us, that approach was a rousing success. It respected nautical absolutism while maintaining the co-equal dynamic of our marriage.

Of course, it did have the occasional absurd result. For example, there was that time in the Red Sea, sailing to the Suez Canal, that we disagreed in a big way on the best harbor for landfall. During my watch, we sailed north toward my choice, and then at the change of watch Alan turned us around and sailed us south toward his choice, and then at my watch I headed north, then at his watch south, and so on back and forth over the same stretch of water until we got over ourselves.

The vast majority of the time, though, life on the boat was a near-perfect reflection of our wildly different but resolvable philosophies. In our land life, for example, Alan hated it when the furniture was moved around. If I so much as re-angled a lamp, he would chafe. I, on the other hand, loved to rearrange the furniture on a whim, and would have been content to move house completely the earlier of every six months or whenever the place got dirty. We realized that what we had in *Heartsong III* was a living space in which the furniture was actually nailed to the bulkhead

(Team Alan), in a home for which the outside environment itself was constantly changing (Team Liza).

Our choice of route reflected that same juxtaposition of preferences. I am more comfortable knowing what the next port will be, and planning for it. Alan would love to prepare for everything, and then go literally whichever way the wind is blowing at the moment. We satisfied both preferences by establishing climate-driven deadlines to be in certain parts of the world – *e.g.*, to arrive in the southern Pacific by the time the mid-Pacific cyclone season started – but then being as spontaneous as he felt like being about the route we took to get to the appointed spot at the appointed time.

Our approach worked for us. I hasten to add, however, that there as many successful approaches as there are happy voyagers. And most voyagers are pretty happy.

CHAPTER 11
PASSAGE TO THE GALAPAGOS ISLANDS

Q: What do you do if the wind stops blowing? Do you have an engine?

A: Yes, we have an engine. We use it sparingly, though, because it requires diesel fuel, which costs money and requires stopping and filling up at industrialized harbors we might prefer not to visit. When the wind stops blowing completely, we often sit still in the middle of the ocean and wait until it starts blowing again. When the wind starts blowing from an unfavorable direction, we usually just tack.

As *Heartsong III* sat with sails flapping, tipping from side to side like a carnival ride with each big ocean roller, Alan and I were sitting in the cockpit surveying our options.

To starboard, about 100 miles away but clearly visible, was the primary border of the Inter-Tropical Convergence Zone, an extensive weather phenomenon that looked like Mordor with its constant lightning and thunder, black and purple clouds, and aura of menace. To port and directly overhead were the gray skies of the outskirts of the ITCZ, and the cloud configuration did not promise any significant wind. Astern was Panama, which we had left at dawn that morning. Dead ahead were the Galapagos Islands, and the wind – to the extent there was any – was blowing directly from there, right on our nose.

"The way I see it, we can either drop the sails and motor all the way to Galapagos, or we can start tacking," I said.

"The way I see it," he replied, "it that it's your watch and your call."

"Thank you, sweetheart, but it's going to take about a week to get there either way, and I feel like we need an integrated approach. Can we go over the data?"

"Sure."

Tacking, by the way, for those who may not know, is a procedure by which a sailboat can make forward progress even though the wind is blowing directly from the destination. Normally, a sailboat cannot make forward progress directly into the wind. If a boat points directly into the wind, all that will happen is that the sails will flap, and the boat will be pushed backwards. For that reason, a sailboat cannot reach a destination if (a) the wind is blowing directly from the destination towards the sailboat, and (b) the boat is pointed into that wind, toward the destination.

A boat moves forward by a combination of the wind putting pressure on the sails, and the rudder holding the boat to a course. If the wind is blowing from the side of the boat, no problem. The sails have plenty of pressure, and the rudder keeps the boat from slipping sideways; so the boat moves forward. If the wind is blowing from behind the boat, again you can configure the sails to let the wind put pressure on them, and bob's your uncle. However, if the wind is coming directly on the nose of a boat – directly from where it is you want to go – there is no way for that wind to put pressure on the sails to make forward progress. If you set the sail out to one side, even a little bit, the wind very happily pushes you backwards away from your destination, not toward it.

Hence the concept of tacking.

When you tack, you aim the boat a little bit off to the left or the right of your destination, rather than directly towards it. You set the sails to be on the opposite side of the boat from where the wind is blowing, so that the wind fills the sails and provides the necessary pressure on them. You sail that way for a while, then you tack – *i.e.*, you turn the boat back across that direct line to your destination, and keep turning it until the boom swings to the other side of the boat, and the sails fill with wind on the opposite side. Then you sail that direction for a while. Then you tack again, back to the original angle.

The upshot is that you zigzag all the way to the destination.

Personally, I like to think of tacking as a metaphor for moving through life. But I digress.

"Here are the pros for motoring straight into the wind," I began, wishing I had a legal pad to jot all of this down. "We will probably get there faster."

I paused. That was actually the only pro I could think of, but it was a big one. I was still in a hurry to get to the South Pacific.

I resumed, "Okay, so here are the cons for motoring straight into the wind. We will use at least" – I consulted my calculator – "three-quarters of our fuel, which means there needs to be a reliable source of diesel in the Galapagos Islands, which there probably is, but we've had trouble fueling other places before, and it is an island group. No mainland fuel supply. Boy, that's a big risk.

"Also, we have beam seas, so if we motor straight ahead, we will wallow like a pig all the way there. Can you think of any other cons?"

"Loud and hot?" he contributed. "Embarrassing to admit in front of our friends?"

"All very good points. Okay, what are the pros for tacking? Smoother ride, quieter, fuel-saving?"

"Yep."

"And the cons?" I ran the numbers. "Even assuming the wind gets up to something reasonable, it will probably take us a full day longer to get there."

"If I was in a hurry, I would have taken an airplane."

I laughed. "And that's the winning argument. Prepare to come about."

So we tacked our way for seven and a half days to the Galapagos, ending up going an estimated 300 nautical miles out of our way, but having a relatively smooth passage. I say "relatively," because the trip was punctuated by a couple of Texas-style thunderstorms, courtesy of the ITCZ, during which, as usual, I stowed our laptops and a spare GPS in the microwave, and hoped for the best. At one point, we had a two-knot adverse current. For a full 12 hours, we sat in one spot with no wind and flapping sails. Then finally spotting land near sunset on the eighth day, we had to stand off until morning light, of course, to negotiate the harbor entrance. However, after listening to woeful tales of other voyagers' passages, we believe we had a more enjoyable time than most.

For example, the trip had several points of interest. One afternoon while I was on watch, and way too early in the trip for me to be tired enough to have hallucinated it, word of honor: a full-sized refrigerator floated by. I will just repeat that. Four hundred or so miles from any land mass, a full-sized refrigerator floated by. It was white.

The next day, we spotted two birds bobbing by on a piece of driftwood. They looked stunned and about to panic, as if they had accidentally fallen asleep on the subway and ended up in Jersey. We thought about trying to get them aboard, but by my calculations the current would get them to South America more quickly than our zigzagging could get them to the Galapagos.

Then the day before landfall, we saw a large seabird in flight off our port bow. When it came closer, we saw that it was a red-footed booby, with its webbed feet and bright blue bill. Wow, we thought, almost reverently. According to the guidebook, not many people get to see one of these, even in the Galapagos. The bird flew down and perched on our forward rail. Double wow, we thought. We took great pains not to disturb him as we tiptoed and whispered to find the camera. Then we noticed a second booby coming in for a landing. Then they began calling their cousins.

When it started looking like a Hitchcock movie, we lost our Greenpeace attitude and started thinking NRA. But we couldn't get rid of them. We shouted; we waved; we luffed the sails and tacked. Their only response was to continue making us painfully aware how very, very much they had eaten that day. Finally, I tied garbage bags to stream and flutter on the rails and lifelines. One by one, the birds departed.

And we made landfall in the glorious Galapagos looking like a small-town parade float with a noticeably malodorous air.

LETTER HOME
ACADEMY BAY
ISLA SANTA CRUZ
GALAPAGOS ISLANDS

Hi all,

We arrived safely at Academy Bay, Isla Santa Cruz, the main point of entry for the Galapagos Islands, after seven and a half days at sea.

We have been eco-touring since our arrival last week. Alan, whose idea of a good time on land was sitting up late watching the Nature Channel, is in heaven. On Saturday, he got to swim with baby sea lions. They were afraid of him at first – that is, until he reared up onto a rock and made alarmingly realistic sea lion flops and honk-barks. Then they were all over him. He was fully and completely slimed.

So far we have seen frigate birds, blue-footed boobies, red-footed boobies, masked boobies, a killer whale, a 12-foot Galapagos shark, brown pelicans, a swordfish doing air gymnastics, land iguanas, marine iguanas, sea lions, giant tortoises, sea turtles, land turtles, wild canaries, Darwin finches, and all manner of fish and lizards.

We had the chance to see several of the islands, including Isla Isabella and its still-active volcanoes. While at anchor in a cove/swampy area at Isabella, we left the boat and spent half a day looking for giant seals on the other side of the island. When we got back to the anchorage, some friends anchored nearby brought us pictures of the giant seal that had, in our absence, hopped and scooted up *Heartsong's* stern steps onto the aft deck to get some sun.

Oh the irony.

Love, Liza

CHAPTER 12
THE PACIFIC CROSSING

Q: What do you do when you are on watch on a long passage?

A: I scan the horizon for hazards; check equipment; futz with the sails; make entries in the logbook; plot our position on the chart; make course changes; commune with the auto-pilot. I hand-steer from time to time to get the feel of the sail-set or to stay awake if I'm drowsy. I make my assigned meals. I eat, read, listen to music, write music; zone out to the sound of the wind in the sails. I watch for dolphins and whales; daydream; think; live in the moment; soak up the solitude.

Q: What was it like to cross the Pacific?

A: It was amazing. It was one of the very best experiences of my life. I felt free and self-sufficient and at one with nature. If I die tomorrow, I will die happy because I did it. But imagine driving in a Winnebago cross-country from San Francisco to Miami without ever stopping or getting out, while bouncing over bumpy gravel roads in the rain at about 10 miles per hour. Landfall, when it came, was quite gratifying.

"Are you ready to depart?" Franz, the captain of our anchorage neighbor *Freiheit* was standing in his dinghy, holding on to our railing, shooting the breeze with Alan while I went over our pre-passage checklist. We were anchored on the southwest side of Isla Isabella. About a half dozen boats, including *Freiheit*, were here staging their Pacific crossings.

"Just about," Alan said. "I wish we had found some fuel. We topped off the tanks in Academy Bay, but our jerry jugs are empty."

We carried ten large jerry jugs that we could fill with emergency spare fuel and lash to the deck for long passages.

"Yes, our cans are empty, too," Franz said. "I have heard there is a commercial fishing boat with spare diesel in this area. Do you wish to see if we can find him?"

"Sure!" The redhead is almost as exuberant about an impromptu field trip as he is about street food. They loaded up all of our and *Freiheit*'s jerry jugs into the dinghies and set out around the point to the south.

Sometime later – and it could have been 20 minutes or two hours, given that I was lost in my checklist – Alan returned and tied up the dink.

"Hey, give me a hand with these jugs. We hit the jackpot."

I set down the clipboard and helped him start moving the five-gallon containers one by one from the dinghy to the aft steps, then from the aft steps to the aft deck, then from the aft deck to the side decks to be lashed securely to the stainless steel stanchions.

"They're all full. Guess how much it cost?" he asked with a grin, as we grunted and hauled.

"Well, let's see. I assume there was a premium for the remote location. We paid $2.15 per gallon for the diesel we bought in Academy Bay. So . . . four bucks a gallon?"

"Nope."

"Five bucks?"

"Nope. Fifty cents a gallon! Whoop! Man, we got a deal."

I was impressed. All around the world, the usual result of our negotiating ability was to talk people down to twice the going rate.

"Wow! Way to go."

Months later, in Tahiti, we heard a voyager telling the tale of the angriest man he had ever seen in his life. It was a commercial fishing captain who returned to his ship in the Galapagos to find that his crew had sold off all of his diesel fuel, for pennies on the dollar.

Yep.

* * *

No two passages are ever the same, but one thing we could pretty much count on was that anything we did not prepare for usually happened. Our checklist got a little longer with each trip.

Because of the length and potential adversities of the Pacific passage, every item on the list got a little extra attention. For example, for any passage longer than an overnighter we liked to prepare food in advance – usually hearty meals like spaghetti or stew, divided into single nukable portions and stored in the fridge for easy access during a watch when conditions were inconvenient for using the stove, and a hot meal was a godsend. For the Pacific, we prepared twice the usual amount.

Another pre-passage checklist item was to ready the built-in couch in the main saloon to be a sea-berth. We covered the upholstery with sheets to protect it from the inevitable salt water spray that would find its way down the companionway ladder from the cockpit, and to protect it from our saltwater-soaked or otherwise non-hygienic selves when we were too tired to clean up post-watch before hitting the sack. Then we rigged a lee cloth to hold us in place on the berth while sleeping in rough conditions.

The lee cloth is a piece of canvas as long as the couch and wide enough to pass beneath the couch cushions and tie via grommets to the ceiling handholds. It makes sort of a stationary hammock, with sides, so that when the boat motion rolls the sleeping crew one way, the padded back of the couch holds the sleeper steady, and when the boat motion rolls the sleeping crew the other way, the lee cloth prevents falling out of the berth onto the floor.

On passages, I loved the ritual of coming off watch (usually pretty tired), climbing and snuggling into the padded sea-berth (oh glorious, thank you), setting the alarm for half an hour before I was due for my next watch, and immediately falling into a deep sleep to the roll and rhythm of the boat.

The remainder of our pre-departure checklist included things like doing all engine and genset maintenance, rigging safety lines, pulling the dinghy out of the water and securing it to the deck, checking safety equipment, checking the liferaft, assembling a "ditch bag" in case we had to abandon ship, checking sails and rigging, pre-setting single sideband emergency radio frequencies, putting fresh batteries into all handheld electronics and flashlights, checking the emergency beacon, and a host of other activities. There is nothing quite as satisfying as checking things off a checklist.

And so, there on Isla Isabella, with every item checked off and preparations complete, and armed with a decent weather window – at least for the few days the weather gurus were able to predict with any accuracy – we departed the Galapagos Islands to cross the Pacific Ocean to French Polynesia.

The portion of the Pacific that we would be traversing is 3,400 miles of open ocean. Unlike the Atlantic, which sees a lot of traffic, both private and commercial, the eastern Pacific Ocean is a relatively empty expanse of water. Indeed, we saw absolutely nothing during our Pacific crossing – not another vessel, not a seabird, nada.

The particular route we chose is called the "Coconut Milk Run." Because of the favorable current and wind conditions, it is the typical route for sailboats traveling from Panama or the Galapagos to the South Pacific. Our particular passage of the Coconut Milk Run took sixteen days and six hours. So for more than sixteen days we were blissfully at sea, out of sight of land, in the arms of the wind and the ocean. At the halfway mark we were, according to our charts, about as far away from land as it is possible to be on the planet.

After the first two or three days, our minds and body clocks, as usual, adjusted to the watch schedule: seven hours on, seven hours off, three hours on, three hours off, two hours on, two hours off, repeat. Time starts taking on a different feel. Without getting too Zen on you, I would say that time doesn't feel like it passes so much as it rotates. The clock exists only as a way to indicate whose watch it is. There's no sensation of a day going by. It doesn't feel like it's Thursday or lunchtime or bedtime or time to do this or that, or that it's getting late, or that it's early. It's either my watch, or it's Alan's watch, back and forth, watch and watch.

Patrick O'Brian, master of the sea novel, describes it much better:

> *The unvarying routine of the ship's day . . .*
> *obliterated both the beginning of the*
> *voyage and its end, it obliterated even time,*
> *so that it seemed normal to all hands that*
> *they should travel endlessly over this*
> *infinite and wholly empty sea, watching the*
> *sun diminish and the moon increase.*

And that's how it came to feel – that we were engaged in a process, without beginning or end.

Not long into the passage, we had our first crystal clear night. There is zero ambient light at sea. All lights on our boat at night are red, including our flashlights, so that our night vision isn't impaired. I came on at 2:00 a.m. for my long watch, and the stars were so concentrated and bright in the sky that I could almost read by them.

On a cloudless night in rural areas in Texas, in the absence of city lights, the Milky Way looks thick and three-dimensional. On trips to Marfa, an artist community in the vast uninhabited expanses of West Texas, I have often marveled at the well-populated night sky, at the depth and breadth of our own particular galaxy. But a comparison is in order. If the West Texas night sky is a skyscraper, then the night sky in the middle of the Pacific Ocean is downtown Manhattan. At sea, the sky pulls one's consciousness up into a three-dimensional vortex of sensory overload.

Gazing straight up, one can occasionally catch a whiff of infinity.

Lying on the side deck, securely hanked on to the safety lines and gazing at the sky one night, I caught my first sight of the Southern Cross. Although that constellation is from time to time visible in the Northern Hemisphere, it is bright and center-stage near the equator and in the Southern Hemisphere. The Southern Hemisphere has no single bright star, such as the North Star, for celestial navigation, but the Southern Cross has for hundreds of seafaring years fulfilled that role.

The Southern Cross appeared low in the sky at first, and then ever higher the farther south of the equator we traveled. My first sight of it, of course, triggered a very raucous vocal rendition of the venerable Crosby Stills & Nash song. I was out there in the middle of nowhere, singing away at the top of my lungs, hurtling forward through the dense darkness of the sea and sky. Not a care in the world. Not one care.

Except, what was that light? Immediately astern was a large white light, no a huge white bow light of a ship running right up our stern. Oh dear lord, I had failed to watch for traffic, and we were about to be run over. I sprang to the radar screen. Nothing. How can that be? But no, not a blip for 20 miles and more. What in the world?

I looked astern again. Still there, even larger. My mind dallied with the thought of a UFO. Then the light lifted higher, and I was freaking sure it was a UFO.

Until I realized it was the moon – a gigantic, full, perfectly white orb rising in the east, casting a gleaming path towards me across the water. The path looked solid and inviting, like I could and should step off the stern and walk it all the way to the sky.

Well, at least I hadn't woken up the redhead to alert him to an alien invasion.

For a good portion of the trip, we had a rough ride. Colliding with the normal six-foot southeasterly whitecaps, which we were expecting, were 12- to 20-foot swells from the south. The resulting large and very confused seas made day-to-day life a challenge. In particular, I wished we had a harness to keep me from being bucked off the marine toilet.

I dutifully added that item to the checklist for further study.

But the wind was steady and perfectly calibrated for a fast passage. We had multiple days of 200-mile runs. All other things equal, a fast passage is a safer passage. One has more control over a boat traveling at speed than over a boat limping through the waves. And statistically, the less time one is on passage, the less time one is exposed to storms and other natural disasters outside the likelihood of rescue. Of course, there are limits to this truism, and there is a sweet spot. If one maintains speed by flying too much sail for the wind and sea conditions, then one puts undue stress on the mast and rigging. Too much stress leads to breakage. Breakage can disable the boat. A disabled boat in the middle of the Pacific Ocean cannot hope for rescue within any reasonable time period, if at all. So a faster passage is a safer passage – but with an asterisk.

On about Day Two, we started flying our gennaker. A gennaker is a huge asymmetrical sail flown off the bow, similar to a classic spinnaker, but slightly smaller and a tad sturdier. It was a thing of beauty, emblazoned with our *Heartsong III* logo – two hearts pierced by a musical note. The point of flying that type of sail is that it is larger than a jib or Genoa. When the wind is blowing from the aft quarter of the boat, on either side, the gennaker captures more wind, propels the boat more swiftly, and makes for a lovely, smooth ride. However, the gennaker is gossamer-thin. It is a fair-weather sail, intended for light to moderate winds. It is contra-indicated in a typical mid-ocean sea state in winds above, say, 15 to 18 knots. It is simply too delicate to withstand heavier conditions.

For our passage, the musical hearts on our gennaker flew for about ten days across the Pacific Ocean swell without so much as a minor adjustment. The wind and seas were so consistent that once we set the sails, we literally did not touch them for more than half of the trip.

Until we did.

One afternoon during the second week, I climbed into the cockpit to prepare for my watch. I gazed for a moment at our colorful gennaker with love and pride. I gave my sweet redheaded husband a faceful of kisses. I glanced at the binnacle to check our course and did a quick scan of the horizon. Then I brought my focus back to the sea in our immediate vicinity.

I could not help but notice that the tops of the waves were getting their little heads blown off by the wind. I turned to my spouse with a look that caused him to register some alarm.

"Um, sweetheart," I said with a bit of an edge.

"What did I do," he said reflexively.

"What is the wind speed right now?"

He looked at the monitors. "Oh, about 18 knots."

"Is that apparent or true?"

"Apparent, why?"

When the wind is astern, one calculates the actual wind speed, on a quick and dirty basis, by adding the reported, or "apparent," wind speed to the speed of the boat. That number is the "true" wind speed. The true wind speed is the wind force that was actually hitting our poor, delicate gennaker.

I continued. "So, the apparent wind is 18 knots, and the wind is astern, and the boat speed is 10 knots."

He checked the monitors again, and said slowly. "Yep, that sounds right." I could tell he sensed a trap.

"So what is the actual wind speed?"

"Well, that would depend . . . ."

"Okay," I managed a forced smile, "I'll accept an estimate."

He laughed. "Oh, about . . . about . . .." Realization dawned. "Uh-oh."

"Uh-huh."

"Sorry."

"Yeah."

"I'll go forward and take the gennaker down."

"Great idea."

"You know, it crossed my mind about an hour ago to do that."

I glared at him. It didn't make me feel better to know that we had been flying a paper-thin, fair-weather sail in wind conditions that warranted having taken it down an hour ago. We were lucky not to have blown it out or damaged the rigging.

Alan struggled at the bow to raise the sock to extinguish the sail. Nothing doing. The wind was too strong. He turned towards the cockpit.

"I'm going to have to release it. Prepare to jibe."

"Okeydoke."

"Jibe ho!"

I took pressure off the sail, and he released it from the forestay. The sail went flying up like a Roman candle, and Alan quickly pulled it in and tucked it away into its sail bag.

Returning to the cockpit to deploy the jib, he ventured a comment. "Well, that went pretty well."

"You're lucky you have a free pass. That's all I'm sayin'."

"I know." Pause. He raised his eyebrows inquiringly. "I love you?"

"Hmmph."

Generally, however, all the planning and preparation paid off. The trip was noticeably devoid of disasters. Not all of the voyagers who sailed to the South Pacific that season were as lucky. In all, we heard of eleven boats that either did not survive the passage or that survived the passage only to sink elsewhere in the South Pacific. Of those, we know for certain of only three whose crew were rescued.

The morning of Day 17, I sighted a blip on the horizon. I had the spine-tingling pleasure of waving to get Alan's attention, pointing forward, and bellowing in the best tradition of seafaring movies, "Land ho!"

It was Fatu Hiva, a southern island of the Marquesas island chain. We were right on course. A few hours later the mountainous terrain was discernible. A few hours after that, we were circling the island's largest protected bay, the Bay of Virgins, looking for a place to park.

The Marquesas Islands consist of two French island groups that are, together, the farthest islands from any continent in the world, about 500 miles south of the equator and about a thousand miles east of Tahiti. After a few course changes en route, we had aimed for the southernmost island of the group, Fatu Hiva, for two reasons. First, it was the destination that allowed us the most comfortable point of sail on our crossing; and second, from there we could explore the remainder of the Marquesas Islands with the wind at our backs.

"Where do you want to drop the hook?" I spoke into the family band radio headset from the helm. There were a half dozen glistening white sailboats at anchor in the bay. Since there is absolutely no way to get to these islands without having crossed the Pacific Ocean, we were safe in assuming that each vessel was fresh from its own Pacific Crossing.

Alan was at the bow, preparing the windlass. He pointed vaguely toward the shoreline.

"Over there between those two white boats."

Sigh. "They're all white, sweetheart."

"Oh, right. What's the depth right here?"

"One-seven-oh."

"Too deep anyway. Let me know when it's at ninety feet."

We were still a hundred yards from shore. As we moved in more closely, looking for water shallow enough to drop the hook, I became mesmerized by the shoreline as it came into focus.

Fatu Hiva is everything you would want a volcanic South Pacific island to be. The jungle starts immediately beyond the beach and is dense with flowers, palm trees, and prehistoric-looking ferns. Towering cliffs guard the Bay of Virgins like primeval gods. So anthropomorphic did the cliff faces appear, we wondered whether they had been carved that way. We expected giants to appear any moment for their daily boulder tossing, or King Kong to show up looking for a sacrificial blonde.

But the upshot of the volcanic nature of these islands is that the anchorages are deep and rocky on the bottom – generally poor holding. We had carted 300 feet of chain all the way from Florida to accommodate these anchorages. You want a 5-to-1 ratio for rope rode for a good set on the anchor. That is, if you are in 30 feet of water, you want 150 feet of rode. With chain, you can get away with a 3-to-1 ratio. We found a good spot at 100 feet of depth, with good swinging room, and we were in business.

Needless to say, we were exhilarated to set foot on shore. But first, we made a dinghy tour of the anchorage and said hello to our fellow Pacific-crossers. We recognized some of the boat names from the Vagabond Net. There would certainly be a party in the works.

Stepping ashore was a little wobbly at first, but solid ground was welcome. Pareo-clad village women, their hair decorated with flowers, traded us grapefruit (called "pamplemousse" here) and crafts for nail polish and t-shirts. Neatly scrubbed village kids trailed us laughing wherever we went. It was like stepping into a previous century to a place where food grows wild and people are productive but undriven and content.

God bless the isolation that keeps these islands safe from the rest of us.

LETTER HOME
MAEVA BEACH
TAHITI, ISLES DE SOCIETE
FRENCH POLYNESIA

Hi all,

We have been exploring French Polynesia. In Hiva Oa, we visited the grave of Tim Gauguin. I have always scoffed at the idea of light being special in any particular place, but I have to agree that the light here does seem unique. It makes me wish I had inherited my mother's talent for painting. In Hana Moe Noa Bay in Tahuata, we put up our brand new hammock and didn't move for a week, except to attend a village festival where the men sang and danced, and the women played bingo.

Sometime before the beginning of cyclone season, we will island-hop across the remaining couple of thousand miles to New Zealand, where we have booked a slip at Gulf Harbour Marina, just north of Auckland, for the America's Cup races.

But for the next couple of months, our destinations are so remote they don't even have a McDonald's.

Love, Liza

CHAPTER 13
BORA BORA TO PALMERSTON ATOLL

Q: Did you have any really bad storms at sea?

A: Yes, several. The most dangerous force in the world is Mother Nature. Human beings, even if they are up to no good, can't hold a candle to her.

"*Tango, Tango, Tango,*" I hailed on channel 16 of our VHF radio, "this is *Heartsong III.*"

"*Heartsong,* this is *Tango,* over," Bella responded.

"Dominoes or cards?"

"I think it's too windy for cards."

"Dominoes it is. Yacht Club in half an hour?"

"Sounds good. *Tango* out."

The yacht club in question was the Bora Bora Yacht Club, which consisted of a thatched-roof open-air hut with a rickety dinghy dock, some even ricketier plastic tables and chairs, and an honor bar. I love honor bars. In this case, it was a half-fridge with beer and soft drinks, a few economy-sized bottles of hard liquor, some plastic cups, a price list, and a screw-top jar to receive payment of one's tab. The existence of honor bars, which we frequented at yachtie hangouts around the world, validates my belief in the basic honesty and goodness of humans. People pay their tabs. If honor bars ever go away, I'll know the human race is in trouble.

We were anchored about 50 yards off the yacht club dinghy dock, in thirty feet of churning white-caps in the lagoon at Bora Bora. It was blowing like stink. We and about a dozen other boats were sheltering as best we could in the lagoon. Most of us were looking for a window to head west to Tonga. One intrepid captain had made a break for it the day before, and we were getting radio reports that conditions were so rough that the crew had not been able to sleep since departure.

All things considered, I planned to hang out at the honor bar and play dominoes until the front lifted. Voyaging is plenty adventurous enough without voluntarily seeking out bad weather. Also, I like playing dominoes. I particularly like the Texas domino game of "42," a/k/a "redneck bridge." My current crusade was to teach it to enough voyagers that I could always find a game, at least in bad weather.

Our time in the Society Islands of French Polynesia had been memorable. The Society Islands are an archipelago of fourteen islands, of which Tahiti is the largest. We had enjoyed and participated in various cultural activities in Papeete (pronounced pah-peh-EH-tay), Tahiti's largest town and main port of entry. We were lucky enough to be there for the Heiva festival, which included competitions by dance troupes of exquisite Polynesian women in traditional costumes, and races among some very manly men in outrigger canoes. Say what you will about the beauty of the French Polynesian islands, the beauty of the French Polynesian people far surpasses it.

From the anchorage, we explored the island by way of local buses, which consisted of flat-bad trucks that slowed down slightly at each stop for one to jump on and off. Our anchorage stop was the village of Faa. That's pronounced with two syllables: FAH-ah. Down the road there was also a stop named Faaa (pronounced with three syllables, as in fah-ah-AH). Slightly further down the road – and I am not making this up – was a stop named Faaaa (pronounced with four syllables, as in fah-AH-ah-ah. It occurred to me to wonder what Polynesians have against consonants. After a nice dinner ashore with some of the island's excellent French wine (one of the many advantages of being a territory of France), we had to focus carefully on the signs to know where to jump off the truck.

From the vantage point of the Papeete town quay, the spectacular island of Moorea (pronounced moh-oh-RAY-uh) is visible about 28 miles distant, an easy daysail. According to some, Moorea was the inspiration for the song "Bali Hai" from the musical *South Pacific*:

> *Bali Ha'i may call you*
> *Any night, any day*
> *In your heart, you'll hear it call you*
> *"Come away, come away"*

> *Bali Ha'i will whisper*
> *In the wind of the sea*
> *"Here am I, your special island*
> *Come to me, come to me"*

And that's pretty much how we felt about it.

The magnificent Cook's Bay, Moorea's largest protected inlet, became our headquarters for exploring Moorea and its surrounding waters. It remains one of our favorite spots in the world.

After settling in to the Cook's Bay anchorage, our first order of business was a self-guided walking tour of the island. This plan was defeated on the first attempt, and at each of many subsequent attempts, however, by our inability to get past the first turn in the road. That turn was the only entrance from Cook's Bay to the paved road that traverses Moorea and goes up the mountain. The problem wasn't the turn itself. The problem was that the turn was guarded by a pig. This pig was not your run-of-the-mill pig. It was a pig the size of a moose. And it wasn't just big, it was ugly. Its head and front half were charcoal gray and menacing. Its back half and tail were normal pig color, but speckled with large black blotches. On its neck were wolverine-like bristles.

"Here, piggy, piggy," Alan called upon seeing it for the first time.

"Leave that pig alone, Alan. I'm serious. It's ginormous, and it looks mean. Maybe it won't see us. Just treat it like a guard dog and don't make any sudden moves."

"No, it's friendly."

"How do you know?"

"It looks friendly."

"It does not look friendly. It looks like one of those hideous evil beasts in a fantasy horror movie."

"Aw, it wouldn't hurt a fly, would you, piggy?"

The redhead approached the pig with outstretched hand. The pig bristled, squealed in a malevolent basso profundo, and wheeled toward us at a dead run.

Alan stood there for about two seconds before he started backpedaling in high gear.

"Run!" he shouted

I was already halfway back to the boat.

For whatever reason, just about everyone else we talked to was allowed free passage by the pig and had nice walks on the island. But not us. Maybe the pig was insulted that Alan called it "piggy?" Maybe it didn't like my ponytail? I don't know. We tried to sneak by. We tried to run the blockade in the company of others. We went in the dead of night. That pig would not let us pass. To see the mountain, I finally had to rent a car.

We fared slightly better with the sea creatures. Around the bend from Cook's Bay was a reef that housed a group of friendly stingrays. Fun fact: the collective noun for stingrays is "fever," so I will amend the prior statement to say that the reef housed a fever of friendly stingrays. For the admission price of raw chicken or fish, the stingrays would swirl around and snuggle up close and eat (or rather, suction) the food out of our hands. Alan wanted to put tuna in his ears, but I drew the line.

The overnighter from Moorea to Bora Bora was an easy sail, but the weather turned on us almost immediately upon arrival. By way of tourist activities, we had walked around the island, and we had braved the dinghy run to the opposite side, which was protected from the winds by the interior mountains but was too shallow for anchoring. There, we snorkeled in water so calm and crystal clear that it was impossible to know for sure without touching it whether the water was even there. The dinghy looked to be magically suspended in thin air over scalloped white sand. On one afternoon when the wind died down to a mere gale, Alan went scuba diving with some of our friends to "manta ray alley," a Bora Bora dive site where they swam and communed with the much bigger brothers of the Moorea fever of stingrays.

But now we were figuratively drumming our fingers. We were ready to sail west.

After a few more days of enforced inactivity, we declared a weather window – or at least, enough of one for two voyagers with cabin fever. At dawn we set sail for a projected week's westward crossing to reach the Vava'u Group of the Kingdom of Tonga.

For the first three days, we had 40-knot winds and 20-foot breaking seas. Those conditions constitute gale force. It was rough out there. From time to time, it was actually dangerous as we bounced and slid down the wave faces.

One of the perils of sailing in relatively large, steep breaking seas with a gale-force quartering wind – the conditions that were present on the passage from Bora Bora to Tonga – is the phenomenon of "broaching to." A sailboat can broach in certain conditions when a strong gust of wind or a turbulent sea causes the boat to turn and present its side, instead of its bow, to an oncoming wave. Broaching can lead to a death roll, or to "turning turtle," in which the mast becomes horizontal instead of upright and then continues to roll downward beneath the water until the boat turns upside down with its mast extended straight downward towards the ocean floor.

This is not a good look for a sailboat.

So when the weather showed no signs of letting up on Day 4, we started consulting the chart for somewhere to duck into for a respite. Anywhere.

"The closest island with a leeward bay looks to be a place called 'Palmerston Atoll.'" Alan said loudly, to compete with the deafening shrill of the wind.

"Do we know anything about it?" I yelled back from a foot away.

"No."

I pulled out the cruising guide for this area of the South Pacific and read for a few seconds.

"It's a really tiny island," I shouted, "but it looks like it might have some decent shelter. It's inhabited – small village. I say we try it."

"What?" he yelled over the wind.

"Let's try it."

"Okay. Changing course now."

Never was there a more serendipitous detour. Palmerston Atoll is a group of half a dozen tiny sandbars connected by a reef and enclosing a shallow lagoon. It is hundreds of ocean miles from anywhere else and visited only by passing sailboats and a supply ship from New Zealand that calls four times a year, plus the occasional Japanese freighter. The houses are thatched-roof huts. There is no running water or electricity, other than individual generators in a few houses and common buildings.

The real story is the people. About fifty souls inhabit Palmerston Atoll. They are all descendants of one man, a 19th-Century British explorer named William Marsters, and his three Polynesian wives, who some say were sisters. Marsters landed here and claimed the island for himself and his wives and, ultimately, their children. To this day, every person on Palmerston has the last name of Marsters. Occasionally, a young adult will leave the island and return with an off-island spouse, but inter-marriage among the three branches of the family is still the norm. The family has a strict rule against inter-marrying within a single branch, of course – although that ship might have sailed long ago.

In the mid-20th Century, the Marsters family received official ownership of the island from New Zealand. The family developed a passport stamp with the outline of the atoll. It is now the pride of our passports. I learned later that some voyagers call in to Palmerston for the sole purpose of getting the stamp.

The family elects officers from time to time, and the highest office is mayor. The mayor presides over the sole industry on the island, which is parrotfish herding.

I'm not making this up.

Every morning, the members of the family who are not involved with subsistence tasks wade out to the reefs with nets and palm fronds to nudge parrotfish into an enclosed watery corral. There the fish remain until the family harvests them to sell to a Japanese freighter that calls in a few times a year for that express purpose. Apparently, parrotfish are a delicacy of Japanese cuisine.

In any event, the workday grind ends sometime before noon. After a nice lunch and a nap, the family employs the remainder of the daylight hours in a spirited game of beach volleyball. At night, they gather around one of the generators, which is hooked up to a television set, and watch DVDs. As a change of pace, sometimes they gather on the beach and sit around a fire and sing.

Alan and I are hoping to be adopted. We would happily change our last name to Marsters at a moment's notice.

With or without adoption, the Palmerston community has developed a symbiotic barter relationship with passing sailboats. While voyagers remain anchored at Palmerston, they are invited ashore daily for a family-style lunch – usually something very tasty grown on the island or caught in its waters, and cooked in palm leaves in underground pits. In return, voyagers leave diesel fuel for the generators, or canned goods or toiletries or clothing. In our case, in addition to the standard offerings, we also left a DVD of an old Dallas Cowboy football game that a friend had sent us from the States. It was a nine days' wonder.

Our final night on the atoll was perhaps one of the best nights ashore of the circumnavigation. The Marsters family invited us to the beach for some music. Before law school, I made my living as a musician and singer. I'm not happy too far away from a piano, so I had made space on the boat to store a battery-operated portable electronic keyboard.

From time to time in a crowded anchorage or marina, I would pull it out and invite people over for a singalong of oldie goldies. It was always a blast. So that evening, we put the keyboard in the dinghy and headed to the beach.

When we got there, the festivities had already begun. A nice bonfire was blazing. Several members of the family, seated on driftwood and folding chairs, had picked up guitars and started to play. One of the larger men – easily 6'3" and 350 pounds – had selected a ukulele and was balancing the tiny stringed instrument on his stomach. As he strummed away double-time, his entire body jiggled in rhythm.

Then they started singing.

It was as if the heavens opened up and an angelic chorus descended. In five- and six-part harmony, the men and women sang with perfect pitch and clarity. They sang Polynesian folk songs, simple tunes that radiated emotion and peace. The harmonies were simple, but rich and luscious. The songs soared in volume, then died to a whisper, then soared again.

They went through several of these soul-moving airs, and then turned to me and my piano expectantly. How in the world would I be able to follow that act?

Well, I represented my culture the best I could with rousing versions of "Heard It Through the Grapevine" and "My Girl." They listened politely for a while, then resumed their angelic chorus with obvious relief.

I tried again later with "Hey Jude" and "Margaritaville."

Tough crowd.

Later that night, long after we had returned to the boat and sacked out, we heard a knock on the hull. It was several members of the family, warning us that the wind had changed direction, and that we were in danger of being blown onto the beach or onto one of the barrier reefs. We could hear and see other family members spreading the warning to the other boats at anchor. Masthead and deck lights started flickering on. The weather front that had sent us to Palmerston had blown itself out. The wind had backed around to the opposite compass direction, and the bay that had been sheltering us was now completely open to the elements. We pulled up the anchor and made a hasty departure to sea before we were blown too far towards shore to get away.

Once at sea, we surveyed what were now calm seas and moderate winds and decided to continue on to the Kingdom of Tonga. We had said our goodbyes and expressed our appreciation the previous evening. I still wonder, though, whether the onshore wind peril was an act of revenge by the Polynesian gods for my having desecrated this unspoiled island culture with pop music and American football.

I hope not. Or, at least, maybe we can make it up to them later.

CHAPTER 14
THE KINGDOM OF TONGA

Q: Do you get to see any whales?

A: Yes. We often see them on shorter passages and near coastal areas. We almost accidentally hit one near the Great Barrier Reef in Australia. He rolled away just in time and gave us a major, whale-sized stink-eye in the process. The best encounter was when Alan swam with a humpback and her calf in the South Pacific.

The Kingdom of Tonga is a constitutional Polynesian monarchy consisting of 169 islands. Only 36 are inhabited. The rest are a voyager's gunkholing paradise.

The Tongan people have two defining characteristics. The first is that they do not like to say "no." They will not say it directly. Instead, they will say "yes" while offering nonverbal clues that they really mean "no." We learned to recognize a click of the tongue and a nod of the head as an indication that we would need to look elsewhere for whatever it was we were seeking.

The second defining characteristic is that they are a very large people – tall and thick and muscular and substantial, men and women alike. Tongans are sought after in the rugby leagues, and more than a few have been drafted by American professional football teams. Nowhere was this brought home to us more than as we were preparing to attend church on the capital island of Tongatapu and needed to shop for clothing for the occasion. It was rumored that the King would be in attendance, and we wanted to make a good impression.

Correct church attire for women is all white. That was no problem for me. Correct church attire for men is a dress shirt, tie, and a tupenu, which is a sarong-like, kilt-like . . . well, I'll just go ahead and say it: It's a skirt.

I felt that Alan should have one if we were going to church, and who knew – perhaps we would be invited to other semi-formal occasions while in the kingdom. And Alan, game as always, said sure why not.

"Where am I going to get one of those skirts?" he asked, as we walked on a rutted sidewalk in the capital Nuku'alofa.

"It's called a tupenu, not a skirt. I think I saw a department store around here somewhere. At least, it was a building and there were clothes hanging on a rack out front."

We paused as two women, easily 6 feet and 280 pounds each, swept by us on the sidewalk. We had to step entirely off the sidewalk onto the gravel road to let them pass.

"Aha," I said. There it is.

We went in to the clothing store, and I made eye contact with a woman standing behind a counter.

"Good morning," I warbled. "It's a lovely day."

"Yes it is. I hear that the weather will be fine for some time."

"That would be nice. It's such a pretty island."

"Thank you. You are very kind."

Niceties concluded, she came down to business. "Are you looking for something in particular?"

"Yes," I said. "My husband is looking for a tupenu. And he also needs a dress shirt and tie."

The lady turned her attention to Alan. Now Alan is a good-sized guy, a strapping 5'11" and 180, but the lady in the shop had him beat by at least an inch and 50 pounds.

"The tupenu is for him?" she asked.

"Yes, for him," I answered.

She pointed towards the back of the store. "The children's department is over there."

"The children's department?"

"Yes, he will need the pre-teen sizes."

So we found the children's department, and sure enough, the pre-teen boys' sizes fit the redhead perfectly. Just for fun, he tried on a man's "small," and it wrapped around him about three times.

Appropriately dressed, we attended church that Sunday. The King of Tonga attended as well, although he appeared to doze off fairly quickly in the proceedings. The choir was the highlight. Their *a cappella* music – reminiscent of Palmerston but more sophisticated – was so transcendentally beautiful that it brought me to tears in the first 30 seconds.

"Thank you for wearing the skirt, sweetheart," I said as we were leaving the church. "I'm not sure the pastor would have been so welcoming if you hadn't."

"No problem. It's nice and breezy."

I looked at him in horror. "You have something on under there, don't you?"

"Of course," he said in an insulted tone. "I'm wearing my Speedo."

I rolled my eyes.

* * *

After anchoring in a succession of picture-perfect Tongan deserted islands and diving so many lovely reefs and walls that we lost count, we decided to spend some time in the main bay of one of Tonga's inhabited islands. One morning as we were doing some boat work, a local boat motored out to us, and to other voyagers anchored nearby, to invite us to a birthday party. We accepted with pleasure.

Getting to the party at the appointed time involved climbing a small mountain made of damp red clay. It was a feat in itself. Near the top was the family's home, made of cinder blocks and repurposed timber. The family members served us drinks and chatted with us and the other guests until dinner was served. The birthday honoree, the family patriarch, made an appearance and was toasted and applauded.

The party was a resounding success in its combination of informality and generous hospitality. At dinner, some of the guests were seated at a low table, until the chairs ran out, and then the remainder of the guests sat on the floor. Food was passed around family style. At one point, a piglet's head appeared to be making its way down the table. I could see that each guest appeared to be dipping something out of the top of the head, and then eating whatever it was they had dipped out.

Oh dear lord, please don't let this be . . ..

But it was. A delicacy of piglet brains, cooked (blessedly) and served in the skull, was heading our way. When it arrived, we looked at each other, smiled appreciatively at the host, and dipped. It was a little slimy, but not as bad as it looked.

Well, okay, it was pretty bad. But the party was great, and we expressed our sincere thanks to our hosts as we left to slip and slide back down the mountain to the bay below.

The next day, we headed out. Our plan was to leave the northern archipelago and island hop our way south. We were perhaps a mile offshore when just beside the boat we saw whale spume, and then a fluke in the air. And then perhaps 100 feet away a baby whale breached and practically danced on its little tail before crashing back into the water.

"Alan," I called excitedly. "Come look."

He was already putting on his mask and snorkel, and had his fins in his hand.

"What are you doing?"

"I'm going to go swim with those whales."

"Seriously?"

"Yes, why not?

I could think of about a thousand reasons why not, but you know what? Life is short.

"No reason. I love you. I'll stay with the boat and be close by if you need me." I dropped the sails to have more maneuverability.

So for the next half hour, Alan swam with a huge humpback whale and her calf. The calf was very curious, but Mom appeared to be leery about letting it get too close. At one point, Mom swam slowly past Alan just below the surface, and for a while, he said later, all he could see was her gigantic eye, close to him, watching him as he snorkeled alongside.

I kept the boat stable and as near as I could to them without spooking the whales. Finally, Alan waved, and I motored over and picked him up.

"All done?" I asked.

"Yes." He was grinning from ear to ear. "That. Was. Awesome."

* * *

It was only a few days later that we heard a Mayday call. We had made a fair amount of progress island-hopping southward in Tonga and were at anchor in the Ha'apai group of islands in the central archipelago. Another boat anchored in the same general area had hailed us on Channel 16 to give us a heads-up that they had heard an emergency broadcast on single-sideband radio, but they did not know where the emergency was.

We tuned into the correct channel on our SSB and started listening in increasing dismay. A boat was hailing the New Zealand Navy for rescue. There were two souls aboard. The man was talking to the Navy, and we could hear the woman screaming and crying in the background. It was horrible.

It emerged that the boat had run aground on a large reef in the darkness. It was about 25 miles from us, three to four hours away in these reef-infested waters – or more likely five hours as night had fallen and it would be impossible to see the telltale signs of breaking water over a deadly reef just below the surface.

The Navy ship gave its position and asked for the position of the distressed vessel. We plotted the position of both boats, and it appeared that the ship was only about 45 minutes away from them.

Alan and I looked at each with visible relief. If we were the closest private vessel willing to help, we would certainly have weighed anchor and done our best to reach them, but the attempt would have been profoundly hazardous. Rescuing people at night from a boat banging up against a reef and in the process of capsizing is a job for professionals, if professional are available. It's like running into a burning building to try to help, when the firefighters are standing right there.

And so we continued to listen with a combination of gut-wrenching sympathy and macabre fascination. The sounds of the boat breaking apart were so loud that it was sometimes difficult to understand the verbal exchanges completely. The channel was left open, so we could hear every bang and boom and scrape. We didn't like to think what might happen if the Navy ship didn't get there soon.

The Navy radio guy told the couple to put on life vests and go sit on the foredeck to wait for them. He told them to take nothing with them other than their identification and an EPIRB, which is an emergency beacon. The woman then came on the microphone and said tearfully that they had a cat, and could they bring their cat.

Alan and I looked at each other in consternation. We were both thinking the same thing: Please don't make them leave the cat!

But the Navy rescued the couple and the cat, and got them all aboard safely. The boat sank completely, almost out from under the voyagers while they were waiting for rescue; and everything else aboard was lost.

It was only then that we heard the name of the sunken boat. It was *Stunner*, the boat with the warring couple that we had met at the Panama Canal.

Alan did not take the opportunity to remind me he had predicted this. The tragedy was too upsetting to personalize. Those poor people. He just shook his head.

In the ensuing weeks, voyagers who knew of the accident were eager to do the post mortem. Had *Stunner* not had proper charts? If not (and it appeared not) and if they were following another boat, had *Stunner* turned too soon, before it had safely passed the reef? If so, why?

A couple of days after we left our anchorage to continue island-hopping south, we passed what might be the saddest sight possible for a voyager to see. At a large reef surrounded by deeper water, we could see the tip of *Stunner*'s mast. The rest of the boat was submerged.

All that remained of *Stunner* was a few feet of mast.

* * *

Our next destination, New Zealand, was high on our list of priorities. People often cite the long plane ride as a deterrent to visiting New Zealand, and indeed it's 12 to 15 hours or so. In contrast, it took us 18 months to get there, plus one more rough passage to get there from Tonga across the waters of the South Pacific.

New Zealand is known as the "Land of the Long White Cloud." It is composed of two large main islands, the North Island (which is the location of the city of Auckland) and the South Island (Christchurch, Wellington). The country's economy is built on agriculture, tourism, and the usual industrial and service activity of a first-world country. New Zealand is a member of the British Commonwealth, so Queen Elizabeth II is the head of state. However, the government is run independently on a parliamentary basis, with executive power held by the prime minister and his or her cabinet.

New Zealand was the first country in the world to give women the right to vote. So far, the country has elected three female prime ministers. I'm just saying.

From the southernmost island of Tonga, the crossing to New Zealand took us six days. It was 1,150 nautical miles of gale-force winds and a blisteringly fast, though highly uncomfortable, sail. We logged our best noon-to-noon distance of 215 miles and our fastest sustained speed of 12.1 knots.

As usual in the Pacific, we never saw another boat or living thing until landfall.

LETTER HOME
WHANGEREI, NEW ZEALAND

Hi y'all,

I don't know where to begin to convey the glory that is New Zealand. The words can't capture the sweeping natural beauty in every direction I look. Honestly, it looks exactly like *Lord of the Rings*, except the greens are perhaps even greener and the blues even bluer. But the vistas, no matter how lovely, can't communicate the simple good cheer of the Kiwi culture.

Checkout person: "Don't buy that here, mate; it's a dollar cheaper across the street."

Store owner: "No, we don't carry that part, but let me drive you down the wholesaler. No worries, mate – he owes me a beer."

Later in the week, we will be having a potluck dinner with the other voyagers who have sailed to New Zealand this season. We are in charge of bringing mashed potatoes for 30 people, and a pecan pie. My plan is to require that each person say the word "pecan" correctly – *i.e.*, peh-CAHN, not PEE-can – before he or she can have a slice. There may be only ten slices, but that's ten more people in the world who won't irritate Texans by mispronouncing our state nut.

We plan to do substantial land travel here – at least six months' worth. It may be that we stay longer than that.

It may be that we never leave.

Love, Liza

CHAPTER 15
NEW ZEALAND

Q: Do you plan to go back to work or are you "done"?

A: When we complete our circumnavigation, we will resume land life and attempt to go back to our careers in law and medicine. We have a few concerns about it:

- Will I become an insomniac in a bed that doesn't move?
- Will Alan walk out naked into the front yard to check the anchor when the wind changes in the middle of the night?
- Will anyone hire us after such a long gap in our respective resumes?
- Will we care if they won't?

We made landfall in New Zealand at Whangarei (pronounced FAHNG-uh-RAY, for no apparent reason), a small city midway down the North Island. The wharf has the look of a Disney village – cute little shops, a coffee bar, a café, a clock museum, a giant chessboard and people-sized pieces, families strolling along the waterfront.

We were eager to explore but needed to spend most of the morning cleaning the boat after the rough passage from Tongatapu. I attacked the saltwater stains on the upholstery and carpet while Alan washed the deck with fresh water from our hose connected to the dock spigot. I cleaned the cockpit and the clear vinyl enclosure while Alan put away the passage equipment and reassembled the main saloon. Working like maniacs, we were finished by noon.

I had seen a sign for what looked like an actual supermarket, and I was chomping at the bit. Also, I needed to find an Internet café to check our email and online bank accounts. Alan was eager for a newspaper and a latte. Civilization! We agreed to meet back at the boat later in the day.

It was a five-minute walk to the supermarket. The automatic doors whisked aside. Whoa. I took a moment to process that magic. Continuing forward, I walked directly into the produce department and stopped short.

Before my eyes was a veritable wall of fresh produce – broccoli, tomatoes, squash of all descriptions, actual lettuce and a dozen varieties of greens, apples, pears, grapes, onions, lovely bright orange carrots with no black rotting patches whatsoever, fresh green beans, bags of neon yellow lemons, limes and peaches and plums, huge washed potatoes, cucumbers. It went on and on, vivid colors, leafy things, bins and bins of them. The tears began to well.

The small woman who had been patiently waiting behind me to enter the store put a hand on my shoulder and gently moved me aside. In a lilting Kiwi accent she asked, with a knowing and sympathetic look: "Off a boat, dear?"

"Yes," I blubbered. "I haven't seen broccoli in . . . in . . . ." I had to turn away. I would go have a nice quiet lunch and then come back fortified to face this sensory overload later. Lord only knew how many varieties of soup and cereal there would be. And maybe even . . . no . . . well maybe . . . . I wouldn't speculate. Time enough for all that later.

I walked around outside for a while to regain my composure and then wandered over to the café – a nook with a wooden counter and outdoor umbrella tables. A quick sandwich would do the trick.

After standing around in the entrance for a while, trying to figure out whether to (a) wait to be seated; (b) just grab a table; or (c) order at the counter, I bellied up and smiled at the spiky-headed, be-nose-ringed female counter-person.

"Chicken sandwich, please, and a Diet Coke."

"Isthlaw?"

"I beg your pardon?" I knew that English was the official language here. I noted that the New Zealand accent sounded somewhat British, but apparently they used entirely different words.

"Isthathelaw?"

"One more time and I'll have it," I tendered optimistically.

"Is . . . That . . . The . . . Lot?" she punctuated.

"Oh," I exhaled, relieved. "Yeah, that's it."

I paid and moved off a little ways down the counter. She took pity on me.

"We'll bring it round your table," she enunciated as if to a five-year-old.

"Oh, thanks," I gushed, and duly sat.

When she delivered the sandwich, nicely sliced in conventionally diagonal fashion, I took a big bite and got through approximately 1.3 chews before I realized it was totally revolting. I sat immobile for long moments, trying to summon the nerve to spit it out. Martyred as usual by my central Texas upbringing, however, I dutifully chewed the bite and, shuddering, swallowed it.

Prodding the remains, I did a quick post-mortem. Bread (check). Butter on the bread (yuck). Actually, thick smears of butter on both sides of the bread (bizarrely yuck). Boiled chicken chunks (check). Lettuce, tomato, grated carrot (check). No mayo or mustard (huh?). Thick round slice of something unidentifiable, burgundy-colored and rubbery, like canned jellied cranberry sauce that had spent a week or so congealing in the sun (huh?).

I flagged down the server.

"Um, what is this?" I pointed to the offending item.

"Be true," she responded.

"I'm sorry?"

"Beet . . . Root," she repeated in exasperation and hurried on.

Ohhhhh. I ruminated for a while on the essence of cultural diversity. Then I took stock. Clearly I couldn't finish this sandwich. Even if I took the beet root off, there were the smears of butter to consider. But international relations were at stake. Would it be ruder to get up and leave with the sandwich uneaten or to re-order something edible? I wrestled for some time with a dilemma which, had I voiced it to any male on the planet, would have gotten me committed. Ultimately I was swayed by the persuasive line of reasoning that I was still starving, and no other source of ready-made food was in sight.

I pushed back my chair and sauntered back to the counter. My plan – brilliant in its simplicity – was to order some French fries (which would supplement but not actually replace the sandwich) and then, pretending I was far too full to finish the sandwich, depart with no one the wiser and with no unfortunate American slur against the local food.

"Hi," I lilted, old friends now. "Could I have an order of fries, too?"

It was her turn to say, "Pardon?"

"French fries," I repeated slowly. "French fried potatoes. Oh wait," I consulted memories of British sitcoms, and inspiration dawned. "I mean chips. You call them chips, right?" I beamed.

Stopping just short of rolling her eyes, the server took my money and asked if I needed tomahto sauce.

I hesitated, staring. I hoped tomahto sauce was ketchup but no longer had the will to ask. "Yes, please," I replied, teetering on the verge of trying to rekindle our former camaraderie by telling her sorry, I'd arrived in the country only this morning and didn't know the lingo yet, hah. Mercifully for us both, I resumed my seat in silence.

The chips came; they were excellent, and tomahto sauce was indeed ketchup, perhaps a shade sweeter. I stirred the sandwich up on the plate and left, vowing to practice the phrase "no beet root, no butter" until it rolled automatically from my tongue whenever I got within ordering distance of a Kiwi café counter.

* * *

All in all, we spent more than a year in the Land of the Long White Cloud. During our travels there, we inevitably were reminded that someday we would need to go back to living on land. At every B&B and rental house we stayed, we considered whether this type of town or city, or that type of house or apartment, resonated with us. And the answer kept coming back "not sure." Until the circumnavigation was complete, or at least imminently complete, those questions would have to remain unanswered. The ocean was our home, and that was all we needed for now.

It is said in New Zealand that there is one boat for every two New Zealanders. I would put the number at closer to one for one. Kiwis love the sea, and so we had a lot in common with the population from the get-go.

One of our best memories is of the America's Cup racing and festivities in Auckland. We spent much time hanging out with all the sailors at the village and marinas, and ogling the super-yachts therein. The enthusiasm among Kiwis for this ocean race knew no bounds. For the first race in the final between Team New Zealand's Black Magic and the Italian boat Prada, almost 200,000 Kiwi spectators turned up. Percentage-wise in terms of the United States, that would be as if the entire adult population of Texas (about 20 million folks) showed up in Dallas for a Cowboy football game. It boggles the mind.

And speaking of mind-boggling activities, we also attended an epic production of Verdi's *La Traviata* in a rugby stadium. There were fireworks, live animals, and beer vendors. In my view, this is the way opera was meant to be.

Several memories sum up the reasons why New Zealand is so very different from any other developed, sophisticated country in the world. First, it is often said that there are ten sheep for every person in New Zealand. Well, that's wrong. There are actually six, down from a high of 20 several decades ago. I don't have a problem with that at all, especially when I am looking out over an impossibly green vista dotted with the fluffy things.

Second, there is virtually nothing in New Zealand that can hurt or scare you. There are no spiders, snakes, bears, mountain lions, scorpions, wolves, crocodiles, alligators, giant pigs, or serial killers. It is a country in which you can walk around barefooted and unarmed and feel perfectly secure.

Third, bad things don't happen, or at least not very often, or at least not with the severity that they happen in

Dallas. I will never forget our first newscast. A few days after landfall, we went out and bought a small, portable television. Alan installed the antenna on the mast, and we fired her up. The only channel we could get was Auckland. The news was on. The anchor, or "news reader," as they are called there, had a very serious look on her face.

She reported: "A gang of three people has again attempted to rob a bank in the city center. This is their second attempt this month. Both robberies were prevented by quick action of the teller. It is hoped that the gang will be caught soon, however. In the second attempt, a member of the gang brandished a screwdriver, and it is feared that if a third attempt occurs, someone may be injured."

Never before have I heard the word "brandished" used in conjunction with the word "screwdriver." Alan and I just looked at each other and nodded. This would be a very nice country to spend some time.

Most of our exploration of New Zealand was by land. I would venture to say that we got to see more of New Zealand than the average Kiwi does. We put the boat on the hard and bought a car and drove to the wine country on both islands, to the Rotorua area, to Bay of Islands, to all of the major cities and national parks, to the whole of the coastal and mountain regions of the South Island.

Deep in the South Island, we hiked the Milford Track. From Lake Te Anau to Milford Sound, the track winds through breathtaking wilderness and over waterfall-ribboned mountains, on paths that sometimes are above the clouds It is a 4-day, 40-mile mountain backpacking adventure that darn near killed me. I'd walk for a while and then whine for a while. Then I'd try to sneak something heavy from my pack into Alan's.

Ultimately, though, it was time to depart – mainly because we ran out of acceptable excuses to keep extending our tourist visas. Whenever anyone asks us what our favorite place on the trip was, we usually say that all fifty-five of the countries and island groups we visited were our favorites. If pressed further, however, we always say, "Well, actually . . . our favorite place was New Zealand."

CHAPTER 16
THE FIJI ISLANDS TO VANUATU

Q: When you are in the middle of the ocean, do you ever cool off with a dip in the sea?

A: We often jump in, whether in a pristine coastal bay or out of sight of land. It is one of the great freedoms of living on a sailboat.

The crossing from New Zealand to the Fiji Islands took exactly six days. We had two days with no wind at all (we motored on a glassy sea); two days with perfect winds (15 knots on our beam); and two days under somewhat exhilarating conditions (25 to 35 knots of wind, close hauled, with 10-foot breaking head seas). After a year on land, we were just a little bit rusty.

The Republic of Fiji is a collection of about 300 postcard-perfect islands and reefs scattered over more than 800,000 square miles of water. Just to keep things exciting, the ocean in that area produces a new island or reef every year or so. The charts are not necessarily up to date in that regard. While daysailing from island to island, we kept a very vigilant watch, with binoculars, at either the bow or a few feet up the mast. Unlike our normal efforts that focus on the horizon, we focused instead on the waters ahead.

To experience all of Fiji would take years. After some debate, we decided to concentrate on the westernmost bit – the Yasawa Group, the Mamanuca Group, and Viti Levu.

Since our next destination would be Vanuatu to the west, this approach seemed to make the most sense.

For about half the time, we hit the tourist areas, which were exactly as represented and expected – glorious in every aspect, with the scent of tropical flowers and umbrella cocktails equally intoxicating. I see why people get married in these exotic islands, and I heartily recommend the practice. If the redhead and I hadn't tied the knot back in 1984, we would have headed for the Fiji equivalent of a Las Vegas wedding chapel.

The remainder of the time we spent in the more primitive outer islands. These islands are controlled by hereditary village chiefs in a culture not so very different today than when Captain Bligh arrived in 1789. Well, ok, the villagers back then probably wouldn't have been wearing Nike t-shirts, but otherwise it's similar.

The Fijians whose acquaintance we made in the outer islands told us that they take much pride in preserving the best parts of their traditional way of life, not behind glass in a museum but in their lifestyle and daily activities. In many of the outlying villages, there is no television or modern conveniences, sometimes no electricity. We were told, and we have no reason to doubt, that the simplicity of the village housing and amenities is not a product of poverty. Instead, villagers affirmatively choose to live simply, often in thatch-roofed, dirt-floored huts. They appear to take joy and pride from a subsistence living off the sea and the land.

* * *

"How much of this stuff do you think we'll need?" I asked.

Before heading off to the outer islands, we were doing some shopping at an outdoor market in the city of Suva, on the island of Viti Levu, the largest of the Fijian islands.

"Oh, I don't know, maybe five or six bundles?"

"They sure take up a lot of room. And they're prickly. Are you positive we're going to need it?"

"Pretty sure."

"Okay," I rolled my eyes. "I don't want to get run out of Dodge for not following the rules. But if we need to store some of this on a berth, it's going on your side."

We were talking about kava – a large, gnarled, dried tropical plant stalk and root. To secure permission to anchor in the waters of a village in the outer islands, and to be welcome ashore there, we would first need to present an unspecified amount of kava root to the village chief. This presentation would occur in a formal ceremony called *sevu sevu*. It was unclear to us whether women were allowed to participate in this ceremony, but whether or not, I was happy to give Alan my proxy.

The reason for my hesitance was that kava root is used to produce a drink – called, appropriately, "kava" – that is reputed to be mildly hallucinogenic. It was our understanding that attendees at a kava ceremony would be expected to partake. I felt that one of us needed to be the designated driver, even if it was only of the dinghy.

On the way to the outer islands, we stopped to spend time at a cruiser hangout – the gorgeous Musket Cove, on Malolo Lailai Island – and to dive a reef or two. We were spoiled by this point with perfect deserted bays and colorful dive sites. But each spot we jumped over the side to dive or snorkel in Fiji had its own amazing experience. We saw huge schools of pelagic fish; many large white tip sharks; a foot long lionfish; hundreds of different species of brilliant reef fish, many of them new to us; rays; giant clams; and vivid plant life large and small. At one coral tower, I saw my first sea snake. All I will say about that is I had nightmares for days and found excuses to avoid swimming for even longer.

Shudder.

"Hey, how'd it go?" I asked.

Alan was approaching the dinghy, which we had pulled up a short way onto the beach outside of our first Fijian village. He looked perhaps a little wobbly, but not unduly so. We pushed the dink back in to the water and hopped in. I made him put on a life vest. Who knew what effect a "mild hallucinogen" might have on the ability to swim, even for a triathlete like the redhead.

Once back in our cockpit, safely out of earshot of the village, I proceeded with my direct examination. Alan stared around the boat, focusing on this and that. I giggled.

"You look a little bit stoned, sweetheart."

"Do I?"

I noticed that he had not returned with any kava root, so assumed our offering had been accepted.

"Did it go okay?"

"Yes, it went fine."

"What happened?"

"There were about a dozen people there, sitting on the floor. The chief had on a t-shirt and grass skirt. I gave him the kava root."

"Was that it?"

"No, no. He also had on sandals. I hope he had on something under the skirt, but I don't know."

"No, I mean did anything else happen?"

"Oh. He clapped his hands three times and said something I didn't catch in sort of a sing-song-y voice. Then he picked up a coconut bowl and walked over to this wooden vat in the corner and filled up the bowl and drank it in one gulp."

"And then?"

"He filled it up again and passed it to me. I figured I needed to drink it in one gulp, too, so I did."

He put his hand up to his face and poked on his mouth. "Hey, my lips are numb."

"What was it like?"

"It looked like dishwater and tasted like mud."

"Yuck."

"But it was okay. Better than piglet brains, that's for sure."

I laughed. "So are we good to anchor here and go ashore or whatever?"

"Yes. We all clapped our hands three times, and the chief said something else I didn't catch, and then we talked for a while. I don't remember the conversation exactly, but it was good. He was a cool guy. There were some other boats there, too."

"Were there any women?"

"Uh, I think so. Yes, there were."

Rats. I might have to go ashore and take one for the team at some point down the island chain.

"But the chief said we could stay, though, right?"

"Oh yes. Well, I'm pretty sure he did."

"How sure?"

"Well, I think he would have said something if we couldn't, right?"

"Did he give you any paperwork?"

Alan looked at me in disbelief and then dissolved in a fit of hooting laughter.

Hmmph.

But all was well. We repeated that procedure on each of the other island villages we visited, and nobody ever chased us away.

When we ran out of kava root (I should have bought more), we swung by a tourist island to see the famed "Blue Lagoon." Spoiler alert: Meh. After checking out of the country, we set sail west for a smooth five-day passage to Vanuatu.

* * *

Vanuatu, known as New Hebrides until its independence from English and French colonial rule in 1980, consists of eighty-two small volcanic islands. The official language is Bislama, which is one of the most interesting languages in the world. It appears to be a combination of pidgin English, French, and Spanish. There are enough words that are similar enough to English that you can almost understand it. It's sort of like watching a British drama that takes place in Northern England. You feel that if you can just hang in there long enough, at some point you will understand the dialog.

For example, "welcome" is "welkam"; and "what's your name" is "wanem nem blong yu?" (loosely translated as "what name belongs to you?"). "Where are you from" is "yu blong weah?" To discover the location of the toilet, one asks: "Toilet I stap weah?" "Thank you very much" is "tangkyu tumas." I could go on and on, but I think you get the charm.

We made landfall at the town of Port Vila on one of the larger islands, Efate. While there, we booked an island tour with several other boats. It was quite hot, and I had on a modest but sleeveless top. As we walked along the Port Vila sidewalk towards the tour van, a Vanuatan man passing by, leaned over and grabbed, then caressed, the back of my upper arm.

I yelped, and he let go and hurried off. I caught up with the tour guide.

"Hey, some guy just groped me."

The tour guide was concerned. "I am so sorry. Would you like to press charges?" He looked around to see if he could spot the offender.

"No, it was weird. He grabbed the back of my arm." And I showed him where.

"Ah," the tour guide said, and no more.

"What." I asked.

"Well," he sighed, "old habits die hard. The man was . . . how do I say this . . . checking out whether you would make a good meal."

"I'm sorry?"

"Feeling the upper arm is traditionally the best way to tell whether a person would taste good. After cooking, that is. It is a regrettable holdover from our cannibal days."

To say I was taken aback is an understatement.

I walked a little further in silence, processing this information. Then it crossed my mind to wonder whether I would or would not be a good candidate for a cannibal menu. There was plenty of marbling, sure, but perhaps a bit too old to be tender? I turned back to the guide.

"So do you think the guy thought I would make a good dinner?"

The guide opened his mouth to laugh, and I could not help but notice the unusually long and sharp incisors.

"Perhaps more like lunch. But yes, ma'am, I am quite sure you would make an excellent meal. If we still practiced cannibalism. Which we do not. It was legally abolished, and it has not been practiced since 1969."

1969? Whoa. There were people still alive here who were part of the old regime. I back-pedaled, to the sound of his continued chuckling, and scurried over to the company of the other voyagers.

"Do not leave me alone for a minute," I panted.

"Why not," Amelia asked?

"Apparently, I look very tasty."

She was puzzled, but in true voyager tolerance of all quirks, she merely nodded her head and did not inquire further.

I chafed for a good hour, though, at the thought that I would not qualify as dinner.

The tour focused primarily on the island's substantial role in World War II as an important military base of observation and operations for American forces. There are stands where one can buy Coke bottles from that era, recovered from the harbor. The bottles have the year and place of manufacture, *e.g.*, "1941, San Francisco." Vanuatu should be, in my opinion, a required visit for World War II buffs.

Several other things stood out for me about Vanuatu and our time there. The first was the traditional clothing and traditions of the northern islands. Upon stepping ashore at one of the northeastern islands, I encountered the eye-popping sight of many grown men going about their normal activities clad only in a namba. A namba is a penis wrap made of straw, decorated with various plants and flowers, and secured by a thin cord around the waist. It does not cover any of the other boy parts down there, and it doesn't even address one's backside.

Alan really, really wanted one. So much so, in fact, that I had to use up a spousal veto to prevent it, in part because I knew that he would have wanted to wear it in places like downtown Sydney. I did not want to have to bail him out of jail.

Later, while anchored at another small, non-industrialized island, we were invited to the "coming of age" party for the oldest grandson of the island's chief. We were told that because of the significance of this particular boy, the occasion would be marked by the ceremonial killing of fifty pigs. I assumed the pigs would be killed by others who were responsible for the feast. But no. The pigs were to be killed by the boy himself, by hand, in a public display of strength.

Poor kid. We declined the invitation with regret. I did not want to have to try to un-see that.

What I will always remember about Vanuatu, though, is our accidental run-in with a dugong. On Efate, we had made the acquaintance of a small contingent from National Geographic. They had been in the islands, they said, for several weeks to find, photograph, and video a dugong, which is listed as "threatened" on the world wildlife list. Unfortunately, despite extensive chasing down of tips, they had been unable to document that the animal could be found in these waters. They were on their way back home to France.

The dugong is a large marine mammal. It is herbivorous, meaning it is not above us on the food chain. I like that trait in a sea creature.

Dugongs are distant cousins of the manatee, many of which call Florida home. One of the visible differences between the two species is that while the manatee has a paddle-like tail roughly similar to a beaver, the dugong has a fluked tail similar to a whale. There are other differences as well, but the bottom line is that the dugong is not just a manatee with a different name. It is an entirely different sea animal.

Dugongs feed on seagrass meadows found on the sandy bottoms of coastal areas in the western Pacific. Their closest relatives, sea cows, were hunted to extinction a few centuries ago. Although dugongs are typically long-lived, usually 50 to 70 years, their reproduction rate is relatively low, usually only one calf every five years.

We received this information with interest from the National Geographic crew, and we wished them a safe trip home.

Two days later, we dropped the hook in a large bay on Epi, a Vanuatuan island just north of Efate. It was hot. We jumped in the water to cool off. There, in about 20 feet of water, serenely feeding on the bottom and stirring up little cyclones of sand, was something that looked to be the size of a small pickup. Upon closer inspection, it was maybe 10 feet long and weighed 800 pounds. We grabbed our snorkels and masks to investigate further.

It was a dugong. We grabbed our video camera and underwater housing. In the ten auspicious minutes before the dugong departed, we shot some mediocre-quality home video that has been used, with our permission, by conservation groups and news teams around the world. Pretty awesome.

The dugong herself had what looked to be a smile on her face the whole time. She was cartoon-character cute, in the manner of that hippo with the tutu. She even had a sidekick, an angel fish that never left her side as she cruised up to the surface for air, and then back down again to the seabed to feed.

We radioed our location to cruisers on Efate, in case the National Geographic folks hadn't left yet. I don't know what happened with that, but we departed northward feeling like Jacque Cousteau.

CHAPTER 17
AUSTRALIA

Q: *Do you ever see any sharks?*

A: Yes, all the time. Even more than in my old law practice.

Q: *Do you ever worry about being attacked by a shark? Do you use a shark repellant, or anything like that?*

A: To be attacked by a shark while swimming in mid-ocean would be similar bad luck, in my view, to being hit by a bus on land, or possibly having a piano fall on your head while you're walking down the sidewalk. As to shark-repellant, we haven't tried it. The question is: How will I know if it works, unless I find out definitively that it doesn't? While snorkeling or diving, I usually carry a dive knife and sometimes a three-foot metal rod with a sharpened point. Having said all that, however, we do avoid some waters as too dangerous for swimming.

On a calm sunny day, after a comfortable passage from Vanuatu to Australia, we approached Sydney Harbour. The harbor entrance is guarded by two dazzling and imposing headland cliffs called "the Heads." To get to Sydney, we would have the unparalleled joy of sailing between the Heads and into Sydney Harbour. To our starboard, a couple of hundred yards distant, we could see two large beaches crowded with people. To port was rugged coastline as far as the eye could see. We were loafing along under easy sail in light beam winds, with nearly flat seas. I pulled out the binoculars to look for hazards, but the entrance was well-marked and looked to be straightforward.

Alan was neatening up the deck in preparation for landfall when I heard him say "whoa" in a hushed but horrified tone.

"Come here," he whispered. I dutifully made my way to the deck where he was standing.

Wordlessly, he pointed down to the water to our immediate starboard side. Lolling on the surface was the biggest shark I have ever seen. It was a great white, called a "white pointer" in this part of the world. He was at least 20 feet long. I could see his entire body, from snout to tail tip. The huge dorsal fin was fully outside the water. He was snaking along with us at our pace. When he rolled slightly and surveyed Alan and me with a cold-eyed stare, I had had enough.

"Let's get back in the cockpit," I shuddered.

"You go ahead," Alan said brightly. "I want to watch him."

"Please, sweetheart, can we both just get back into the cockpit? I'm a little freaked out."

"Okay." He pulled himself away from the deck edge and stepped over the coaming into the safety of amidships. "How long do you think it would take this guy to swim over to that beach?"

Oh dear God. "Not long."

We looked at each other in horrified silence. I vowed at that moment not to go into the water for the duration of our stay in Australia. I mentally added the entire country to my very short list of no-swim areas: South Africa (which we would not be visiting this trip), the Galapagos, and now Australia.

And it wasn't just sharks that were behind my general swimming boycott of Australia. Further north, up and down the Queensland coast, very large saltwater crocodiles, or "salties," live and breed in inlets and estuaries. If they were confined to those inlets and estuaries it would be one thing, but no. They roam freely for several miles into the ocean and out to coastal islands as well. The saltie is the largest reptile on the planet. Males can reach 23 feet in length. Both genders are aggressive and dangerous, and I didn't want any part of them.

In Cairnes, on the Queensland coast, a park ranger had ordered Alan and his kayak out of the water and had been more than annoyed that we were not appropriately respectful of the danger. Swimming or kayaking anywhere within 10 miles of shore in northeastern Australian waters is just plain risky, no matter how briefly one is in the water.

For example, it is standard operating procedure for voyagers to "swim the anchor" after dropping the hook. One or more of the crew dives into the water and swims to the point on the surface immediately above the anchor to view its position. The reason for that maneuver is to make sure the anchor has a good "set" – that is, that it has securely grabbed the ocean bottom and is likely to stay there until the crew pulls it back up. If an anchor does not have a good set, it is likely to drag. If the anchor drags across the bottom, the boat moves from its intended position, usually in the direction the wind is blowing. That movement is bad enough if the wind is blowing one out to sea, and there are no hazards along the way. But if the wind is blowing onshore, or if there is a reef or other boats along the drag path, then Houston, we have a problem.

So one way to minimize the risk of dragging is to swim the anchor. In shallow enough water, one can often dive the anchor as well – that is, free dive or SCUBA down to the bottom to make sure it is set properly.

To swim or dive the anchor on the Queensland coast, however, is folly. And folly thy name is "saltie." While anchored in the Whitsunday Islands, we heard a news report of a man who was taken by a saltie while swimming an anchor, while his wife watched helplessly. So no. If we dragged anchor on the Queensland coast, then so be it.

I had not really thought about the Sydney area being problematic, because it does not harbor any saltie fugitives from up north. But after seeing that shark, I was a believer. Just during the time period we were in Sydney, several shark attacks occurred – one in the harbor itself. Around the corner closer to Melbourne and Adelaide, on the south coast, there were several more. One involved a pro diver using an electronic shark-repellant device. The diver was attacked by a huge Pointer, which bit off his leg at the hip. The company that manufactured the repellant device issued a statement that the device was old and obsolete. But presumably it was originally marketed as effective, or no one would have bought it, right? Am I missing something here? I think that shark repellant technology may still have a way to go.

And as long as I'm venting: How can it be that shark experts and conservationists promote the idea that only a handful of shark attacks occur worldwide every year? Those numbers appear to me to be exceeded annually in Australia alone.

We experienced only one quasi-dangerous encounter ourselves, and on the other side of the world. In Tobago, while snorkeling, we had been approached by a black tip shark. It had been relatively easy to keep it at bay with my long metal pole as it swam beside us while we swam back to the boat. However, other voyagers of our acquaintance had not been so lucky. One man had lost a lot of skin and had broken both ankles while scrambling up onto a reef to evade a group of white tips that charged him while he was snorkeling in French Polynesia. Another acquaintance had been bitten badly and had lost part of his arm and shoulder while swimming in an island group north of Vanuatu. Only the quick action of his wife had saved him from dying of blood loss.

But as long as we stayed out of the water, I loved living in Sydney Harbour. It is without question the most beautiful urban harbor in the world. No matter how many times one has seen the Opera House and the Harbour Bridge in photographs or on television, sailing past them takes one's breath away.

Sailing in Sydney Harbour is simple in some ways and challenging in others. Most of the shoreline is steep to, and all hazards are clearly marked. Navigation is therefore no problem. The sheer number of boats and ships underway, however, is daunting. By law, Sydney ferries have absolute right of way over all other vessels. Word to the wise: The ferry captains just assume you know you're supposed to stay out of their way.

By custom, any boat engaged in a regatta also has the right of way, over everything but ferries. Sydneysiders love their regattas. On a fine Saturday, the harbor is teeming with racing pylons and all sizes of sailboats, the crews of which are engaged in hoarse shouting and constant motion – tacking, changing sails, jibing, grinding winches, jumping from one side of the boat to the other. I don't think we would garner much respect in that crowd if I were to mention the days on end we sometimes go without changing course or touching the sail-set.

In all other things, though, we became enthusiastic Sydneysiders. For example, we became loyal fans of the Sydney Swans, our local Aussie Rules football team; and we attended as many major events as possible, including the annual LGBT Mardi Gras Parade.

Aussie Rules football, if you have never watched it on cable, is played on a huge oval field by large, muscular, helmetless blokes wearing short, tight shorts and a flimsy jersey. As far as I can tell, the phrase "Aussie Rules" is a euphemism for no rules whatsoever, which would fit in well with the national ethos. This sport requires maximum toughness. Players run flat out, smash, punch, and kick nonstop – and that's when they don't have the ball. Play is suspended every 15 minutes or so to set a few of the worst fractures and allow the crowd to get another beer. As for scoring, it appears to happen continually, and the best defensive strategy is just to knock the other guy down. A goal is worth six points. A "behind," which is a near miss, is worth one point. In one nail biter we attended along with about 30,000 other fans, the Sydney Swans free-kicked a clutch goal at the buzzer to beat the North Melbourne Kangaroos 103 to 100. Major celebration ensued.

In contrast, the LGBT Mardi Gras Parade had much better outfits. Sydney is second only to San Francisco in having the largest openly gay population of any city in the world. The parade was somewhat risqué, but all in good fun. My favorite was a male marching troupe from Canada wearing copies of Royal Mounties regalia, but only from the waist up, while wearing thongs below and carrying the banner, "We always get our man." Like good comedy satire, there was something to offend everyone.

The crowd was even more entertaining than the parade. For example, I snagged a great spectating spot next to this huge tattooed bearded biker-looking guy, who, being Australian, immediately offered me a beer from the cooler at his feet. After accepting the beer and chatting for a few minutes, I couldn't help but notice that he was wearing nothing but black lumberjack boots and a pink tutu. Nice guy. Accountant from Wagga Wagga.

All other events paled, however, against the spectacle of the New Year's Eve fireworks in Sydney Harbour. We decided to anchor in a little bay off the Sydney Zoo well in advance to get a good spot.

But first there were Boxing Day activities. On every December 26, thousands of vessels gather in the harbor to send off the annual Sydney Hobart Yacht Race. The race covers 628 nautical miles and, because of the treacherous waters and weather, is often described as the most grueling ocean race in the world. This year, we joined the fleet – the spectators, that is, not the racers. We motored alongside the sleek yachts with their foulie-clad crews until they were all properly sent off. Then we eased over to the zoo anchorage, dropped the hook, and popped a cork.

From this vantage point, we would have a ringside seat for the fireworks, which are set off famously every year above the Harbour Bridge. From our cockpit, the Bridge, Opera House, and a large portion of the main harbor were visible. Short of tying up at the Opera House itself, which was not allowed, we had the best seat in the house. Even better, the bay itself was deserted except for us and a small unoccupied boat bobbing on a mooring. And it stayed that way for the next four days.

Then came the morning of December 31. Alan took his morning coffee up into the cockpit and yawned loudly, then exclaimed: "What the heck?"

He continued his exclamations with a "whoa" and a "you need to see this" designed to get me up to the cockpit. I complied.

What had been vacant expanses of water since the yacht race sendoff were now chock full of boats of every description. Some were maneuvering, some were already at anchor, some were engaged in shouting matches as they fended each other off or vied for the same spot. There were super-yachts alongside fishing dinghies alongside ski boats alongside daysailers. By lunch it was topsides to topsides, and Alan and I were both armed with a boat hook and keeping other boats at bay. By mid-afternoon, we gave up, put out all of our fenders, and rafted with a couple of Aussie boats.

By happy hour the shore, too, had filled up with spectators. We read a news article the next day that the crowd was estimated to be a million people. This was not a crowd of just any million, however. This was a crowd of a million partying Australians, who, as far as we could tell, wake up with a beer in one hand and a cigarette in the other.

Like all other Australian parties that we had the privilege to attend, the Sydney Harbour New Year's Eve spectacle did not disappoint. First a fleet of schooners, Christmas-lit to the tops of their masts and the ends of their rigging, sailed a pattern through the harbor. When it was dark enough, the fireworks began – primarily over the bridge but also at strategic points on the water – and continued for what seemed like a full hour. Alan and I sipped an excellent Australian shiraz and oohed and aahed with everyone else.

Then we sat up until dawn to make sure nobody plowed into us as they departed the scene.

* * *

Before we left Sydney, we planned and performed the strategic legwork for the next leg of the trip. We also splurged on a few techno-goodies. Included on that list was a satellite telephone. It was hideously expensive to buy, and even more hideously expensive per minute to actually use, but we felt it was a prudent move for the reputedly dangerous waters ahead, in Southeast Asia and the Middle East.

The next leg of our trip would be from Sydney up the eastern coast and over the top of Australia, through the Torres Strait to Darwin. From there, we would cross the Timor Sea to Bali, and then sail the Java Sea to Singapore. From Singapore, we planned to traverse the Strait of Malacca along the coast of Malaysia, which we hoped to explore at some length. Then we would spend as much time as possible in Thailand waters before departing westward across the Indian Ocean.

All of this itinerary was driven by the familiar voyager phrase: "Phuket by Christmas!" That catchphrase is code for getting the timing right on the route we were taking. To have the most advantageous seasonal weather to cross the Indian Ocean to the Red Sea, to transit the Suez Canal, and to have adequate time to enjoy a full Mediterranean summer, conventional wisdom dictates that a voyager must reach Phuket, Thailand, by Christmas.

As we departed Sydney, we were keeping a weather eye on the clock.

LETTER HOME
NORTHERN COASTAL WATERS OF AUSTRALIA

Hi all,

As I write this, we are nearing the end of a most pleasant five-day passage "over the top" of Australia to Darwin. It's 4:20 a.m. local time, well before dawn. Alan is asleep, and I'm on watch. The radar screen is completely blank – no other boats within 24 miles. We are ghosting along in the Arafura Sea, flat calm with just the hint of a following swell, and winds are a very light six to ten knots east-nor'east. There is no sound but the occasional flap of the jib and plop-whish of a wavelet. The Australian mainland is still in sight and immediately south of us, to port. To stay on course, due west, all I have to do is follow the glittering yellow wake of the giant full moon dead ahead.

As we sailed north through the Great Barrier Reef and along the treacherous northern Aussie coast, we explored deserted mountainous coastlines and rainforests, shallow turquoise waters, and reefs and rocks unchanged – perhaps untouched – since Captain Cook negotiated the same arduous route in the 18th Century.

Of course, he had the advantage of a large crew. On the other hand, our plumbing is much better.

We look forward to negotiating the entrance lock to Darwin and seeing something of the Northern Territory. Then on to Bali!

Love, Liza

CHAPTER 18
SECURITY AND FIREARMS

Q: Did you carry firearms on the boat?

A: Yes. We carry a Mossberg Mariner 590 shotgun and a Remington 30-06 rifle. Although the chance of attack at sea is small, the chance of rescue is even smaller.

In the almost six years we lived afloat on *Heartsong III*, our boat home was never violated. We never lost a single item to theft, aboard or ashore. And apart from attempted piracy in areas where everyone expects it, and apart from a handful of isolated and insignificant incidents of hostility, we were never physically threatened in any way. I continue to be far more wary of Mother Nature than of my fellow humans.

Still, as with all things on a voyage, planning and preparation are the keys to good fortune. Nobody wants to spend time and energy being paranoid. It was our policy to minimize the risk of attack as much as possible with reasonable effort, and then to go about our business without worrying about it.

Essentially, there were three situations for which we had a defense plan:

- at sea, against pirates;
- at anchor or dock, against individual sneak-boarders; and

- on land in high-crime urban or resort areas, especially for me, a female, while ashore alone.

Against piracy on the high seas, the goal is not perfect defense, which is impossible against a determined attack. The goal is to be the least attractive target in the area. We found the best strategy was mainly to pay attention. After observing thousands of local boats around the world, we can say unequivocally that a local "fishing boat" with more than two or three guys on it is not engaged in fishing. It is either a ferry, in which case it will not deviate from course; or it is up to no good.

Upon sighting such a boat – and certainly if it begins a pursuit – it is advisable to maintain top speed, even if it means motor-sailing and/or changing course, to keep it at a distance. Another effective measure is to plan to sail in company in the few areas of the world known to be the absolute riskiest – *e.g.*, Indonesia, the Malacca Straits, the Gulf of Aden, and mainland Venezuela.

We carried a shotgun with "bang mortars" that exploded mid-air at a relatively high volume of sound (although much more quietly than we originally hoped when we bought them). The point was to warn pirates off before they got close enough to board. Our rifle was a thirty-ought-six with armor-piercing bullets. We felt that a direct hit at or below the waterline of a marauding vessel would sink it. At least, we hoped it would. Before entering high-risk areas, we spent a few minutes refreshing our firearm skills and practicing with both guns, and luckily those were the only times we had to fire them.

Against a sneak-boarder, the best defense is simple: Close and lock all hatches and companionways whenever you are asleep and whenever you leave the boat. Some of the worst attacks we know of took place during the day when lock-averse cruisers were napping or when they returned to the boat and surprised a thief belowdecks.

On *Heartsong III*, we had enough porthole cross-ventilation that we did not need to leave human-size hatches open all the time. An option for those who like or need to leave hatches open while they sleep below is a lockable metal grating, which unlocks from below. The risk of not being able to unlock the grating quickly enough in the unlikely event of a fire is insignificant in comparison to the certainty that from time to time a local criminal will check your defenses.

Simply locking up will eliminate the vast majority of risk of an intruder. In addition to locking up, though, we also installed a hidden fuel line valve that, in the "off" position, would prevent anyone from starting the engine and stealing the whole boat.

As for protection ashore, we practiced normal urban caution, such as paying attention to our surroundings, never flashing our money, not wearing nice jewelry, and not discussing where our boat was located – since it was clearly unoccupied if we were ashore. In addition, I carried a small canister of pepper spray in my bag. Pepper spray is strictly illegal in most places, but I would do so again without qualm.

With these low-effort precautionary measures in place, we felt free not to worry about being attacked and to enjoy our interaction with the local population, the vast majority of which constitutes zero risk of theft or violence.

There are some downsides of carrying guns, of course. For example, checking in to a country when you have firearms on board involves significantly more trouble and expense than if you carry no firearms.

First, most countries will want to "store" guns and your ammunition for "safekeeping" while you are in the country. When you get the firearms back, you may notice that a fair amount of your ammunition is gone, and that the guns have been fired. That particular issue can be prevented by installing a trigger-lock and refusing to surrender the key. There is no protection, however, against the firearms and/or ammunition becoming mysteriously "lost" while in official custody. These losses are not uncommon.

Second, on departure you must clear out of the exact same port at which you originally cleared in to retrieve the guns; or in larger countries, you can pay a small fortune to have them shipped to your exit port, after giving several weeks' notice, which still does not guarantee timely delivery. These things must be factored into route planning and budget.

Third, some countries – notably Singapore – levy a non-refundable customs fee for mandatory gun storage that is roughly equal to the value of the gun itself.

Fourth, if you carry guns and decide not to declare them, you are risking a heavy fine, jail time, and/or confiscation of your boat. In Malaysia, gun-running is punishable by the death penalty. In Tobago, our anchorage was searched and one poor French cruiser was carted off and gone for three days until he could raise the US$2,000 fine that was levied for failure to declare his rifle.

Fifth, unless you buy a "marinized" gun, it will rust unless you take very good care of it.

Sixth, the situations in which you would want firearm protection are virtually nil. Almost every encounter you will have with local boats and citizenry will be at worst harmless and at best unmissably rewarding.

With regard to handguns, special considerations apply. Having a handgun for close-quarters protection is, in my view, a very bad idea on a cruising boat, even if you like them and would have one at home as a matter of course.

For starters, if you declare a handgun, it will always be confiscated for the duration of your stay; and it is even less likely to be returned unfired, if it is returned at all. Moreover, handguns are small enough to be concealed on a person's body. They are thus more likely to go missing from your boat in general. If a crime is committed with your handgun in a foreign country, you might be able to clear the situation up, if you have declared it and are meticulous about your paperwork, but you will suffer some stress and loss of time and money in the process. And of course, there is always the possibility, looming in the minds of us more paranoid folk, that an ineffective or malicious constabulary might pin the crime on you anyway. After all, it was your gun.

Most countries treat handguns far more stringently than rifles or shotguns. A failure to declare is usually a serious enough crime to land you in jail. Moreover, handguns are virtually useless in pirate situations against a half dozen guys with Kalashnikovs. The downside outweighs the upside by a landslide.

As a substitute, flare guns are actually a pretty good weapon in close quarters.

To minimize the bureaucracy of it all, consider postponing your gun purchase until the first-world country just before a danger area. For example, if you are circumnavigating from the west coast of the United States, wait until New Zealand to buy. Then you'll have your guns for the high-danger areas of Southeast Asia and/or the Gulf of Aden but won't have to hassle with them while island-hopping across the Pacific. You will need to investigate in advance which countries allow firearm purchases, but this exercise will take a lot less time than carting your guns back and forth every time you make landfall throughout the safer areas.

If you have guns on board, no matter what type, it is imperative that you keep excellent records. Create and make many copies of a Firearms List, which details your guns, type, serial numbers, ammunition type and amount. Yes, you need to count the bullets. Make spaces for your boat stamp, your signature, the date, port, time of gun surrender or sealing on board, the customs official's signature, any fee that will change hands, and anything else official-looking you can think of. When you check in, make the customs guy sign off on two copies and keep one for yourself. Read and fill out their own paperwork carefully, and make sure you have a first-class paper trail. For example, in the fine print of some customs entry forms, flare guns are listed as a declarable firearm. The bottom line is that you need to be able to document (a) your compliance with local law, and (b) your lack of access to your gun in the event that a shooting crime is committed nearby.

Practice firing. Take your guns to a range and fire them many times until you are comfortable with them.

But even more important than the firing range is to run drills on your boat while underway. Things feel a whole lot different on a rolling, bucking boat than on dry land. It's a good idea to practice evading and firing under all points of sail and in daytime and nighttime. Take enough ammunition that you can run some drills with live fire.

Be careful not to do what a friend of ours did, though. While practicing with his rifle off the coast of New Zealand, the poor guy fired aft from the cockpit and severed his backstay. I'm not sure he'll ever live that one down.

If you carry guns, it is important to have a heart-to-heart with your crew. There is no point in having guns if you are not prepared to use them. Decide whether you think you could kill somebody. Decide beforehand whether you will fire to protect property, or only if your personal safety is at risk. For pirate situations, decide whether you will fire only to prevent them from boarding, or whether you will continue to fire once they are on your vessel and/or whether you will continue to fire if they appear to be leaving. Debate the line between self-defense and vigilante-ism, and decide where it lies for you. Think through what actions might indicate whether men in a local boat are honest fishermen (99.999% of the boats you will see) or marauders.

You will benefit by talking to a lawyer, or looking up the laws in your home country and state regarding what force is allowable for self-defense and for protection of property, and what actions on the part of an intruder would indicate their intent. Regardless of what law (if any) would ultimately apply to any actions on your part, you will at least have some guidelines to begin your own personal debate on these issues.

CHAPTER 19
INDONESIA TO SINGAPORE

Q: *Apart from the Somalian pirates that everybody has heard of, are there still pirates out there?*

A. Why yes there are. We're still probably a whole lot safer at sea than on a Dallas freeway, though.

Q: *Did you ever have to sail the boat singlehandedly? Isn't your boat too big for that?*

A: Alan and I both were called on at various times – usually because of illness or injury – to sail the boat for an extended period of time without help from the other. Just about any size boat, short of a superyacht, can be set up for singlehanded sailing. In my view, voyagers should always plan their equipment so that in an emergency, the physically weakest crew member can get the boat safely to port alone.

Near the equator at twilight, the sea and sky melt together at the edges — silver-blue, shiny, hazy. In calm weather, the sun reflects the same pinks and oranges to the mirror seas as it does to the sky. The effect can bring on vertigo and a sensation of falling. Without a horizon to orient yourself, the effect is as disorienting as flying a small plane in the clouds. At moonset, the whole spectacle is repeated, except in glowing variations of white.

On just such a night, after just such a moonset, I saw my first pirates.

We had seen many an Indonesian fishing boat in the South China Sea, as we sailed from Darwin, Australia, on a course to Singapore. Indeed, I spent most of every night watch slaloming among Indonesian fishing boats, trying to stay out of their way as they plied their trade.

Some of the boats were lit, some were not. Some were just big enough for one old guy, a sail, and presumably a fish or two. They looked more like painted wooden surfboards with sides and a mast than a proper boat. They had neither engines nor lights. But the owners go all out on the sails. Each is a different bold design in bright colors, presumably to identify each other from far away. They look like little resort pleasure crafts zipping around. True, they cause more than a little navigational headache, especially when they stay out after dark. On a moonless night, I once came within about two feet of one, and the only reason I saw and was able to avoid it at the last minute was the frantic flickering of the owner's Bic lighter. But during the day they were delightful to watch and be among. As we left Bali, one old guy ventured close enough to signal us he was thirsty, and Alan tossed him a canned Coke. He saluted in thanks with a huge gap-toothed grin in a wrinkled walnut of a face. Multi-cultural harmony was achieved. And it would have made a heck of a commercial.

Other than spending a fair amount of energy trying not to run the little boats over, I gave them no thought as safety hazards. Similarly, the large metal commercial vessels – well lit, and stationery for long periods of time – were no threat. These were making far more money scooping up massive quantities of fish than they could possibly hope to score by stealing a handful of American currency and electronics, or even our boat herself. We were small pickin's to legitimate commercial fishermen.

It was the local medium-sized boats that were worrisome. In that part of the world, they even look sinister — wooden and metal, about thirty feet long, painted with bands and symbols of multiple bright colors, with a sharply curving prow like a scimitar blade. These boats, when peaceably fishing, were usually home to two or three guys. Any more than that on board and nobody made enough money to justify the diesel. That's the quick and dirty of how you know when they're fishing and when they're up to no good.

We had been warned to keep a weather eye out for these local boats, especially at night. Every time I saw one appear on the horizon, I tended to hear Movie Indian Music in my head – you know, the open-fifth chords that film composers used in mid-20th Century westerns to announce the presence of marauding Apaches.

At about 3:00 a.m. on the first night out on passage from Bali to Singapore, such a boat caught my attention, about a mile off our starboard beam, unlit. The radar showed its little blip moving on a slow converging course. The boat was too far away and too dark for me to be able to see how many crew it carried, but I altered course ten degrees to port to stay clear.

I assumed I had inadvertently entered this guy's fishing zone, which the mid-sized boats tended to patrol in a box pattern, dropping nets then going back around to pick them back up. I did not want to enter a fishing zone for two reasons. First, it was just plain rude. These guys are making their living, and I can certainly go around. Second, if I were to snag a net with my propeller, it could not only damage the guy's net, it could disable us.

So I changed course. The local boat altered its course as well, and continued to converge. O . . . kay. Still probably not a problem, probably coincidence. I gave the engine a little more gas to speed up to seven knots. He sped up. I turned thirty degrees to port, a move that emphasized a clear intention to stay out of his way. He moved back to a converging course and sped up. My heart did little fluttery things. The chase was on.

I put the boat on auto-pilot and dived below.

"Hey, sweetie," I lilted, giving him a big smack on the cheek to wake him up. "I think we may have our very first pirates. Up and at 'em."

While I was down there, I grabbed the shotgun, which along with the rifle we had been keeping on the sole of the saloon within easy reach while in these waters.

Was this guy just curious? Bored? Was he out of cigarettes and looking to trade? I didn't want to stick around to find out, but he was closing on me fast. I took the poor engine up to max RPM and prayed it wouldn't overheat. It whined and grumbled and gave me ten knots over the flat-calm sea. I showed the pirates my stern and crouched on my knees in the cockpit with the gun handy. If they get within fifty yards, I told myself, I'll fire a warning shot.

Alan crawled into the cockpit. He was carrying our spotlight.

"I'm going to stand up and see what they look like, on the count of three."

At "three" I stood up as well, and looked aft.

"Holy crap."

We both sat back down on the sole and looked at each other, shaken. A line of about a dozen men had been visible. The men were crowded at the bow, and one held what looked to be a grappling hook. Another held what looked to be an automatic weapon. The visual had been too brief to see anything else.

But the Apache movie music was blaring in my head. They were definitely pirates.

The benefit of having run our pirate drills now became apparent. We each went about our assigned tasks without having to talk or think. I marked the distance between the two boats on our radar screen. We would know with exactitude whether they were gaining on us, or whether we were the faster boat. Their boat was heavier, wooden, and smaller – so I hoped that meant it was relatively slower. Of course we had no idea what kind of engine it had.

Alan organized the guns and spare ammunition in the cockpit to be within easy reach of both of us. He scanned the horizon to make sure we weren't running towards a second boat that might be working with the first one. There was nothing at all ahead that we could see visually or on radar. So that was good.

He fired our flare gun to signal distress. In sixty seconds, he would fire a second blast. If any voyagers were out there, we were confident they would come to our aid. Perhaps a commercial boat might do the same.

I hailed on channel 16 that we were a sailboat under pursuit and requesting assistance. It was too early for a Mayday. I would broadcast that only if it became apparent that we could not avoid being boarded.

It was too early to check the radar for a relative distance measurement.

We waited. Alan fired the second flare.

Fewer than five minutes had elapsed since I had woken Alan up. I had a passing thought that it's good that things happen very slowly at sea.

Alan stuck his head up for an instant and looked aft.

"It looks like they are at the same distance," he whispered.

"Why are we whispering?" I whispered. He grinned.

And we waited.

At ten minutes, I checked the radar. Oh thank God. The distance between us had increased measurably – less than a tenth of a nautical mile, but measurably.

We waited. Alan checked the engine temperature and nudged the throttle up a little.

As the night wore on, we continued to put distance between us. When the radar screen told us we were half a mile to the better, we moved up to the cockpit coaming and looked around.

The boat was gone.

It's time like these that a girl wishes she had some ice cream in the freezer, I can tell you. I made do with a Kit Kat, and Alan went back to bed.

* * *

The next day, Alan came on watch with a frown and started rubbing his stomach. I put it down to the excitement of the night before. I was feeling a mite peaked myself.

"Are you okay?" I asked.

Alan hanked himself on to the safety lines and climbed out on deck. In response to my question, he grabbed a stanchion and threw up violently over the side. He then looked at me in absolute terror and ran below to the head.

A vision came unbidden into my head. It was the redhead on the day we left Bali, stopping at a local street food vendor for some mystery meat on a stick, with all the fixin's.

Several hours later, he was moaning on the pilot berth. I had continued on watch. I had also scoped out the nearest anchorages on the chart. They were not plentiful or particularly protected, and, in any event, I was pretty gun-shy about stopping in this area after our experience of the night before, especially with my big strong man out of action. I decided the better part of valor was to continue on and play it by ear.

I did a scan of the horizon and went below.

"Here, sweetie, drink this." I was holding a squeeze bottle of Gatorade.

"I don't want it," he groaned.

"Okay, but you are going to have to drink something soon."

"Okay, okay."

I went to the forward bilge and pulled out the bag that contained an I.V. needle, tubing, and saline bag. There were no instructions. It occurred to me that if I became seriously ill, I was covered. With my lack of medical skills, Alan was kind of out of luck.

I went back up to the cockpit to check our course and sails.

Twelve hours later, I had gotten him to drink some Gatorade, some of which actually stayed down. He was sleeping but looked to be in pretty bad shape.

I went into the galley and took another No-Doz.

A little later, I woke him up. "Sweetheart, I am going to have to depend on you to assess your medical condition, okay? Can you do that?"

He nodded.

"Do I need to put in ashore and get you a doctor?"

He shook his head no, forearm over his eyes.

"Do I need to start an I.V.?"

"No."

Well that was a relief.

"Here, have some more Gatorade."

He gamely took a few sips and fell back asleep.

The next morning, he looked a little better but was still clammy and had been back and forth to the head all night. He kept down some broth, though – hallelujah.

Late that afternoon, after 36 hours on watch, I simply could not stay awake any longer. It had been a long time since a law school all-nighter, and I was out of shape. Thank goodness the sailing had been easy, and the weather, though rainy, had not been severe. I went below and shook him gently.

"Sweetheart, I'm so sorry, but I need for you to sit up in the cockpit and stand watch for a few hours while I take a nap."

"Okay, no problem." He immediately fell back asleep. I shook him gently again and helped him up. We propped him up on cushions in the cockpit with a bottle of Gatorade, some crackers, and the watch alarm. He gave me a sickly grin.

I climbed into the pilot berth and hoped the redhead could stay awake enough to keep us from being plowed under by traffic. But at that point, I didn't care one way or the other. I fell instantly into oblivion.

A few hours later, as I relieved him and sent him back below, Alan felt well enough to look sheepish. He knew that I knew what had caused this debacle. He still looked alarmingly ill, and to my credit, I hesitated for a moment before seizing my advantage. But only for a moment.

"Raise your right hand and repeat after me," I intoned.

He raised his right hand.

I continued. "I hereby swear or affirm . . ."

"I hereby swear or affirm."

". . . that I will not under any circumstances . . ."

"That I will not under any circumstances."

"Eat anything whatsoever from a street vendor . . ."

"Eat anything whatsoever from a street vendor."

"For so long as we both shall live."

"For so long as we are in Indonesia."

I laughed. We would be leaving Indonesian waters the next day, and he knew it. He was going to be okay.

CHAPTER 20
SINGAPORE TO THE MALDIVES

Q: Is the voyaging lifestyle too demanding for someone of retirement age?

A: The lifestyle can certainly be physically demanding at times, but if you're in decent shape you'll be fine. Although most voyagers of our acquaintance are between 45 and 60 years old, there are many voyagers in their 70s, and some in their 80s. Rather than youth and strength, the qualities required of a successful circumnavigator are more in the nature of good judgment and endurance. It's a marathon, not a sprint.

Q: Do you do any SCUBA diving?

A: Yes. We dive pretty often. We are both certified SCUBA divers, and we carry all the gear, plus a compressor to fill the tanks, plus "brownie" regulators for tank-free diving (and cleaning the hull). Alan holds a rescuer diver certificate.

We pulled into Yacht Harbour Marina in Phuket, Thailand, at noon on Christmas Eve. Phuket by Christmas? It was down to the wire, but we made it.

I cleaned up the boat after the overnight passage from the Malaysian island of Langkawi while Alan went off on a mission-critical task. We had no turkey, dressing-making ingredients, or cranberry sauce of any kind. His quest was to find a restaurant or hotel where we could have Christmas dinner the next day.

The trip up from Singapore had kicked our butts. Singapore is a country consisting primarily of one highly sophisticated city on an island at the tip of the Malaysian Peninsula. Directly south of the city is the Singapore Strait, which is a commercial shipping lane. Directly to Singapore's north is mainland Malaysia. Singapore is a lovely place and a consumer paradise. It also is the birthplace of a delightful cocktail called the Singapore Sling, which we sipped at every opportunity.

Rather than stay at a marina in Singapore, we headquartered south of the city, on the other side of the Strait, in Nongsa Point, Indonesia. It was easier and less expensive to take the ferry across the Strait to the city every day than to figure out Singapore's gun regulations and to pay the steep marina and registration fees. And Nongsa Point was lovely. Also, it had a fraction less smog.

With an eye on the calendar, we stayed long enough to get the flavor of the city and its famous street food (Alan was a happy guy) and then continued on. Continuing on meant that we had to cross the Singapore Strait.

The Singapore Strait is about 10 miles wide and 65 miles long. It goes east and west. That is, there is a shipping lane that travels east, and a shipping lane that travels west. There are complicated rules to join this marine freeway, and complicated rules to exit. It has its own radio frequency. On any given day, approximately 2,000 commercial ships traverse its length in the ordinary course of business.

To get to Thailand, we needed to go north. That is, we needed to cross the 10-mile width (about a two-hour undertaking) at right angles to the traffic, then join it for a while in the westbound lane before departing to the north – all without getting run over and sinking. The task was akin to walking across a busy eight-lane freeway.

We pulled out from Nongsa Point and watched the Strait for a while to get a feel for it. We went over our plan. Alan was on watch and thus captain for this venture.

"I think a zig-zag approach is our best bet. We will make as much progress as we can north, then stand and let traffic go by, then cut behind them, and play it by ear until we get across the east bound lane to the west-bound lane. Then I think we should join the west-bound lane and just sort of work our way to the far right, and exit as soon as we can. I'm not going to raise the sails at all. We'll do the whole thing under power."

So we zigged and zagged and swore and dodged and prayed and made no friends among the commercial captains. But two hours later we were sailing up the western coast of Malaysia towards places with enticingly exotic names like Malacca and Penang and Kuala Lumpur.

Sailing in the Malacca Strait, we encountered the worst electrical storm of the trip. The thunder was deafening, You know the "one-Mississippi, two-Mississippi" counting thing after a lightning strike to determine how close the lightning is? We never got past "one-Mississ." One strike hit the water only a few yards behind the boat and lit up the mast like a signal beacon. The whole boat – all 28 tons of it – rocked with the impact. And yes, the laptop survived unscathed in the microwave. However, the most harrowing part of our Malaysian experience was the bus trip we took up into the mountainous interior of the country to see Kuala Lumpur and to visit an elephant sanctuary, where rumor had it we could actually swim with the elephants. The roadside cliffs were so steep and the bus driver so clearly stoned that I finally just put a blanket over my head and went to sleep.

All things considered, we were very happy to arrive in Phuket.

I was wiping off the cockpit's clear plastic protective side curtains when Alan arrived back at the boat with good news about Christmas.

"Guess who I ran into?"

"Who?"

"*Orion* and *Fair Wind*. Amelia has organized Christmas lunch for tomorrow and said they can make two extra places if we want to join them. I said yes."

"Perfect."

"Also, I heard that *Sea Spirit* is here. Princess Katie has some party invitations to some buffet thing tonight we are supposed to go to."

"I presume details will be forthcoming? Like – where it is?"

"Oh, somebody will know."

Sigh.

"Also, I rented us a jeep, just in case."

"Excellent."

"It doesn't have a floor, but other than that, it's not bad."

"Great."

"Also, I got some intel on pirates off the coast of Somalia."

"What have those rascals been up to?"

"Well, actually, what I have is a description. Some boats have already gone through the Gulf of Aden to the Red Sea this season. They were traveling together. They told the Net that they ran into a group of three boats that approached them and fired shots. I'm not sure how they got away, but they said there was one large boxy-looking boat and two speedboats with blue tarps covering the front."

"Okay, good to know."

"They gave a latitude and longitude, too, and don't let me forget to get that from Jerry tomorrow."

"Okeydoke."

I climbed down the companionway stairs and moved to the nav station. Once there, I picked up the radio microphone and tuned in the hailing channel.

"*Sea Spirit, Sea Spirit, Sea Spirit*, this is *Heartsong*." I repeated the call twice more before I got a response.

"*Heartsong*, this is *Sea Spirit*. Channel six-eight."

I obediently moved to Channel 68, which is a working channel for conversations. To change frequencies for an extended conversation leaves Channel 16 open and uncluttered for hailing and emergencies only – which is as it should be.

I proceeded on Channel 68. "Hey, Kate, it's Liza. I understand there's a party this evening, over."

"Yep. About 6:30. It's a huge buffet and dance at that white hotel on the peninsula by the smaller marina. Fifteen dollars each. Is that okay with you, over?"

"Sure, that's fine. We'll be there, over."

"There's a talent contest, too. Somebody told me you can sing, right? Over."

"Well, technically, yes," I laughed, "but I don't know about being in a talent contest. Over"

"Okay, well we'll play it by ear tonight. Do you have a car, over?"

"Yes, over."

"Can you bring *Salamander* with you, over?"

"No problem, assuming they're okay with a car that doesn't have a floor. See you there." *Heartsong III* clear Channel 68.

Later that day, Alan and I walked into the hotel with the *Salamander* crew, more or less on time. Princess Katie approached us with our tickets. We handed her thirty bucks, and she waved us out into the back garden toward the tables she had reserved.

The hotel's back garden was festive – strings of overhead lights, round banquet tables with white tablecloths, a 10-piece band on the bandstand, waiters taking and delivering drink orders. It looked as if the hotel was expecting a good crowd.

After claiming our seats and introducing ourselves at a table of voyagers, we looked around. Other than the people in our group, all of the partygoers appeared to be local. Cool.

After we had worked our way through the ample buffet and were on our second glass of wine, Kate approached me.

"Hey, they're starting the talent contest in a few minutes. I signed us up. What should we do?"

"Are we sure we want to do anything?" I stalled. "I mean, what's the prize?"

Kate raised an eyebrow. She looked at me in amusement.

"More than we have if we don't do it."

I laughed. Good point. I love that girl.

"Okay," I capitulated. "Let's do something fun, like 'The Lion Sleeps Tonight.' Can you round up a back-up section that can sing the 'oh-weem-a-way' chorus?"

"Done."

"And we need to run through it once before we go on."

"Done and done."

For the record, our performance was creditable. And bless the Thai judges, they let us win.

* * *

After the Phuket Christmas and New Year's festivities had been enjoyed to their fullest, we explored the area for a few weeks before continuing on our route. We anchored among the standing stones of Phan Nga Bay and took the dinghy into water-filled caves open to the sky. The sea was so warm that we had to scrape barnacles off of our propeller on a regular basis. The Phi Islands were one of our favorite stops, with small brightly painted wooden fishing boats moored off expansive white sand beaches surrounded by jungle.

Paradise was marred only when the day came that we could no longer deny that we were both feeling quite ill. We discovered that we had contracted the parasite *giardia lamblia*, most likely while swimming with those magnificent elephants in that dang Malaysian river. Given that more than one voyager came down with the far more serious dengue fever during that time period, we felt lucky. But by the time we finished a course of antibiotics and were fully recovered, it was time to leave for what turned out to be a smooth and fast 1200-mile westward crossing of the Indian Ocean.

* * *

"I'm going to drop the sails and run the engine," I said as we approached the entrance to the Port of Colombo, which is the commercial capital of the island country of Sri Lanka, off the coast of India.

"How come?" Alan asked as he hoisted himself into the cockpit from belowdecks.

"Look around. We appear to be in a major shipping channel here. I may need to maneuver quickly."

"Okay, sounds good."

The engine turned over, but when I put her into gear, she started overheating immediately.

"Hey sweetie, we're overheating."

Alan emerged from the engine room after checking the water level.

"There's plenty of water, and everything looks fine down there. I wonder if we've fouled the propeller again."

Running the engine in shipping lanes had proved to be a problem before. The amount of trash in the water is excessive, and all it takes to stop us is one large, strong piece of floating detritus, like a metal cord or a ripped tarp, wrapping itself around our prop. For example, when we arrived at Nongsa Point, the prop had become fouled by thick shredded plastic, and we had limped into the bay under the power of our dinghy outboard attached to a very ingenious platform dreamed up by the redhead and attached to *Heartsong*'s stern steps.

I took stock of the situation. We were disabled and drifting in commercial traffic. Not good.

"Raise the mainsail, please, and let's take her out a bit into open water."

"Aye, aye cap'n."

I rolled my eyes and unfurled the jib.

About ten minutes later, in safer waters, we dropped the sails again and sat there with bare poles to assess the situation. Thank goodness it was a calm day.

I looked at Alan. "I hate it, but I think one of us is going to have to go over the side and take a look."

"I know. I'll do it. If the prop is fouled, we'll have to cut whatever it is away with a knife."

"Thank you, sweetheart," I batted my eyes at him. "You're so strong and brave."

He gave me a suspicious look, but put on his snorkel and flippers. I attached a safety line to his waist, and he jumped feet first over the side. I continued to look for traffic and to broadcast on Channel 16 our location and that we were temporarily disabled.

Alan hoisted himself onto the stern steps. "Yep, there's a big heavy net with metal things on it, and it's wrapped around the propeller and the shaft."

I had already started assembling the "brownie" gear – *i.e.*, a regulator on a 30-foot hose attached to a SCUBA tank nestled in the middle of a float. It would allow Alan to stay underwater to work on the prop, rather than have to free dive it. We had never used it at sea, though. Even in calm conditions, the boat was thumping up and down and wallowing a little with each wave. I started worrying about the boat hitting him in the head while he was down there. We had a solution aboard for situations like these: a bicycle helmet.

"Hey, do you mind wearing the bike helmet?" I asked him as he deployed the brownie.

"Do I have to?"

"Yes."

"Okay then. You're right," he sighed.

He dove down, and I kept an eagle eye on his air bubbles as well as on the horizon. I had called two commercial vessels approaching us to ask them to keep a wide berth, and even though they did not answer, they had very politely complied.

It took a good hour for him to free us from the net. When he finally hoisted himself and his collection of knives aboard the stern steps, his face had gone that chalky pallor that indicated exhaustion. I thanked him profusely and started the engine to give us some way and to make the boat's motion a little more comfortable. The prop was back in action.

I had been cogitating in the meantime. I helped him pull the brownie back aboard and get it stowed.

"Sweetheart, I have been thinking."

"Uh-oh."

"I'm thinking we should just continue on to the Maldives."

"Really." He paused to think about it. "Why?"

"Well, you must be exhausted, and you could get some rest now if we did that. If we go into Colombo, we'll have to be dodging commercial traffic and docking and stuff. Also, when we were near the entrance, I looked in, and I don't know, it didn't grab me. I'd like to see something of Sri Lanka, but the port itself, not so much. Also, they are still recovering from that mine or bomb or whatever it was that exploded in the harbor. The Maldives will have beaches and pretty water and protected anchorages, and we can spend more time there this way, instead of dividing our time between two spots."

"Okay, sold."

I kissed him.

"Thank you for saving our prop. You're my hero."

This statement sounded flip, but it was true. There is no way I had the muscle strength to cut that net and free the prop. If I had been out there alone, I would have been at the mercy of a tow operator.

Also, there is a place deep down where my sweet redheaded husband knows and appreciates that I regard him as a cross between Captain America and Iron Man.

"I love you," he said brightly. "Let's hoist the sails."

* * *

We made landfall in the Maldives on Valentine's Day. Alan was born on Valentine's Day – which actually explains a lot.

We pulled into a perfect tropical anchorage on one of the northern islands shortly after lunch. As usual, I was on the wheel, and Alan was at the bow, preparing to drop the hook.

"Where do you want to anchor, Birthday Boy" I spoke into the hands-free family band radios.

He pointed in the general direction of shore. "Between those two white boats over there."

"Sweetheart, they're all white."

"Oh, right. Sorry."

I noticed something approaching us from one of the boats already at anchor. As it came closer, I saw that it was a line of a half a dozen dinghies. As it got closer, I could hear some singing. They arrived, and I recognized some of the occupants as close friends. I waved. Everyone was smiling and laughing between lines of the song as they motored around our boat.

They were singing "Happy Birthday" to Alan.

Aww.

Later we hosted an impromptu birthday happy hour for everyone in the anchorage. Although a few had not yet made the decision whether to turn right (towards the Red Sea) or left (towards the Seychelles or East Africa) when they departed the Maldives – and some had already decided they might just stay here for an extended visit – the conversation inevitably turned to Somalian pirates.

"I heard on the Net in Colombo that several sailboats have been attacked this season," Allie of *Daytripper* said.

"Yeah, and it's always the same. Three boats, one big and boxy, and two smaller boats with blue tarps on the bow," Henry of *Terra Nova* chimed in.

"One British couple was kidnapped and ransomed. I don't know whether it was this year or not, though." This tidbit was from Stella of *Heart Beat*.

We sat in silence for a while and sipped our wine or beer. I handed around a plate of hors d'oeuvres.

Alan spoke. "Who has guns?"

Some did, but most did not.

"We decided it was too much trouble to have to declare them everywhere, and we didn't want to risk going to jail if we didn't declare. And also, we just don't like guns. So we aren't carrying any," Maggie of *Serenity* said. They were a Canadian family cruising and home-schooling their teenage daughter.

"Who else has kids?" Tim of *Serenity* asked.

"*Daytripper* and *Fair Wind* do," responded Evelyn. Nobody else spoke up. It was clear, however, that Somalian pirates were a major concern to all.

Another dinghy pulled up to join the party, and the conversation became more general. Did anyone want to dive the reef tomorrow? Some boats were leaving the next day to go further south. Some were planning to call in to the capital, Malé.

The Maldive Islands are an independent country consisting of about 1,200 coral islands grouped in 26 atolls. The country has a population of about half a million people. The chief industry is tourism. The average height of the islands is about four feet above sea level, and the highest point on any of the islands is less than eight feet above sea level. The effects of climate change and rising sea levels, if not solved or at least mitigated, will completely wipe this lovely, pristine archipelago off the planet.

The island at which we were anchored was a small, remote one. There are no tourist accommodations here. The village families live in cinder block homes, some with sand floors. The walls and fences are covered in lush, brightly colored tropical flowers. The beaches are perfect, and the water is every possible shade of blue, banded according to depth over colorful reefs and bright white sand. The village people and officials are Muslim. We got a preview here of what would be a standard experience in the Red Sea countries: Calls to prayer are broadcast publicly and very loudly on large outdoor speaker systems. It took some getting used to, but once we got used to it, we kind of missed it when we left the Muslim world.

However, I will just say that it's definitely weird to see a toddler walking around wearing an Osama bin Laden t-shirt. For the entirety of the trip, we proudly flew an oversized America flag from our stern. It occurred to me that perhaps we should keep a closer watch here and other countries coming up along the route, in case a crazy person decided to take offense.

When we checked into the island, Alan as usual communicated that he had medical expertise. The customs official thanked him and mentioned that the island's doctor had retired last year and moved off-island. They had not yet been able to replace him.

"However," the official continued slowly, "it is of course not allowed for our people to receive medical treatment from a doctor who is not of the Islamic faith."

This was news to me. However, different groups had different rules, and we always tried to respect local customs.

"Okay," said Alan, nodding his head. He accepted the stamped papers allowing us to enter the country. "Also, we need to declare our firearms. Here is the paperwork. The firearms are on the boat, if you would like me to go get them."

We never took them in with us initially, until we found out what the standard procedure was. The rules were many and varied around the world, sometimes within the same country.

The official replied, "No, I will send someone out to pick them up."

And he did, and everyone was very professional, and we thought no more about it. We proceeded to spend lovely days and nights enjoying the perfect weather and the island paradise.

When it came time to leave, Alan went ashore to check out of the country while I began checking items off the departure checklist. He returned with the stamped paperwork, but no guns. I was below, plotting our course through the reefs.

"Didn't they give you our guns?" I asked.

"No, he's sending someone out with them."

"Ah, that makes sense."

We completed the checklist and were ready to go. No guns. We waited. After an hour, we started getting concerned.

"Did he say when someone was coming out?" I hazarded.

"No, but it sounded like it would happen pretty quick. He knows we are trying to get away this morning."

"Maybe he forgot. Should we go back in and ask?"

"I don't want to do that. But, on the other hand, waiting around isn't getting us anywhere either."

I saw some movement ashore and picked up the binoculars. On a small beach around the corner and out of sight of the customs office, a group of people were arriving. Some of them carried folding chairs. Some of them sat on driftwood or on the sand. Some women were wearing hijabs with western street clothes, and some wore full traditional burkas. There were several children. A couple of dozen all told had arrived. They appeared to be waiting for something.

"Huh. I wonder what those people are doing?" I said idly, still surveying the shore with the binoculars for any signs of activity from the customs office.

"It's not time for prayers."

"No. Ferry, maybe?"

"No, the ferry comes to the main dock. I saw it yesterday."

"Picnic?"

Alan took the binoculars. "Well, if it's a picnic, it's an odd one. They don't appear to have any food. Hey!"

He pulled the binoculars away from his eyes and turned to me. "One of the men just waved at me."

We looked at each other. What in the world . . .. But this did look a lot like the lines that often formed on the beach when Alan did an informal clinic on remote islands.

I was processing this when Alan said: "Do you think they want me to come ashore?"

"I was thinking the same thing. But the guy said you weren't allowed to treat anybody."

"He also said that they haven't had a doctor here since last year."

I was worried. I remembered the bin Laden t-shirt. Could this be entrapment of some sort?

Alan was already putting his medical kits into a backpack. We hadn't deflated the dinghy yet in case we needed to re-visit customs to get our guns. The dink was in the water, ready to go. I knew better than to try to stop Alan from offering medical care, so I put on shore shoes to go with him.

"Actually, I think you should stay here," he surprised me by saying. "Just in case there's a problem. You need to be able to go for help if we need it."

"What, you don't need someone to hold the flashlight for you?"

He laughed.

"No, you're right." I was proud of him for going, and proud of him for recognizing and acknowledging the potential danger as well.

I watched the beach with the binoculars for the next two hours, as Alan saw each and every one of the persons who needed help. Finally, he got back in the dinghy and motored back out to the boat.

"We were right," he shouted from the stern, as he tied the dinghy up. He climbed into the cockpit, where I now had the binoculars trained on the customs building to make sure they weren't sending out the militia.

He continued, "Sorry that took so long. I had to go through interpreters for most of it. They had a lot of questions."

"Anything serious?"

"Yeah, a couple things that I recommended they go to Malé to the hospital to see about. Otherwise, just normal stuff – a broken ankle, a staph infection, measles, a laceration that needed stitches and antibiotics."

"I am very proud of you," I gave him a kiss and picked the binoculars back up. "Aha!"

"What."

"If I am not mistaken, here come our guns."

And indeed, the customs boat pulled up, and the men aboard gave us our guns and some paperwork and, with a smile and a wave, wished us a safe trip.

CHAPTER 21
THE ARABIAN SEA AND GULF OF ADEN

Q: *While traveling, do you always have communication with other cruisers, or are there times when you are out there all alone with the ocean?*

A: We strongly prefer to be out here alone. For us, that's part of the joy of the trip. A notable exception, however, has been when we are sailing dangerous waters in which there is safety in numbers.

Heartsong III was bobbing adrift in the Arabian Sea, about a hundred miles east of Socotra, which is an island well off the northeastern Somalian Coast. We were there because we said we'd be there, at this exact spot, at this exact time. A couple of months before, in Thailand, we had made a (somewhat drunken) pact with a few of our best voyaging buddies that we would band together to traverse the dangerous route through the Gulf of Aden to the Red Sea. I don't remember the night particularly clearly, but it's possible that a few choruses of "That's What Friends Are For" may have been sung.

As one traverses the Gulf of Aden on a westerly course, the northern coast of Somalia is on one's left, and Yemen is on the right. It's about eighty to a hundred miles across the Gulf. That doesn't seem like a lot of room when there are pirates.

Yes, pirates. We had seen some fairly scary ones in Indonesia, of course, but those were probably ordinary fisherman, moonlighting. The pirates in the Gulf of Aden were serious pirates – people-smuggling, murdering, boat-jacking, scary individuals, armed with automatic weapons and not bearing even a passing resemblance to Johnny Depp.

The only way to minimize the risk of an attack from these career criminals was to be like the person in the bear joke. You know: As the grizzly approaches, one friend says to the other "Why are you putting on your running shoes? You can't outrun the bear." And the other friend says, "I don't need to outrun the bear. I just need to outrun you."

And so it is with pirates. The best way to avoid attack is be the least attractive target on the water in the general vicinity. For this particular tiny area of the world, we had heard of other voyagers adopting a "safety in numbers" approach, and it seemed like a pretty good idea. We would form a flotilla of half a dozen or so boats, and sail through the Gulf of Aden together, until we could safely turn the corner into the Red Sea.

So we left our happy hour in Thailand a couple of months previously with high-fives (and I seem to recall some "I love you, man" tears) to go our separate ways with our separate interim routes and destinations – but with a promise to be at a certain longitude and latitude, on a certain date, at a certain time, a couple of months later.

Heartsong was the first to arrive at the appointed spot, and I was feeling a little foolish that I had expected anyone else to show up. With all of the uncertainties of sailing, and all of the changes of mind and plans that might have intervened, it now seemed ridiculous that we had busted butt, after our usual excessive lingering in Phuket and the Maldives, to arrive at the designated time.

Alan, ever the optimist, was scanning the horizon with binoculars.

Whenever people ask me about sailing, one of the first questions they ask is whether we would do it again, now that it is "more dangerous" – *i.e.*, after all the highly publicized pirate attacks that have occurred off the coast of Somalia in the years since we returned to land. The answer is that it has always been dangerous for mariners in that part of the world; and there have been attacks on yachts and ships in the Arabian Sea and Gulf of Aden for decades, probably for centuries. What has changed is that the pirates are better armed now. They have boats that can venture farther from shore, at faster speeds; and they have abandoned the notoriously inaccurate Russian Kalashnikov for more modern weapons of war.

From my perspective, this change has happened in a logical progression, sparked by the chaos of the civil wars in that area of the world that have been raging for the past twenty or thirty years. How can a handful of guys in third-world watercraft hijack a freighter on the open sea, people ask me. The answer is simple: The owners of said freighter have historically been more afraid of mutiny than they have been of piracy. Ergo, to keep weapons out of the hands of the crew, virtually none of the commercial ships carry weapons on board. Forty unarmed crew are no match for a half dozen boarders spraying automatic fire.

So one successful robbery finances another, with more guys and improved weaponry, which finances another, with more boats with improved speed, etc. Eventually, they have enough of a force to take a military ship unaware; and then they have real weapons. And so it goes.

Sailboats are in an odd position. We move more slowly and are far more vulnerable to attack; but on the other hand, the reward for a successful hijacking is much less than on a freighter with valuable cargo and a safe full of wages for a large crew. Moreover, unlike commercial vessels, many voyagers, including us, carry firearms and aren't afraid to use them. A sailboat for pirates is sort of like beef jerky. It will do if nothing else is available. If a nice juicy steak is visible, however, it's unlikely they will go for something that's going to be tough and chewy.

After the episode in Indonesia, Alan and I spent some time talking through how we would handle a serious attack. In any situation, we would be seriously outnumbered. The primary goal, then – really the only strategy that has any chance of succeeding – is to keep attackers at the farthest distance possible, and at all costs, to keep them from boarding.

In short, the best option is, like Brave Sir Robin, to run away. We had three distinct stages of operations. Plan A: Fire into the hull of the attackers' boat with our armor-piercing bullets. If we can sink their boat, or cause the crew to stop and patch it, we can then create time to run away. Plan B: Fire the shotgun onto the decks, beginning at as far a range as possible. If we can injure them, or at least make them re-think their cost-benefit analysis, we may be able to run away. Plan C: If boarding is inevitable, toss the firearms into the drink, so they can't be used against us or someone else.

Plan D: Well, we never really formulated a Plan D, as it would seem a waste of time to do, but if we had, it would probably involve praying.

For this particular little stretch of Somalian pirate jurisdiction, we were hoping for friendly reinforcements. And so we waited. And waited.

"Hey, I think I see something," Alan pointed due east with his free hand, while still holding the binoculars to his eyes. "No, sorry, just a wavetop."

He continued to scan. Ten minutes later, he sat up straight.

"I think that's something," he practically shouted with excitement.

I squinted. Yes, that might be a mast.

Alan swept the binoculars along the horizon further south. "And there's another one."

And then there was another, and then another. And another.

Half an hour later, six sailboats were dropping sails and circling each other out in the middle of bloody nowhere, laughing and launching dinghies, standing and chatting at each other's topsides, woohooing, comparing routes, and applauding each other's effort. Provisions were exchanged; fuel was shared from the larger boats, which had bigger tanks, to the smaller ones. We ran a few pirate drills and formulated our basic strategy.

The plan was that we would sail in a modified diamond pattern – one boat leading, three in a line behind it, two bringing up the rear in the gaps between. We would try to maintain a distance of a quarter of a mile between boats. The slowest boat would lead, and the fastest two would bring up the rear. That way, in the event of a problem, the faster boats could close the distance more easily than if one or more boats had to turn back. *Heartsong III* took her position at the back, on the port, or Somali, side.

Upon approach of a suspect vessel, we would all close the gaps to within a few yards and circle the wagons in tried-and-true frontier style – the unarmed boats and boats with children would move to the center, the larger and armed boats (including *Heartsong* – and remember also, our hull was made of twaron, which is bullet-proof) would take up stations on the perimeter. It was a decent plan.

Judging from our results in practice, though, our main danger wouldn't be from pirates but would rather be from ramming and sinking each other while we tried to maneuver. It is not easy to move in close quarters on a sailboat in any kind of seaway and wind.

Another key component was communication. From listening to the various single sideband nets, we knew that pirates were able to find their prey in a vast expanse of thousands of square miles of water. How? Luck? Radar had limited range, and we all knew from close calls with freighters that sailboats don't show up all that well on radar in any event.

Could it be VHF radios? The rule of thumb is that VHF signals are line-of-sight, typically about twenty miles. Most sailboats, however, mount their VHF and single sideband antennae at the very top of the mast, thus maximizing reception. It was possible that sailboat communications were being heard and monitored at a much farther distance – maybe three or four times the norm. We resolved, therefore, not to use our primary VHF radios on each boat, but rather to use only our handhelds. Maximum range for a handheld VHF radio is about five miles; and we would stay off the normal hailing channels. We would have to stay close to be able to talk, but we would minimize the possibility of a marauder picking up our chatter. Also, although it was strictly against the international rules of the road, we would run without lights at night.

Okay, what else. Oh. We would all have to go at the speed of the slowest boat. Absolutely, no problem. That tenet seemed so obvious and so easy to commit to in theory. But after a couple of days of standing on the brakes, I can't say that I didn't start having second thoughts about the whole sailing-in-formation thing. *Heartsong* was down to no jib at all, and a handkerchief-sized main, and we were still having trouble not overrunning the boats in front. The devil sat on my shoulders during my watch: "Surely it would be safer to go as fast as possible. We could scout ahead and radio back if there's any danger." Yeah no.

The bad weather was actually a blessing, however. One thing you can count on about pirates: They are lazy. They do not come out in a blow.

At the same time, there is something you can count on about voyagers. Although loyal, we are not particularly compliant. That is, we are each used to doing things our own way and having complete autonomy on our own boats. The defining characteristic of a voyager, assuming there is one, which there isn't, is that we like the adventure of being in charge of our own destiny. That's one of the reasons we are typically out there alone in the first place. Keeping that diamond formation in any kind of shape, and with any kind of regular distance between those boats, took an act of congress. But we persevered, and in the main we succeeded. With a few notable exceptions of people temporarily going off the reservation, and I will name no names (cough, *Tango*), we all did a pretty darn good job. Okay, *Heartsong* got reprehensibly impatient from time to time as well. I hope that Amelia of *Orion* will speak to me again someday.

So we set out in the Arabian Sea in our diamond pattern. That first evening the seas were flat and the winds were moderate, and the sailing was lovely. The setting sun turned all of the water bright gold, and we could see the other boats' silhouettes, black against the gold of the sea.

Early the next morning, the wind picked up and the skies became threatening. The seas responded accordingly, and sailing in formation became more difficult to maintain. But we persevered, and it was a good thing we did.

It was on day three, in weather turned fine, that Alan and I saw in the far distance a boat that made us say "hmm." Our straggly flotilla was heading more or less due west, and the boat in question was coming toward us, heading due east, a mile or so to starboard of the starboard-most boat of our little fleet. It looked to be a fairly large local boat, not military, too large to be a fishing boat, not large enough to be commercial. While we watched, it continued slowly on its course. A local ferry, maybe?

. Still. I picked up my handheld. "Y'all see that boat to starboard?" I asked. Everyone reported in the affirmative.

"What do you think?"

Serenity, the starboard-most boat and thus the closest boat to the stranger, came on the air. "I think it's probably fine. He's not coming toward us."

And just as *Serenity* finished speaking, the boat did indeed make a visible turn in our direction. Um . . ..

Daytripper chimed in, with a deliberately calm cadence: "I think just for fun we should practice our drill."

"Excellent idea."

And so we all headed straight for *Serenity*, closing ranks. As if on cue, the strange boat made an immediate big sweeping turn toward Yemen and directly away from us. We watched for a minute or two, all the while continuing to close up the distance among us, but he was definitely departing the area, and then definitely gone.

Well that was easy.

I picked up the handheld to say a word of congratulations, and then just happened to glance to port.

There they were.

Our attention had been so intent on the boat approaching on the starboard side that we had failed to keep a general watch. Now I could clearly see three boats, still more than a half mile away on our port beam, but close enough that I could make out the boxy shape of the large one. With binoculars, I saw two speedboats with blue tarps covering each of their bows.

The open-fifth Apache movie music sounded in my head.

Pirates. Somalian pirates.

I already had the radio in my hand. "Ladies and Gentlemen," I breathed, "we have visitors."

We had closed ranks considerably in response to the first boat's approach, but within about two minutes we were in such close formation that I think I could have jumped onto *Daytripper*'s decks if I had felt the need. *Heartsong* was still on the portside perimeter, closest to the pirates, and our tightly packed wedge formation continued at the best speed we could collectively muster, under supplemental engine power now, on a course due west. I put *Heartsong* on autopilot and tossed the autopilot remote to Alan, as we took our positions on the forward deck. We showed our weapons, Alan with the rifle, me with the shotgun. And we waited for them to make a move.

For what seemed like hours, but was probably thirty minutes or so, they kept their same distance, paralleling our course. We kept our formation and by some miracle nobody ran into anybody else. My arms got tired from holding the shotgun, and I shifted it to the other shoulder, then rested it on the lifelines. Also, and nobody seems to mention this in pirate stand-offs, I really wished I could ask for a bathroom break.

Gradually it seemed to me that they started dropping a little behind, then definitely a little further behind; then next time I shifted the shotgun, I lost them in a wavetop. And then they were gone.

I set the gun down and started shaking. I sat down on the cabin top, and Alan moved back to the cockpit. There were no words. We all moved our boats a bit further apart for safety, but stayed close enough for comfort. The radio was silent for a good hour. After that, we communally decided, in few words and serious tone, to change course a bit to make us less easy to find if they were going to try to track us. We ran without lights again that night, and with little sleep; and at dawn the horizon was clear.

A couple of weeks later, after we had been anchored for a while in Masawa, Eritrea, the first port of entry on the Red Sea, we fired up our single sideband radio to listen to a net, and heard the sad news that a 30-foot sailboat was overdue and presumed missing. They were last heard from in the Gulf of Aden, perhaps a half-day behind us, sailing alone with a crew of husband and wife. Neither the boat nor its crew were ever found.

Whenever someone tells the bear joke, the joke stops long before the bear catches the slower runner. It seems to me that the faster runner, no matter what the circumstances, will always have a hard time living with that.

* * *

Our adventures in the Red Sea did not end with the pirate episode. The very next night, I woke Alan up at about midnight. As usual, he sat up, instantly alert.

"Problem?"

"We're going to die," I said. "I figured you'd rather be awake."

We were still sailing in formation in the Gulf of Aden on a thickly overcast night with moderate winds and a sloppy sea. A few minutes before, I had hailed *Tango* on the handheld VHF.

"*Tango, Tango, Tango*, this is *Heartsong III*.

"Go *Heartsong*," Bella replied.

"Bella, I think my radar must be malfunctioning. I see a solid mass at about 20 miles dead ahead, which can't be right, because we have nothing but open ocean for at least a hundred miles."

"Hang on, let me look." Pause. "Wow, I'm getting the same thing. It's more than a mile across. What on earth?"

We confirmed that everyone was seeing the same thing, and went to a more alert status.

"Whatever it is, it's not an oil rig or anything else permanent. It's moving towards us at 25 knots," I said. "I'm switching to Channel 16 on the main VHF to hail them."

"Eastbound ship, eastbound ship, eastbound ship, this is sailing vessel *Heartsong III*," I called. "We are five American-flag boats under sail and one Canadian-flag boat under sail, in your path, moving westward at about five knots." I detailed the latitude and longitude of each the six sailing vessels.

No response.

Jerry came on the handheld, "We're turning on our lights."

"Good idea."

Across the quarter-mile of ocean that we were occupying, we could see each of the flotilla's boat's running lights flicker on. We did the same.

For the next several minutes, I repeated the call continuously on Channel 16, changing the locations of our boats as the locations changed.

The problem was that even at top speed and even if we had taken immediate action upon first seeing the radar blip, we could not have gotten out of the ship's path in time. Whatever it was, it was coming at us too fast and was too broad across. We couldn't possibly get around it. Our only chance was to maintain our positions so the ship at least knew where we were. Unless something changed, and changed quickly, this would not end well. If whatever it was had any mass at all, it would plow us under in about 35 minutes.

Alan came up into the cockpit to join me. He looked at the radar and listened to my summary of events so far.

"It's bound to be military," he said. He got on the handheld with the other boats, as I continued to broadcast our positions. Our flotilla-mates had reached the same conclusion as Alan. This was a military convoy, and it was running on radio silence and with no lights. The ship on the starboard wing of the convoy would have to be an aircraft carrier to show up so massively on our radar screens.

Did it help to know what it was that was about to run over us? Not really. I continued to broadcast.

Amelia, Beau, and Tim had crunched the numbers, and we all agreed on strategy. Getting out of the convoy's path was impossible. We would hold our course. If we changed course now, we risked interfering with the convoy's attempt to avoid us – that is, if it was a convoy, and if there was a radio operator who was listening to my broadcasts on Channel 16, and if whatever and whoever it was gave a flip about our continued existence.

Was it a U.S. convoy? Was it Russian? Chinese? British? We had no idea. All we knew was that a wall of metal was coming towards us.

Maggie came on the handheld. "Twenty minutes to contact."

I continued to broadcast to the convoy on Channel 16, now putting emphasis on the Canadian-flag sailboat. Surely nobody wants to kill Canadians, right?

"Fifteen minutes to contact."

At that moment, a spotlight burst from above onto *Daytripper*, illuminating the boat as if on a Broadway stage or in a police shakedown. We could hear the whir of rotary blades and could make out a vague silhouette.

"It's a Blackhawk!" Alan shouted. "They're American."

The Blackhawk proceeded to spotlight several of the other boats in our flotilla, and then was gone. Our handhelds sounded of whoops and laughter. At least the convoy knew who and where we were. At least it was "ours."

I stopped broadcasting. I had probably been driving them crazy, and now that I knew they were aware of us, further broadcasting was pointless.

We waited in silence.

"Twelve minutes to contact."

The convoy was close enough now that if there had been a moon, we would have been able to see shapes and motion. But the moon, if it had risen yet, was tucked behind a thick layer of cloud cover. It was pitch dark. The convoy was still running without lights. We couldn't see a thing.

Sam came on the handheld and in an even voice said, "Does anyone else see motion on the radar? It looks like the formation is changing."

Beau said, "Yes, I'm seeing that, too. What are they doing?"

"No idea."

I gripped Alan's hand. "I love you."

"I love you," he responded.

"Ten minutes to contact."

We waited.

Our attention shifted back and forth between the radar display and the opaque darkness surrounding the boat. On the radar display, it began to look as if the ships in the central part of the convoy might be slowing and shifting. Then we could see clearly that some were moving to port and others to starboard. The course of the carrier changed slightly on the convoy's wing.

They were creating a path for us to sail right through the middle of them.

Two minutes later, the radar told us it was clear dead ahead. Four minutes later we could hear engines and rotors roaring loudly all around us in the stillness of the night. Five minutes later we were hit with a passing wake that bounced us around like a bath toy in a jacuzzi. We held on for dear life and let out some sail to stabilize the boat. We also let out our breath.

And then it was over. The convoy had passed. Nobody in our flotilla said anything for a long while. Then Amelia came on the handheld.

"Let's do a quick roll call. *Orion* is here."

"*Heartsong* is here."

"*Tango* is here."

"*Serenity*."

"*Daytripper*."

"*Grace* is here."

We had all made it.

As we passed through the *Bab al-Mandab*, or Gates of Hell, into the Red Sea, our little flotilla broke up. Alan and I said our goodbyes and set a course for Massawa, Eritrea.

Several of the boats decided to stay together for a while. Later, we heard from them that we had missed an exquisite introduction to the Red Sea countries, a metaphor for the distinctive environment and culture we were about to enter.

The evening after *Heartsong*'s departure, the smaller flotilla had passed a hilly offshore island. As they sailed by in the light evening breeze, a line of wild camels crossed the highest hilltop and was perfectly silhouetted against the giant red orb of a setting sun.

LETTER HOME
MASSAWA, ERITREA

Hi Folks,

Since leaving Thailand, we have sailed 3,700 miles. Twenty-six of the last 31 days have been spent at sea. In truth, we are somewhat fatigued.

A few days ago, we entered the Red Sea. We are now safely anchored in Massawa, Eritrea.

It's hot and dry here. Sand and dust cake the skin and make the air thick and scratchy on the throat. The only colors in sight are shades of brown and gray. Herds of camels roam the roadside. Buildings are bombed out from decades of a war for independence with neighboring Ethiopia. Armed soldiers patrol the streets, which are mainly rubble. People smile, greet us in English, introduce themselves, and take us by the arm to help us find the market or their cousin's tiny cafe. Small children herd goats into the desert that crowds the edges of town. A curly-headed ten-year-old orphan and self-described "businessman" sells packs of gum and cigarettes. Women in traditional clothing carry firewood on their backs.

Ships in the main port unload endless gunny-sacks of grain marked "USA Relief." I came very near to losing my camera by recording what looked to me to be unauthorized interception of some of those bags onto small local flatbed carts. The port authorities were not amused, and I was lucky to get away with surrendering the memory stick containing the photos. I plan to notify the organization behind the relief effort, but I have officially abandoned a career in international sleuthing.

We depart for Sudan in the next few days, after leaving behind medicine, many pairs of reading glasses, old Levis, photographs, children's books, crayons and toys, and, by request, CDs of "American rock and roll."

This just in: Alan has returned to the boat after having coffee with a new local friend in the man's family home. Two things made this seemingly normal interaction a little out of the ordinary. First, the man's home was built during the Ottoman Empire, in approximately the 15th Century. Second, "having coffee" in this instance involved choosing one's beans, roasting them over coals, grinding them, savoring frankincense wafted one's way, and then drinking a thick, sweetened tiny demitasse of the actual liquid.

Eritrea continues to be a fascinating destination. We are taking a taxi up into the mountains tomorrow to explore Asmara, the capital, before we leave to sail up the Red Sea towards Egypt.

Love, Liza

CHAPTER 22
THE RED SEA TO THE SUEZ CANAL

Q: Do you ever get lonely?

A: No. We miss our family and land friends, but we stay in touch by email, and some have come to visit. Plus, we have made many close friends among the cruising community. The bottom line, however, is that Alan and I love having so much time together. There is nowhere I would rather be than alone with the redhead.

Anchored in shallow water about five miles off the coast of Sudan, just north of Eritrea, Alan and I were dressed and sipping Diet Coke well before first light. There was total silence. I knew Alan was thinking the same thing I was – what an amazing thing it was for two regular old Texans to be sipping sodas at dawn while anchored off a reef five miles off the coast of Sudan.

The sand islet crescent where we had passed a peaceful night lay just beyond the reef, maybe a cable's distance east. A small surf washed soundlessly onto the beach. On the other side of the sky, a moon just past full hung on to the horizon, and the pearly haze on the water was a cinematographer's Oscar nomination. The air was muggy, yet clean-smelling. For the moment, the anxiety of being in the Middle East was at bay, and we exchanged a look that started at the eyes and worked itself into a grin.

The storm that had curtailed our progress yesterday had blown itself out overnight. The barometer was steady. We would venture out once again. Alan slurped the last bit of his drink – so much for silence. Crumpling the can, he raised his eyebrows in the silent question, "ready?"

A few minutes later, the anchor and chain came up off the bottom with the usual loud grinding metallic, lurching, start-and-stop thrilling sound. That sound always makes me feel like a dog must feel when the front door opens and someone says the word "walk." I shiver and prance and wag my tail, and I don't mean figuratively. Every single time, there's a brand new world out there. When we drop anchor again, it will be in a different place, different water, maybe a different country. In this instance, however, adventure wasn't the goal; it was the enemy. We hoped only to have a nice uneventful overnighter to Safaga, Egypt.

And the day passed obligingly. We had calm water and six knots of wind, which barely ruffled our hair much less the sails. In a bid to make headway towards Egypt, we motored in a direct path to windward. In a Red Sea transit, one must go northwest practically the whole time, and practically the whole time the wind blows from – of course – the northwest. When the wind blows very lightly, one motors directly into it on course, as we were doing. When the wind blows like stink, one looks for shelter. When it blows moderately – actually, it almost never blows moderately, but when it does – one tacks at the closest possible angle off the wind, back and forth, making perhaps a mile or two in the direction of the goal for every eight or ten miles one sails. When the wind is from the northwest in the Red Sea, one does well to hold a course of north-northeast, followed by a course of west-southwest, repeat de capo. By aiming at two o'clock for a while, then turning and aiming at 10 o'clock for a while, one makes slow but steady progress towards 12:00.

Normally, *Heartsong* relishes going to windward and can sail a tight angle to the wind – often pinching smoothly at 30 degrees. We had smoked boats similar to ours on the tight windward haul to New Zealand from Tonga. In the Red Sea, however, we were doing well to average a 60-degree close reach. The reason is that in the Red Sea the waves are steep, close together, and on the nose. The boat slides off wave number one and stops dead in her tracks at wave number two. The resulting leeway is worse than anywhere else in the world we have sailed.

The pathetic mileage one gains towards one's goal can be assisted by running the engine, or "motor-sailing," to keep speed up the face of waves and therefore reduce leeway and improve one's angle on the wind. Once past Eritrea, the engine gets a workout, and all one can do is be grateful for cheap Middle-Eastern fuel. And hope for a dead calm. The engine will probably be running no matter what. At least in a dead calm there is no headwind, and one can make better time to the northwest. Calm was what we wanted, and calm was what we got for most of that day.

Just after midnight in Alan's watch, something changed. Asleep in the pilot berth, I noticed the sound of the engine working a little harder than it had been, changing its pitch in a rhythm that suggested laboring up a wave and then sliding down it. Then I heard Alan adjusting the mainsail. I felt the boat change course a bit. In whatever realm of mind one registers such things when sound asleep, I deduced a blow.

As indeed it was. In the course of twenty minutes, we went from gliding along on a motor-yacht excursion to being a bath toy in the jacuzzi. By 0130 the wind was thirty knots true, gusting thirty-five, and the seas were fifteen-foot skateboard walls. I returned to full consciousness just in time to be bucked out of the berth onto the teak floor.

"I have got to stop being too lazy to put up the lee-cloth," I mumbled, rubbing my elbow. Looking up the companionway, I noticed frenzied activity in the cockpit.

"Blowing thirty-five knots," Alan shouted above the wind. "Sorry about the rough ride." His cheerful face wore its usual storm overlay of confident terror.

Alan is, blessedly, not a poker player. The federal judge for whom I worked as a law clerk always used to say that Alan has an "affidavit face." Whatever the redhead is thinking, it shows. Right now he had the look of a poker player who has bet every penny of his net worth on a straight, but isn't completely sure what beats it. He was moving back and forth across the cockpit, adjusting the sails, adjusting the course, controlling the boat whenever a wave hit us full on, trying unsuccessfully to mask his deep concern at the conditions.

With only a few minutes remaining before my watch officially started at 0200, I decided to forego brushing my teeth and instead crawled to the nav station to take a look at the chart. There was no shelter nearby. Nothing, zip, nada. We could either press on to Safaga, or we could turn back to El Quseir.

There is only one thing a voyager dislikes worse than tacking in a steep seaway, and that's Turning Back. So I relieved Alan and we pushed on, flying and pounding, falling off the wind on a heading that was nowhere near the direction we wanted to go. We took bathtubsful of green water over the bow and into the cockpit. The whitecaps blew off their wavetops over my head. My ears were assailed by shrieking wind and hissing, boiling, slapping, roaring waves. Three hours later I was drenched and cold and had serious muscle fatigue from bracing. The boat was heeled over at about forty-five degrees. At one point, I tacked just because my downwind leg couldn't take it anymore.

As the first hint of dawn lightened the horizon, I could see for the first time what I had been hearing all night. And I immediately threw in the towel. This was not good. I carefully wore the boat round to a course that would take us downwind to the harbor at El Quseir. Although we had passed that tiny place more than seven hours of constant tacking ago, it was only about ten miles behind us. With the wind and waves pushing us from behind, we did that ten miles in well under an hour. Every foot of hard-won northwesterly progress was erased. But it was the correct decision.

In retrospect, I should have turned back when I came on watch. In less than an hour, we would now be able to rest and eat and check the rigging for damage; and then we'd have another go northwest when the seas abated. Approaching the harbor entrance, I realized I had just spent hours trying to ram through a solid brick wall that I didn't really need to get past, at least not today, or even this week for that matter.

In that moment of exhaustion and discouragement, I had an epiphany: Apparently, I have no actual sense. I guess it's just as well to know.

The town of El Quseir is an adobe village semi-circling a dirty, shallow roadstead bay with only the merest hint of shelter from the elements. The swell pours in from the Red Sea and rocks the anchored boats every few minutes so wildly that one can never put anything down without fear of its flying across the saloon or the cockpit. The wind blows a steady roar that precludes normal conversation. After being out in open water all night, however, it felt like the most protected of lagoons.

A few hours after we arrived, Egyptian immigration officials bounced out in a covered dinghy and accepted the customary entrance fee – a pack of Marlboros and some cash, for which an official receipt was not available. We set the alarm for midnight to check the anchor and the weather. Safaga was a mere eighteen hours away.

And thus began a pattern of sneaking northwest during daylight in anything resembling reasonable conditions, and then ducking into any little bay offering reasonable protection for the night. After just such a day of sneaking and ducking, we encountered the sailing vessel Zephyr.

We had noticed a small sailboat tucked in at anchor on one extreme side of our intended layover site. Like most of the small bays so far on the Red Sea coast, this one was uninhabited and appeared not to have any structures or other signs of life. Thinking we would give the fellow sailor his privacy, if he were friend, and keep our distance, if he were foe, we headed for the other extreme end of the bay and dropped the hook. At twilight, we heard a knock on the hull.

Alan and I looked at each other. He headed up into the cockpit while I stood on the companionway steps holding the shotgun out of sight. Our visitor was a thin man in a dinghy. He looked European, and when he spoke it was in English with a Germanic accent.

"I am sorry to disturb. Do you have a radio?"

"Yes, we do," Alan replied. "How can we help?"

"I was blown here in a storm eight weeks ago. I had damage that I have been trying to repair. I think nobody knows that I am here. Perhaps you would be able to get a message to my wife to let her know I am well?"

He had said the magic words. Alan invited him into the cockpit, and I handed him up a beer. The man's name was Alex, and he was from Switzerland. He was sailing solo up the Red Sea to the Suez Canal, where his family was supposed to join him. His 25-foot sloop had been dismasted in a storm, and all of the antennas that had been on the mast were lost or damaged. He therefore had no functional radio, and he had been unable to communicate. There was no road ashore. He had no engine. We were the first people he had seen for two months.

"Actually," I said slowly, "I think we can do better than a radio message. We have a satellite phone on board. We can try, if you like, to telephone your wife directly."

Alex eagerly accepted, and we fired up the phone. Alan dialed the number. When it started ringing, Alex moved to the edge of his seat.

A woman's voice answered, "Hallo." Alex teared up. Alan handed him the phone, and we slipped down belowdecks.

It turned out that Alex was indeed missing and presumed lost. His wife had exhausted every avenue available, beginning when he was two weeks overdue, to get the authorities to search for him. She was tearful and grateful that he was alive. My German is not great, but I could tell from what I could hear that she was very happy to hear his voice.

Alex offered to pay us for the call, but we figured he had enough problems. We then called a couple of marinas north of us and arranged for someone to come down to help him figure out how to get the boat to a port where repairs could be effected. We had offered to take him north with us, but he was unwilling to leave the boat unattended. Now that his wife knew he was safe, he was happy to wait for help and then continue his voyage. We packed a couple of bags of groceries for him and gave him some jugs of fresh water, and he rowed off, a happy camper, towards his disabled boat.

Have I mentioned that the satellite phone was expensive? Well, that little encounter made it worth every penny.

We continued to bay-hop north and eventually made it to a lovely marina in El Gouna, from where we planned to do some land travel – the pyramids! the Sphinx! Nile cruise!

We left the sea storms behind, but, it turns out, we traded them for Sahara sandstorms. While we were living on board at the marina, sand blew across the open land in opaque sheets. It buzzed like a power saw. It would undoubtedly have blasted the skin off our faces if we had walked out onto the dock mid-storm. On even a normal weather day, powdery sand would coat our decks and skin, and probably our lungs as well. My pockets and backpack were always full of the stuff. I became pretty sure that the traditional female attire for the area was originally designed not so much for religious purposes but for the weather. Long robes and a hajib are eminently practical for the conditions, and I usually adopted a facsimile myself – in part out of respect for local custom, in part for self-protection, but mostly to keep my hair clean.

I no longer wonder how the desert has managed to swallow up huge ancient tombs and monuments over the centuries. The real mystery is how you'd find your car if you left it by the roadside overnight. They must sweep the pyramids every couple of weeks to avoid losing them altogether.

But oh, the land travel was glorious. And even more entertaining was the sight of the redhead whooping it up while galloping on a camel.

* * *

After the Egyptian land travel, the Suez Canal was the only thing that separated us from the Mediterranean Sea, our next and highly anticipated destination.

The Suez Canal is a manmade waterway that connects the Red Sea and the Mediterranean Sea. It is about 120 miles long and 673 feet wide. Its average depth is about 79 feet.

The canal is lined on both sides for most of its length by tall, rolling sand dunes. For part of the way, the canal becomes a divided highway, with high dunes also adorning the median strip of land. About halfway through the Suez Canal transit, in one such divided stretch, I looked over to port and saw a scene straight out of *Lawrence of Arabia*. A large freighter passing us in the opposite direction looked for all the world like it was sailing through the sand dunes instead of on water – exactly like the ship that Lawrence saw when he arrived at Suez after crossing the Sahara Desert.

Traveling through the Suez Canal takes two full days for a small boat like ours, broken up by a marina at the halfway point, at which one can stay for as short or long a time period as one would like. The marina is quite near the city of Cairo, and many of us took the opportunity to spend some time in that fascinating city – particularly to visit the Museum of Egyptian Antiquities and various highly recommended local restaurants.

Unlike the Panama Canal, the Suez Canal has no locks. It's a straight shot. One does not need extra crew, or extra lines, or any of the things that make Panama so complex.

Like the Panama Canal, however, a boat in transit must take aboard a local canal pilot. The canal pilot is responsible for interfacing with the Suez Canal Authority, and for making sure that the canal rules are obeyed.

Our pilot for the first day was great. Our pilot for the second day was great at first, until he mentioned that it was customary to offer one's canal pilot some whiskey. We didn't think that sounded right, but the implied threat was that he could turn us around if we were not sufficiently hospitable. So we complied with reasonable grace, and the day proceeded without further incident until the very end.

When we were perhaps a few miles from the terminus of the Canal, we were approached by a military-looking boat with armed men in uniforms. Perhaps it was the Canal Authority, but we didn't know, as the signs were, of course, in Egyptian. Our pilot, expansive at this point, spoke with them for a bit, and then turned to us. He told us to provide the men with a token of our appreciation for their protection. For this, we were prepared. A "token of our appreciation" meant a carton of cigarettes per man, which, after quizzing other voyagers on the Net, we had on hand, ready to go. Alan tossed the cartons to the Egyptian boat occupants, who had tied their boat loosely to our stanchions amidships.

The commander of these troops then came aboard. This was unexpected. He clapped his arm around Alan's shoulder in exaggerated bonhomie, and said, "Do you have a gift for me?"

We were a little confused and thought he might be kidding. We had already observed the proprieties. And now we had an additional obligation? Moreover, it was demanded by a uniformed man supported by armed troops on a speedboat?

Alan handled it well.

"Of course we have a gift for you, my friend." He looked around, hoping for inspiration. "Perhaps you would like a bottle of wine from Australia?"

The man, still with his arm around Alan's shoulders, said, "Ah, sadly, alcohol is forbidden.

"We have some nice American ballcaps with the boat's name on them," Alan tendered.

"I have been favored with many ballcaps, no, thank you. By the way, what a nice watch you are wearing."

Alan, bless his unsuspecting heart, brightened and said a sincere thanks. He showed the man his watch more closely and demonstrated its capabilities. "See, it's a calculator watch, and it's also waterproof – very handy. I really like it."

Standing outside of the man's field of vision, I got Alan's attention and pantomimed taking the watch off and handing it over.

He watched me for a few seconds before he got it.

"Oh," he exclaimed. He turned his attention back to the man. "Perhaps you would accept this watch as my gift to you."

"It would be my pleasure. Many thanks."

And with that, the man took the watch and departed in his boat. An hour later, another similar boat approached us. Our pilot waved them off, but they proceeded to follow us for a while and approach again. Our pilot waved them off again. At that point we reached the termination point of the Canal, and the pilot pick-up boat arrived to take our pilot back to shore. We handed him the envelope of cash we had pre-prepared.

Before he left, he gave us some additional instructions. We were to proceed to the anchorage immediately past the end of the Canal. The entrance for sailboats would be to starboard. There we were to take a mooring ball for the night and wait for customs to check us out of Egypt the following morning.

"I believe we have already checked out of the country," I said dubiously. In fact, I knew we had, and I had the paperwork to prove it.

He smiled broadly and somewhat disingenuously, and he looked away and said that yes, perhaps so, but this was an additional formality.

Hmm.

Our pilot jumped aboard the pilot boat and left us. We waved and smiled with gritted teeth until he turned away and was out of sight.

It was my watch. I took the wheel and steered a course, still under engine power, for the channel that marked the end of the Suez Canal. It had taken us all day to do the second half of the canal, and it was nearing twilight. I looked to starboard and spotted the entrance to the anchorage to which we had been directed to go.

I gazed at the entrance and at the dozen or so sailboats obediently bobbing on mooring balls in it. I moved the boat to starboard towards the entrance. And then I blew right past it and headed for open water.

Alan, still sitting in the cockpit, turned and looked at me with raised eyebrows.

I shrugged and said, "So. Would you rather go to Turkey or Cyprus?"

He thought about it for about five seconds. "Turkey, I think."

"Please set a course, if you would be so kind."

He grinned and went below.

I spent the rest of my watch dreaming of the Greek Islands, of Istanbul, of Corfu, of Italy, but mostly of the Dalmatian Islands of Croatia. We had visited the Dalmatian Coast by land, back in the days when it was part of the old

Yugoslavia. I couldn't wait to get there to explore that area at leisure and by boat.

CHAPTER 23
THE MEDITERRANEAN SEA

Q: Did you enjoy the remote islands more, or the civilized areas more?

A: Both. There is nothing comparable to dropping the hook in a perfect bay with perfect, clear water and a perfect white beach on an uninhabited South Pacific island – and then staying for a week or two or three without seeing another soul. On the other hand, the opportunity to use the boat as home base to tour the sophisticated destinations of coastal Europe is incomparable.

We checked into Croatia at a little town just south of Dubrovnik. The official name of this country is actually "Hrvatska." The reason I continue to call the country "Croatia" is that saying "Hrvatska" causes an accidental tonsillectomy.

Before arriving in Croatia, we had spent some time gunkholing Turkey and Greece. In Turkey, we rented a car with *Tango* and traveled around the interior of the country, especially the Cappadocia region. The landscape there is like nowhere else on earth. Volcanic upheavals have created a fairyland of hollow towers and rounded caves from soft porous stone. Early Christians excavated complex underground cities that one can still explore.

Cappadocia is now home to many artisans, miles of hiking trails, and enchanting cave hotels built right into the stone.

If I had to put into words what we liked most about Turkey, though, it would be the good humor and robustness of the Turkish people. Turkey is one of the few countries in the world that is a net exporter of food – and that's after its own citizens have all gone back for seconds.

Turkey has been a republic only since the late 1920s when Attaturk, widely revered as the father of his country, propelled it from an Ottoman medieval subsistence economy straight into the 20th Century without passing "go." Noticing that, unlike the western world, nobody in Turkey had a surname, Attaturk required every Turkish family to pick one. So everybody just picked a last name. Then this amazing leader instigated a democracy; he crafted laws requiring the government to be secular and not run by religious leaders; he began building an up-to-date infrastructure; and finally he completely overhauled the language, standardizing it from Arab script to western script. With its abundant resources and impressive work ethic, Turkey has morphed into a largely modern country in what is possibly the shortest time on record.

On the other hand, Turkey still retains its rural charm. One can still see farmers working their fields by hand and taking vegetables and flowers to market in mule-drawn carts. At one pension where we stayed, every morsel of food at the breakfast table (bread, tomatoes, olives, eggs, honey, cheese, butter, yoghurt, and cucumbers – the typical Turkish breakfast) came fresh from the owners' farm.

After the somberness of the Red Sea countries, it was good to see young men and women talking and laughing together and strolling hand in hand again. Flowers bloomed everywhere we looked. Children looked well-fed and joyful at play. Turkey is a fertile, colorful, happy country; and during our time there, we regained contentment.

The Greek islands in the Aegean Sea were next along the route. We had chartered there early on in our marriage, and Alan was stationed on the island of Crete while in the Air Force. So these islands were old friends. We explored the white labyrinthine villages and swam in waters that are always that particular shade of Aegean blue. We spent many an evening in the cockpit with fresh olives, feta, bread, tsatziki, rich sweet local tomatoes, and a sunset unsurpassed – until the next night.

"Is that it?" I asked. We were sailing from the island of Kea to the tip of mainland Greece on the way to Athens.

"It looks like it, but I'm not sure."

We crept closer under full sail and barely-there winds. I pulled out the binoculars.

"That's it! That has to be it."

We were talking about the Temple of Poseidon. It sits high atop a hill overlooking the bay at Sounion. We turned the corner, and the bay was deserted. Directly below the temple, we dropped the hook. I broke out a bottle of Australian shiraz we had been saving. We took our plastic wine glasses out to the foredeck and gazed up the hill.

Alan broke the silence. "Do you remember when we anchored here before."

"I do. It was on a charter boat. What was the name of it?"

"Mr. Holiday."

"Mr. Holiday. And we anchored here, and there was a full moon that rose behind the temple. How long had we been married?"

"I don't know. Maybe three or four years."

"That sounds right. And we sat here and vowed that someday we would come back. On our own boat next time."

We clinked our plastic glasses together in a silent toast.

"And here we are," he said.

I sighed. "Do you remember what else we vowed on that trip?"

"No," he looked puzzled. "What else did we vow?"

I lowered my voice to a whisper and moved closer to him. "That we would never, ever . . ." I paused.

"Never ever what?"

I snuggled up. "Never, ever drink the Grappa. Ever again."

He laughed. "Words to live by."

We clinked our plastic glasses again.

After Athens, our route took us through the Corinth Canal, which is a manmade short-cut with glacier-colored water between the Greek mainland and the Peloponnese Islands. At the end of the Canal, we made our way up the coast and to the island of Corfu. From there, it was an easy sail to Croatia.

In Croatia's Dalmatian Islands, the breeze carries the scent of pine trees, lavender, and clean blue ocean. The traditional music is unique – male choruses in four-part *a cappella* harmony, belting out a rousing anthem and then crooning something simple and sweet. While we were at lunch one day at a small café in Korçula, about eight old guys eating at the table next to us just started singing out of nowhere, and it was gorgeous. This was in spite of, or possibly because of, all the empty wine bottles on the table. Theirs, not ours. Well okay, one of the bottles was on ours.

We wandered around the fascinating old city of Dubrovnik; hiked and swam on pristine Mljet Island; and spent time soaking up the medieval walled island towns of Korçula and Hvar. We brought the boat inland as well, up-river to Skradn and the Krka National Park for some great waterfall hiking. Our only criticism of the whole country is that they should (1) export more of their excellent wine; and (2) use the proceeds to buy some vowels.

Or maybe they could just trade a few consonants to Tahiti. Win-win.

Although the islands are a vacation paradise virtually undiscovered by North Americans, the place is hopping with Italian, German, and Austrian tourists. The vast majority of these swim and sunbathe in the nude – young and old, male and female, of all possible body shapes and sizes from drop-dead gorgeous to beached white whale. I was by turns appalled, amused, sanctimoniously disapproving, envious at their lack of inhibitions, entertained, astounded at their nerve, and then back to appalled. Alan mainly just stared and laughed, and it was all I could do to keep his clothes on him most of the time.

In Croatia, we finally mastered the art of mooring onto a marina dock or town quay. Almost every marina and town quay in Croatia is "Med-moor." That is, instead of dropping anchor or pulling into a marina slip, you must back your boat up to the dock and tie it up there, facing out.

There are two types of Med-moor – traditional and modified. In traditional Med-moor, you drop your anchor well off the quay, on a straight line extending to the berth where you intend to end up. Then you back into the berth while letting chain out as you back. Once close enough to the quay, you toss two stern lines to secure the stern to the quay. Then you tighten your anchor line to keep the stern off the quay. The end result is that the boat is stern-to the quay, suspended between its anchor and the docklines.

In modified Med-moor, you still go stern-to the quay by backing into the berth as above; but you do not ever drop your anchor. Instead, you pick up the marina's mooring line. The mooring line has one end anchored beneath the water a long distance in front of the quay, and one end secured to the quay for retrieval. The dockmaster will pull this line up off the bottom when you approach the berth so that you can snag it with a boat hook. You attach the line to your forward cleat via the anchor roller; then you back into the slip and secure your own stern lines to the quay. The mooring line runs forward from your bow cleat to the ocean floor. It functions as your forward anchor, holding your bow in place and your boat off the quay.

In both scenarios, there will be boats on either side of you and no finger piers in between. You will be topsides to topsides, sardine-style.

Modified Med-mooring has two big advantages over the traditional version. First, your anchor stays clean and dry (Alan rejoices). Second, when it's time to go, you simply drop the mooring line and the stern lines and drive away. In traditional Med-mooring, in contrast, you must pull up your anchor to be able to depart. Pulling up the anchor is always problematic. It is virtually impossible to avoid having crossed anchor chains with either an earlier or a later arrival. Departure is always high drama, often involving dislodging another's anchor (which must then be reset) or being unable to retrieve one's own with the neighbor's 200-pound Bruce having been dropped directly on top of it. Many an exchange of invective has been known to happen by captains standing on their respective foredecks during the traditional Med-moor departure process. In olden days, it probably started wars.

Modified Med-mooring is definitely the way to go, even though it means trusting the marina to inspect and repair the mooring lines – sort of the same level of trust one gives mooring-ball operators in the Caribbean and South Pacific.

The modified Med-moor procedure is a learned art. I offer here a brief primer, in 18 easy steps. Okay, that's a lot of steps; and also I may not be telling the whole truth about its being easy. But here are the instructions. They assume you have only two people aboard (the "helmsperson" and the "linesperson").

STEP 1: Prepare well in advance of entering the marina area, which will be small and crowded.

- Station the linesperson on one side of the boat, near the stern, with a boat hook. If you want to pass yourself off as Europeans, ensure that this person is wearing few, if any, clothes. A cocktail in hand gets extra points for style.

- Attach your longest dock lines to your stern cleats on both sides of the boat. Run the bitter ends outside and over the stanchions (so not to trap the lifelines or stanchions between the boat cleat and the dock cleat), and coil the line to prepare to throw it ashore.

- Put out every fender you have, on both sides of the boat, and hang one or more of your largest fenders over the stern.

STEP 2: Upon approach to the marina, the helmsperson should hover the boat expectantly near the entrance and look for a man with a whistle around his neck. The man will look you over and assign you a spot. With a whistle chirp, he will motion you in the right direction and go over to the berth to help you moor. Everyone else on the quay will stop what they are doing and watch you come in. They won't help you, of course, but they serve an important judging function.

STEP 3: Do not expect finger-piers or a "slip" such as is known elsewhere throughout the world. Expect instead a space that looks ridiculously small and impossible to get into. The space will be between two expensive mega-yachts with inadequate fenderage and no visible occupants. The other yachts' mooring lines will extend in such a way that they appear to obstruct the entrance to your spot. You will have zero maneuvering room inside the marina. Do not panic, however. Your national reputation is at stake. Do not raise your voice. Do not run. The trick is to . . .

STEP 4: Go very, very slowly.

STEP 5: The helmsperson should position the yacht so s/he can back straight, or at least reasonably straight, into the slip. If you are the helmsperson, take a deep breath and start backing. If you hesitate at this point, the wind will take your bow, and you will be toast. If that happens twice, you will probably need to leave the port and try again down the coast where they don't know who you are.

STEP 6: The dockmaster will have retrieved the slimeline from the bottom. It will be "floating" on the top of the water now (extending in a straight line out from the quay), ready to be snagged with your boathook. The dockmaster will begin giving you instructions. This next part is critical: Ignore everything the dockmaster says. The only boat the dockmaster has ever moored himself is a 15-foot power launch with a bow-thruster and seven crew members. The dockmaster has no clue what you need to do. Smile brightly and tune him out.

STEP 7: The slimeline is your key to success. The linesperson must snag the slimeline at his or her earliest opportunity. Everything depends on getting that slimeline aboard. Take the line in your hands (eeewww), set the boat hook down, and immediately walk the line hand-over-hand forward to your anchor roller. Run the line through the anchor roller; quickly pull it aboard until you start feeling a little tension on the line; and then quickly cleat it off on the forward-most cleat. Don't get it too tight yet. There should be enough slack to allow you to back up to the quay. But don't let it be totally loose either, as it functions to control your bow as you back. I will pause at this point and just clarify that there is no bitter end to a slimeline. When you pull it through the anchor roller, it will still be attached both to the anchoring spot well forward of the boat's bow and also to the dock. So you will just be pulling the middle portion of the line aboard. It may seem odd, but you will get used to it.

STEP 8: The helmsperson is still backing very slowly, with just enough speed to maintain some semblance of control. S/he is also casually hopping out of the cockpit from time to time to fend the boat off the neighbors, as your stern enters the space between them and starts pushing them aside so you can snuggle in.

STEP 9: The linesperson, after cleating off the slimeline forward, now strolls aft. A short pause to scan and admire the beauty of the area scores optional points. When the boat comes within line-tossing range of the quay (and not a second before), toss the windward stern line to the dockmaster. The linesperson may need to fend off from time to time, too, to preserve the next-door mega-yacht's paint job, but the next most important thing after securing the slimeline is to get that windward stern line ashore. Trust your fenders (gulp) and your helmsperson (no comment).

STEP 10: Once the dockmaster has the stern line, he will not – repeat, will not – tie it off on the dock. This is important: He will run it through a metal rung on the quay and toss the end back to you. Be prepared for this toss. He'll do a head fake and then blindside you. The linesperson should catch the line on the first try, feed it through the stern chock, take up all slack, and cleat it off on the stern cleat. To be clear, I will summarize the net result: the stern line is looped through a rung on the quay, and both of the line's ends are cleated off on the boat. The rationale for this configuration is that you will be able to depart the dock without anyone having to uncleat the line from shore.

STEP 11: The linesperson should then meander to the other side of the stern and repeat the "toss catch and cleat" there – all the while nodding, smiling, saying good morning in as many languages as s/he knows, accepting a beer from the next-door captain, and continuing to ignore everything the dockmaster says. The linesperson will then begin a bobbing maneuver – moving from one side of the aft deck to the other, taking up slack and re-cleating the stern lines as the boat backs further into the slip.

STEP 12: When you are more or less into the slip but still a safe distance from the quay (maybe about eight to ten feet), the helmsperson should go into neutral or possibly even give a little forward propulsion to take the reverse way off the boat and maintain a safe distance from the quay, which is concrete and will saw your stern right off if you hit it. By the way, don't worry about being in forward gear against taut and straining docklines for a short period of time. It always looks like you're either going to pop the lines or take the dock with you, but we have done it often enough now to say with some conviction that if you have good quality lines, it's not a problem.

STEP 13: The linesperson or helmsperson should then amble to the bow, where s/he will wrap the slimeline around the windlass and use it to tighten the mooring line as tightly as humanly possible. If the helmsperson performs this task, the linesperson should step into the cockpit in a sort of tennis doubles court-covering strategy. Whoever is in the cockpit should be prepared to give occasional short bursts in forward gear to stay off the quay. Those stern fenders often come in very handy at this point in the action.

STEP 14: When the slimeline is as taut as the windlass can make it, the helmsperson should go into reverse and take the boat as close as necessary for the gangplank to reach the quay. Significant RPMs will be required to move the boat backwards at this point. This is what you want – maximum tightness forward and aft, with your boat suspended in between the slimeline and your docklines. When the boat is close enough to the quay for the gangplank to reach, the linesperson should tighten and re-cleat both stern lines while the helmsperson remains at the wheel in case of emergency.

STEP 15: If the quayside spectators now resume their activities with an air of disappointment, you will know that you did a good job.

STEP 16: After setting the gangplank, you might consider staying aboard until you are absolutely certain that the dockmaster does not intend to squeeze yet another yacht alongside.

STEP 17: While so waiting, you will probably be treated to the spectacle of at least one other boat docking within your view. If you are lucky – because pure entertainment is so rare – it will be a charterer. The helmsperson will be banging into neighboring boats; the crew of six will be pounding up and down the decks yelling and cursing; someone will fall overboard; the dockmaster will be trotting like a dog up and down the dock, whistle shrilling; and inevitably the yacht will go into full reverse before the slimeline is secure, hitting the quay with a sickening crunch of fiberglass. Permit yourself the luxury of exchanging a raised eyebrow with the nearest fellow observer. You are, after all, a member of the cognoscenti.

STEP 18: By the way. If you stay a while, you might just check for chafe at all points of line contact on the boat and the dock every day. Please don't ask me why I know this is important. We don't talk about it.

* * *

From Croatia south to the boot of Italy, one traverses possibly the bluest, calmest, most enjoyable stretch of water to be found anywhere – the Adriatic Sea. Navigated by the ancient Greeks and Romans thousands of years ago, this sea is home to many marine preserves along bordering coastlines.

As usual, we were in a hurry to get to our next destination (in this case, the Amalfi coast and environs, and up to the northern coastline), so we skipped the coastal marine preserves and plowed straight down through the middle.

On one beautiful afternoon, however, about a day before we turned west to go around the boot of Italy and through the Strait of Messina (which cuts between the mainland and Sicily), a marine preserve came to us.

I was on watch, wandering around on deck, taking care of some tasks, enjoying the sun and the sea; and Alan was in the cockpit reading. As I stared out across the water, I suddenly got the urge to sing. But what song would be appropriate in these waters? Hmm. Opera, perhaps? Yes, I decided that would be the correct genre. After all, we were heading to Italy, birthplace of Verdi, Puccini, Donizetti, Bellini, and Rossini.

I moved to the side deck and addressed the waters on our port side. I began an *a cappella* version of Cavatina's aria, "So anch'io la virtu magica," from Donizetti's *Don Pasquale*. Holding on to the shrouds, and of course securely hanked on to the safety lines as well, I gesticulated grandly as I made my imaginary debut at La Scala as a leading soprano of my day.

The high note was approaching. I took a deep breath and hit it squarely with everything I had.

In the water directly in front of me, about twenty dolphins suddenly jerked their heads up and stared at me open-mouthed. I nearly fell off of the boat.

We had no idea they were even there. They proceeded to accompany us *en masse* for about an hour. I tried other arias, but they had become a lot more interested in surfing our bow wake than in my operatic efforts.

These were large gray bottlenose dolphins. They can reach lengths of around 13 feet, and an adult typically weighs around 600 pounds. Among the most intelligent of mammals, they have been studied at the Croatian and Italian marine reserves for decades. Apparently, each dolphin has a unique whistle that identifies him or her to other dolphins. It is said that they can remember the whistles of members of their pod even after twenty years of separation. Bottlenoses communicate with whistles and pulsed sounds. To find food and to navigate, they use a form of sonar, in which the dolphin produces sounds and listens for echoes.

Lord knows what they thought I was saying to them. Whatever it was, however, gave us a jubilant hour in their company.

And then, just as suddenly as they had appeared, they were gone.

CHAPTER 24
GIBRALTAR

Q: *What in the world do you do? With all your*
      time, that is?

A: Apart from regular chores (which take a lot
      longer to accomplish when you live on a boat
      in mostly remote areas) and apart from boat
      maintenance, I spend my time doing the
      things I always said I wished I had time to do
      – like read a lot, write a lot, spend time with
      Alan, learn how to do stuff, go ashore and
      sightsee, talk to people with lives wildly
      different to my own, and get enough sleep.
      Believe me, there's rarely any time left over;
      and when there is, I sit around and do nothing
      at all.

After an uneventful double-nighter on a south-
southwest course, *Heartsong III* rounded the corner of the
Spanish coast.

For a few weeks we had explored the amazing Italian
coast. Who knew that Rome had a port? Well it does, and
it made for an ideal headquarters for a daily train commute
into the city and points beyond.

We then made a beeline for Spain, where we
gunkholed the Balearic Islands. What a joy – particularly
Mallorca and Ibiza, which has an Alan-friendly clothes-
optional beach policy. We sailed up and down the rugged

northwest coast of Mallorca and added yet another bay – Cala de Sa Calobra – to our list of the world's most spectacularly beautiful anchorages. Life has been pretty good in Mallorca and Ibiza for a very long time, I would say, and we soaked it up.

Now as the sun came up astern, the Rock of Gibraltar appeared before us like a cloud-capped mirage. Never has any natural feature looked so out of place. It is a perpendicular lump of clay. The insurance marketing slogan of "solid" is indeed the first word that comes to mind – followed closely by "ugly" and "barren." But the town itself is delightful. We found a tiny slip snug against Queensway Quay, and we were soon enjoying ourselves amid familiar British accents and really good scones.

Strategically placed at the narrow entrance to the Mediterranean Sea, Gibraltar has been a colony of Great Britain since the early 18th Century and figures prominently in the naval history of the western world. As a Patrick O'Brian fan, I was enthralled with the place. Over the course of five hundred years of European history, this port came under siege at least fourteen times. Its ability to withstand such sieges was, I am guessing, a large part of its mystique of strength.

During the wars against Napoleonic France, Gibraltar served as a Royal Navy base sending out various blockading fleets. Later, Gibraltar was a critical player in naval battles against the French and Spanish, including one spectacular disaster in which two of Spain's largest warships each mistook the other for the enemy, fired on each other, and exploded, killing nearly 2,000 Spanish sailors. Gibraltar served as a base for Lord Nelson prior to the Battle of Trafalgar, at which Nelson was killed. As a colony of Great Britain, the town still has a large contingent of resplendent red-coated military – and, as I say, very good scones.

Alan, on the other hand, mainly likes Gibraltar for the hundreds of wild Macaque monkeys that live all along his jogging route up the mountain. I won't let him carry food for them in his pockets, though, for fear of a monkey-mugging.

The plan was to stay here until the official end of Atlantic storm season, and then to depart for our Atlantic crossing. An optional extra was to do a little land travel – maybe a few weeks or so in the interior of Spain, with which Gibraltar shares a border. My basic land goals were (1) to hear some really good flamenco music; (2) to avoid being taken to a bullfight; and (3) to visit the Prado Museum in Madrid. The Prado was the final item on my lifetime want-to-see museum list.

We gave some thought to doing a Spanish immersion course, too, but when Alan found out it did not involve a bathtub filled with Sangria, he lost interest.

The other goals were easily accomplished. The flamenco was riveting. I was able politely to avoid the bullfight. The Prado Museum had mounted, in addition to its normal gallery, a breathtaking Manet exhibit. And we had time to hang out in Toledo, where we felt as if we were inhabiting a painting by El Greco.

As always, our land travel was on a strict budget. For the most part, we stayed in hostels and paradors. Alan's repair and maintenance skills translated to shore as well as to sea. At our hostel in Madrid, he repaired various pieces of furniture and appliances for the recently widowed, tearfully grateful elderly female owner. Not that it reduced our room rate, of course, but the redhead has to be happy with the state of his karma.

However, even after our fill of land travel and after a fair amount of passage planning, deep provisioning, and cruiser socializing, we were still in Gibraltar, waiting. Specifically, we were waiting for appropriate weather to cross that last big body of water on our route – the Atlantic Ocean. The U.S. government Internet weather forecast models showed a low pressure area lurking off the Straits of Gibraltar, with wave heights of thirty to fifty feet and variable winds of gale force strength. In short, there was a heck of a big storm out there. To me, adventure does not mean pointless risk and masochism. So even though we were eager to get away, we decided to sit tight and give the Atlantic Ocean some time to think about itself.

Oh, but I could not wait to be back at sea.

The route we were planning was the classic Great Circle tradewind route. That is, we would catch the prevailing easterly winds that circle the earth from about 30 degrees north of the equator to about 30 degrees south. Although the route across the Atlantic by the Great Circle route is technically longer than the crow flies, it is far shorter in terms of time – at least, it should have been. More about that later. The total distance looked to be about 4,000 miles, more or less, with an estimated time en route of about 20 days. Again, that's what it should have been.

Catching the tradewinds is more of an art than a science, and it's often more luck than art. Basically, one sails south until the trades materialize and then turns right to put them in proper position abaft the beam, where they, in combination with the healthy current that also prevails east to west across the Atlantic, will usually send a sailboat to the Americas whether it wants to go there or not.

The trick is to "find the trades." Much has been written in sailing lore about the horse latitudes – a band of irregular and unreliable winds and calms that overlap with the trades to the north and the south of the equator. By the same token, much has been written about the doldrums, which are dead calm areas at or about the equator itself. Sailors who get stuck in the horse latitudes or the doldrums are out of luck unless they want to motor all the way across the Atlantic, because once you are in those bands, you are pretty much stuck there. So one is aiming for that glorious band of predictable moderate tradewinds blowing from east to west somewhere between the areas of calm.

It was with those aspirations that we watched the weather intently. This would be our final crossing to conclude the circumnavigation. We wanted to get it right.

And sure enough, the day finally arrived that the low pressure area at the mouth of the Straits of Gibraltar lifted northeast across Spain, and a decent weather window emerged. Like hundreds of years of seafarers before us, we caught the dawn tide and made a course for the Straits.

Like hundreds of years of seafarers before us, and also like virtually every vessel that had been stuck like us in Gibraltar waiting for weather. It was like the start of the Kentucky Derby. A supertanker passed us to starboard at about 200 yards while an enormous container ship crawled up our stern and then passed us to port. The water was peppered with small craft, commercial fishing boats, superyachts, and tugs. It was all I could do to hold course and give a decent stink-eye to other sailing captains when they tried to grab my wind.

But we were off.

As usual at the start of a major passage the boat was so heavy with fuel, water, and supplies that our waterline stripe barely showed. Alan has been known to fill every receptacle in sight with diesel prior to a long passage, and I made the usual mental note to check my shampoo bottle before I poured it on my hair. As a tanker's stern wave bounced us around and we wallowed a mite precariously in our overloaded state, I started rethinking all of that Diet Coke and Spanish wine in the bilge.

Alan sat on the foredeck, securely hanked on and meditatively eating a buttered scone from yesterday's final bakery run. Ah civilization, we will miss thee.

As we left Gibraltar Bay, I felt the first slow rolling massive Atlantic swell. A pod of about 50 small gray dolphins gave us an escort for a few minutes, as our course coincided with their feeding route. We crossed the Gibraltar Straits shipping lanes (no problem, compared to Singapore) and came to course five miles off the coast of Morocco, under full sail in a light wind.

Somewhat worrisome was the two-knot adverse current that threatened to make this part of the passage a slow one. According to the charts, the current would switch to our favor at some point, and in any event before we picked up the tradewinds. Traffic had thinned out – most of it barreling through the Straits on commercial Atlantic routes, some turning right to sail up the Iberian peninsula, a few like us moving to a more southerly route. I inhaled a deep breath of clean sea air and set about my usual on-watch tasks.

After sunset and a nice hot dinner, Alan and I were sitting in the cockpit, wrapped in hoodies and blankets against the North Atlantic chill. The wind danced with the sails to the multi-part chorus of the rigging, and they all kept the beat of the hull slicing through the waves.

We sat in silence, each lost in our own thoughts. The silence was companionable and also more than that. It was a shared silence, a communal silence. It was the mental version of holding hands, touching without touching. It crossed my mind to hope that this state of consciousness would survive the conclusion of the circumnavigation and would continue to be possible when we returned to land life.

Would we return to land life? At that moment, I would certainly have voted no.

Alan finally spoke. "Isn't tonight the lunar eclipse?"

"Yes." I smiled.

"Mind if I stay up and watch it with you?"

"I would like that."

We had sailed before on a moonless night, but the lunar eclipse seemed to bring its own brand of darkness to the sky. Sailing on a pitch-dark night is a lot like running blindfolded at top speed down the middle of a football field. There's probably nothing out there to hit, but still. Caution is not possible. One hurtles headlong as fast as one can into total darkness. Merely continuing forward is an act of abandon and a leap of faith. There is a moment when fear departs and exhilaration arrives. It was in that moment we lingered as the moon disappeared.

When the full moon finally emerged after the eclipse, she seemed bright as the sun had been lately in these latitudes. The water was gun-metal grey, Reynolds-Wrap silver, and moonbeam pearl.

As we continued to sail south, still looking for the tradewinds, the weather started to get a little warmer and a little drier. For the first few days, it was get-dressed-under-the-covers cold and damp. Alan had actually been wearing clothes.

After a few days at sea, my shoulders usually gravitate south a good three inches, and my heart rate slows to my usual at-sea beats per minute that Alan says he likes to check every few hours to make sure I'm still alive. The air has substance. It's thick, for want of a better word. My breathing automatically slows down and savors each lungful.

Since there was no sign of the tradewinds yet, we decided to call in to the Canary Islands briefly as we passed. To avoid arriving in the middle of the night, we reduced sail.

With Venus already bright in the twilight sky, I headed to my berth to get some sleep. Alan was happily crawling around the bilge ports trying to figure out why the main bilge pump kept running.

When the sun came up the next morning, Mount Tenerife was fine on our port bow. The peak is a perfectly symmetrical cone – like God used a mold and a straight-edge. This morning the peak towered above a collar of concentric oval clouds, as if a volcano had risen in the middle of the Indianapolis 500 racetrack. We kept the sails reefed until there was enough light for photographs and then continued on to the island of La Gomera. There we made landfall in the very harbor from which Christopher Columbus set sail to discover the New World.

LETTER HOME
PUERTO DE SAN SEBASTIAN
LA GOMERA
CANARY ISLANDS

Hi y'all,

People have asked us at various points what our favorite places have been on the circumnavigation, and what our toughest passages were, and so on. Now that we are nearly at the end of the trip, we have compiled a very subjective "best of" list for posterity. They are listed in no particular order.

Favorite Anchorages
- Bay of Virgins, Fatu Hiva, Marquesas Islands, French Polynesia
- Cook's Bay, Moorea, Society Islands, French Polynesia
- Secret Harbour, Grenada
- Musket Cove, Fiji
- Palmerston Atoll, Cook Islands
- Skopea Limani, Turkey
- White Bay, Jost Van Dyke, British Virgin Islands
- Cala Calombra, Mallorca, Spain
- Farm Cove, Sydney Harbour, Sydney, Australia

Favorite Marinas
- Gulf Harbour Marina, Whangaparaoa, Auckland, New Zealand
- Netsel Marina, Marmaris, Turkey

- CrewsInn Marina, Trinidad
- Porto Turistico di Roma, Port of Rome, Italy

Best Places for Bareboat Charter
- Caribbean: Virgin Islands or the Grenadines
- Indian Ocean: Phuket, Thailand
- South Pacific: Vava'u, Tonga
- Mediterranean: Dubrovnik, Croatia; or Kos, Greece

Favorite Local Food
- New Zealand lamb
- Grenada callaloo soup
- Singapore street food
- Turkey salt-encrusted whole fish
- Bali nasi goreng
- This list could go on for pages

Love, Liza

CHAPTER 25
THE CANARY ISLANDS

Q: *Being together constantly in such a small space, how do you and your husband avoid killing each other?*

A: We do really well together. In fact, most of the married cruising couples I know are particularly close. What I don't know is whether cruising brings a couple closer together, or whether a couple needs to start out extraordinarily close to survive the experience.

In the small-world category, we stepped ashore at Puerto de San Sebastian on La Gomera Island and ran into about a dozen voyagers we have met at various places in the world, all congregated here to catch the tradewinds for Florida or the Caribbean. There was *Serenity* and *Tango*, who had been part of our Gulf of Aden flotilla. There was *African Queen*, *Windsong IV*, *Second Chance*, *Sail Away II*, *Gloria II*, *Escape*, *Alter Ego*, *Narwhal*, and others.

Lunch was at a tiny local restaurant – the kind of place where Mom doesn't so much take your order as tell you what you'll be having. Dad brings ceramic pitchers of red wine dispensed from an ancient wooden barrel in the corner. Then Grandma delivers the food from the kitchen. Some of us spent several hours there at gingham-covered tables exchanging weather information and radio frequencies, planning the crossing, and trading sea stories. I live for afternoons like that.

One point we could not deny. It was a Friday. As every sailor knows, it is the worst possible luck to leave harbor for a voyage on a Friday. Not one of us believed it. Not one of us left harbor either.

Alan spent most of the evening in his quest to figure out why the bilge pump kept running. It turns out that water was seeping into the main bilge from the anchor locker – not good. If we were to take significant green water over the bow for an extended time during the passage, a leak like that could actually sink us. Yikes. Once again, Alan's vigilance and refusal to let things slide may have saved our lives (or at least prevented many hours of pumping out the bilge underway).

While Alan and Sam of *Tango* were working hard to repair the leak, I strolled around the Saturday market in San Sebastian town square and topped up our fresh provisions – fresh bread, oranges, tomatoes, peppers, all lovely. I sat and listened to local musicians busking on the street corners and rewarded them suitably, in some cases for their talent, and in some cases for their courage to perform in public anyway.

We were planning one more passage departure celebration with other voyagers, and then we would set sail. Our course would follow the wake of Christopher Columbus – southwest until we picked up the tradewinds, then due west until we hit something.

* * *

It was in the Canary Islands the night before departure that we faced up to the fact that the trip was nearing its end. At dinner Alan was uncharacteristically silent, almost morose. He had spent most of the day with Sam repairing a leak in our anchor locker. For several hours they had contorted themselves into the tiny unventilated space, inhaling epoxy fumes, sweating. He was looking a little pale.

"You OK?" I asked him.

"Yeah, fine." Silence.

Uh-oh. Problem? I initiated the usual line of questioning that I call "an exploration of feelings" and he calls "cross-examination."

I opened casually: "Are you feeling sick at all? Those fumes were pretty strong. You probably have oxygen starvation."

"No, I feel pretty good, maybe a little stiff. Remind me to stretch after dinner. Here's the position I was in all day." He proceeded to hunch over with his neck on one side and his elbows tight against his waist. "But I tell you, if Sam hadn't been here, it would have been impossible to fix. He brought his [some tool – I didn't catch it], and it made the job go about eight times faster. We got the locker sealed up, though, and pumped dry. It's the best shape it's been in for years." He took another bite and stared off into space.

Hmm. Many words, spontaneous flow. Implies problem is unrelated to the day's events. I tacked.

"Do you think we're ready for the crossing?"

He brightened a little. "Pretty much, don't you? I still have to check the lifelines and rigging. But I can do that tomorrow. Is there anything else left on the checklist?"

"Nope. I did fresh provisioning today and checked all the stowage."

"Then all we have to do is get fuel, which I'm not looking forward to. I'm thinking I might ask *Serenity* to ride over there with us if there's any wind at all. If we get athwart one of these canals there's nowhere to go, and we'll need help fending off."

I nodded in agreement. The marina was a maze of narrow canals densely packed, at this time of year, by yachts preparing for Atlantic passage.

"Yeah, I walked over to the fuel dock earlier today, and it's rough concrete with no bumpers. Also, there were a couple of boats tied up to it that look like they were berthed there, so we'll probably have to parallel park between them. The depth looks OK, though."

He stretched his shoulders back. "Yep. If we don't get bad news on the weatherfax tonight – and right now the window looks pretty reasonable – I think we could leave tomorrow."

"Agreed." Okay . . . doesn't sound as if what's bothering him is related to the crossing itself, or to getting away from the dock. I tacked again.

"It's amazing to think we'll be home in another month or so."

"Yeah." Silence. He stared off into space.

Bingo.

I chewed my Spanish bread dipped in Spanish olive oil (both delicious, by the way) and took a sip of Spanish Chardonnay (well, two out of three's not bad). Is he just sad that the trip's on the last leg? Or is the problem "re-entry"?

"Have you been thinking about what it'll be like to go back to medicine when we get back?"

"Some." Silence. Bite. Stare.

Ooh, getting warm.

"It was incredible of your group to keep your job open for you. It's amazing to think you might be able to just slot back in as soon as we get back."

That was pretty much as far as I could lead the witness. If I pressed further he would notice what I was doing and make some joke about practicing my lawyering skills. And then the moment would pass, and he might never get it out, whatever it was. I waited, vowing to say nothing at all until he spoke again. Assuming I had identified the correct topic, then silence – however difficult to maintain – would be the most effective tactic. I felt the urge to speak, so I stuffed bread into my mouth. Slowly I chewed. Alan fidgeted into a different sitting position. He did the tiny head bob he does sometimes before saying something important. I held my breath and swallowed.

"I kind of feel like I'm behind, though."

Aha.

"What do you mean, 'behind'?

"Just behind."

I spoke reasonably, trying not to spook him. "You worked in Sydney to keep your skills current. Lord knows you've practiced medicine the whole trip, and I'm betting you saw medical conditions that nobody in Dallas will ever see in their lives. Plus, you did about a thousand times better than I did keeping up, reading journals, doing your CME."

"Yeah, no. I'm not worried too much about my skills. I feel OK about my knowledge level. It's not that."

"What is it then?"

"Oh, never mind."

"Don't 'never mind' me. What is it?"

He inhaled and blew it out. "Well, everybody else has spent the last six years working hard, and saving money, and all I've done is nothing."

"Do you call sailing around the world 'nothing'?"

"No . . .."

"Do you call spending these years alone with your wife who adores you 'nothing'?"

"No . . .."

"Do you call fulfilling a dream that we have both had for as long as I can remember 'nothing'?"

"No. Stop it. You know what I mean. I'm behind. I should have been earning money and putting it away. I should have been working hard while I was still young. What if something happens to me now? We've spent most of our savings, and you'd be stuck with nothing, plus a boat payment, plus upkeep on a boat that may take years to sell."

"So it's me you're worried about?"

"Yes."

"Oh-kay. Well (a) we still have our emergency fund left, and (b) we've paid our insurance premiums, and (c) I will try to overlook the blatant insult that I can't support myself."

"I didn't mean it like that. Look, I just feel like everybody has gotten ahead of me, and I'm behind now. And I'll get over it." He stacked the dishes and took them into the galley.

I sat there and thought for a minute. First, if I just sat there, maybe he would go ahead and do the dishes without noticing I wasn't helping. Second, I was trying to figure out something to say. Was he really worried that he had somehow let down the team? No, that couldn't be it, because he knew how I felt. There was nothing I would rather have had in my whole life than these glorious years.

So what was it? The old Type A personality? Feeling "behind" implied a race. Had the old competitive spirit risen from the dead? Before we left to go sailing, a strong reflexive undercurrent of "keeping up" had defined, or at least colored, almost every decision we made. We didn't think about it, but it was there. We lived in a nice neighborhood, drove nice cars, owned the latest gadgets, enjoyed going out. We had just recently talked about it, laughed at ourselves about it. I knew that Alan had embraced these recent years of not knowing about trends, not caring what anyone else had. Yet he still felt like he was "behind."

I walked over and put my arms around his back. "You know, if life is a race," I whispered between kisses to his neck, "you have already passed the finish line." I thought for a minute. "Now I guess you'll just have to start lapping the field."

He laughed, but his face cleared.

CHAPTER 26
THE ATLANTIC OCEAN CROSSING

Q: Did you keep a journal of the trip?

A: We kept a log. A logbook is part journal, part maintenance record, part navigation aid, part random notes. It is a crucial part of a voyager's life at sea. Reading a logbook is the best possible way to understand an ocean passage.

From the
LOGBOOK OF *HEARTSONG III*
Canary Islands to the Americas

Day 1: Sun 16 Nov
Ship's Time: 1830 (12:30 p.m. CST)
Position: 27°43.26' N, 017°42.65' W
Course & speed: SW @ 11.9 knots through the water, 10 knots over ground

Journal Entry and Notes: If I were at all diligent about checking my bio-rhythms or horoscope or numerology or feng shui or whatever, I would have known that today they all must have been in agreement that I should attempt no activities whatsoever. This has been the toughest single afternoon of the entire circumnavigation.

We left harbor at the crack of noon, our usual early start – so far so good. Two hours out, though, Alan's toilet backed up and started leaking in gushes. Just about the time he fixed the toilet and we got everything cleaned up and the carpet hung on the lifelines to dry, the wind started howling and the waves started growing. We turned to the immediate issue of reducing sail. About that time, a high-speed inter-island ferry on a collision course got our full attention. When it became clear he had no intention of either responding to our radio call or changing course, we made an emergency jibe and then increased sail to bear off more rapidly.

After he passed and our heart rates slowed to normal, we reduced sail again, and it was a darned good thing. Not twenty minutes later we were in the worst gale I had seen since the Red Sea. Erring on the side of understatement, Alan and I agree that we had twenty-foot breaking seas and sustained true winds of forty-five knots. The foam blew horizontally off the top of the waves, almost two stories over our heads. From the cockpit, we were looking straight up at green water breaking over the dodger.

After about two minutes of this, we abandoned our course and turned to run due south with the wind and waves directly astern. Having double-reefed the sails at the outset, we reduced them further to the smallest scrap of main and jib, then to a scrap of jib alone to keep pressure on the bow and reduce the chance of pitch-poling. After an hour, we took her all the way down to bare poles. And still we were flying along, propelled by the seas and the windage of our freeboard and dodger.

Nothing about the weather forecast this morning hinted at any possibility of high winds. The gale must have been a freak effect of a low-pressure area well north of us in combination with a "wind acceleration zone" common to the Canary Islands. At least, that's our working theory.

Whatever it was, it was localized and lasted only a couple of hours. At 1830 now we are still running under triple-reefed main and jib in case of a repeat performance, but we're back on course in less than thirty knots of wind and in reasonable seas. I regret to report, however, that the newly cleaned carpet that was hanging on the lifelines is long gone. Also, we are missing some plastic fuel jugs that were lashed to the deck. And of course, we have the usual bumps and bruises and saltwater-drenched clothing. No broken bones, no bleeding, no leaks. Not a bad tally, all things considered.

At 1900 I go off watch. First, I plan to spend a full minute under a really hot shower. Then I will find some fresh warm dry clothes and socks. Then I am heading to my lee-berth and will attempt no activities whatsoever until it's time for my watch at 0200.

All will be well in the morning.

Day 2: Mon 17 Nov
Ship's Time: 1900 (1 p.m. CST)
Position: 26°21.7' N, 020°12.2' W
Course & speed: 253° T (262° M) @ 8.5 knots
Wind: NE 15 knots

Journal Entry and Notes: Well, yesterday's gale is long gone, and the sailing has been excellent today. We made a thorough inspection, and there's no damage that we can see apart from the carpet and fuel jug casualties.

Because the wind is directly astern, we have gone wing and wing.

That is to say, we have attached the Genoa to a whisker pole and extended it all the way out to starboard. Then we released the boom and mainsail all the way out to port and secured it with a preventer to avoid an accidental jibe. The effect is a full press of canvas spread from port to starboard, all the way across the boat. It is one of our favorite points of sail, not least because it's so darn pretty. It is also stable and comfortable. The boat sits nearly flat. The wind pushes it along steadily from behind, and the waves appear to flatten at the boat's approach. Honestly, I could sail wing and wing forever.

This afternoon about a dozen small gray spotted dolphins kept us company for half an hour. They leaped from the tops of the highest rollers and gave little wiggles mid-air before belly-flopping back into the water. Alan and I were out on deck hooting and laughing our fool heads off, watching them. What a show.

It is sunset now, and the horseshoe of horizon ahead is spotted with clouds and curtains of rain. I see clean decks and full water tanks in our future.

All is well.

Day 3: Tue 18 Nov
Ship's time: 1800 UTC (noon CST)
Position: 25°46.7' N, 022°30.36' W
Course & speed: 231°T/241°M @ 3.2 knots
Wind: ENE @ 7 knots

Journal Entry and Notes: Today two rainbows formed, one of them horizon to horizon with both its feet in neon white cumulus. It looked like the entrance to Heaven, and we passed right through.

Then at about two o'clock this afternoon, we blew out the clew of our mainsail. A noble performer for 30,000-plus nautical miles, our mainsail today showed unparalleled courtesy in waiting for calm seas, light winds, and clear skies to part company with the boom. Had it happened in high winds, the mainsail would surely have flogged itself to shreds before we could have gotten it under control.

Alan is now suspended from the mast effecting the repair, which involves replacing the kevlar mesh connecting the clew to the clew block. The repair would take an hour in a sail loft with a heavy-duty sewing machine, but looks to be about two days' worth of work by hand underway. In the meantime, without our mainsail we are drifting along in light winds under jib alone – very, very slowly. But then – if we were in a hurry, we would have booked an airplane.

All is well.

Day 4: Wed 19 Nov
Ship's time: 1615 (10:15 a.m. CST)
Position: 24°15.5' N, 24°31' W
Course & speed: 242° M @ 6.2 knots over ground
Weather conditions: Sky 50% clear, 50% cumulus
Status: Motoring at 2200 rpm for max fuel efficiency

Journal Entry and Notes: Well there's not a breath of wind out here – which is just as well, considering we have no mainsail. The clew repair is nearing completion, though, and we've started whistling for a breeze. A weather report on single sideband radio called for possible easterlies in the vicinity of twenty degrees north latitude, thirty degrees west longitude, so we're motoring in that general direction until Alan completes the repairs.

I wish I were able to help with the repair, but I don't have the hand and arm strength required to force the needle through the thick layers of canvas and kevlar on the clew. I can't force it through even once, much less the hundreds of times necessary to make the fix hold in high winds. So Alan has been sitting on the boom by himself all day, power-sewing. My contribution to the effort has been to stand his watch in addition to my own, and to feed, dress, and undress him when required. When he finally called it quits last night and went below for a shower, his arms were so numb with fatigue he couldn't raise them over his head to get his t-shirt off. His fingers and hands are bruised and bleeding. My poor redhead.

Today saw more small spotted dolphins, more rainbows, more limitless gently rolling rippling shiny dark blue water. Rain showers peppered all horizons, but only a few crossed our path.

There is an ancient and more insightful version of "have a nice day" that goes "may no new thing arise." And today, blessedly, none did.

All is well.

Day 5: Thu 20 Nov
Ship's time: 1800 (noon CST)
Position: 22°44.31' N, 026°27' W
Course & speed: 243° M @ 5-8 knots
Wind: E @ 6-12 knots
Weather conditions: Mostly clear sky, 71° F

Journal Entry and Notes: Oh glorious. Conditions became perfect today to fly the big asymmetrical gennaker. We are skimming across the surface of a calm sparkling sea. It feels like drifting in a hot-air balloon — weightless, silent, thrilling. Billowing ahead of the bow, the sail draws us forward like a sustained note on a violin, like a glider under tow. This light easterly breeze may not last long, but today's progress put me in mind of all the things I love about sailing. Did I mention that it's glorious?

Today's wildlife count includes one seabird fishing a very long way from home, one lone tiny flying fish, and yet another large pod of spotted dolphins, who raised themselves up out of the water and cocked their heads to watch us as we moved around the deck setting the gennaker this morning. It is of course possible that this pod of dolphins is actually the same one we saw yesterday. For all we know, it may be the same one we saw just off the Canary Islands three days ago. In our experience, however, dolphins seem to detect our presence and swim with us for only a limited amount of time, as if they are escorting us through their territory. For an hour they may be playing all around us, surfing our bow wave, watching everything we do; and then all of a sudden they are gone. The effect is of a friendly dog who runs up and down the fence as you pass and then goes back to pressing business elsewhere.

A couple of hours ago, though, I started hearing some odd noises – whistling, grunting, a succession of haunting sonorous calls. I was reminded of — could it be — whales? For twenty minutes I raced from one side of the cockpit to the other with the binoculars, scanning for spume, for flukes. Nothing. I finally gave up and went below, where the noises became louder. It was Alan on the pilot berth, snoring away.

All is well.

Day 6: Fri 21 Nov
Ship's time: 1800 (noon CST)
Position: 21°22.1' N, 028°17' W
Course & speed: 243° M @ 6 knots over ground (motoring at 2000 rpm)
Wind: 0-2 knots variable
Weather conditions: Sky 100% overcast, scattered light showers

Journal Entry and Notes: No wildlife today. Nothing at all, as a matter of fact. Apart from that [expletive deleted] ferry in the Canary Islands, we haven't seen another boat or ship or evidence of human existence since we departed

La Gomera last Sunday. I have come to crave the total isolation one can achieve at sea, the sensation of limitless space. For many hours every single day, I am alone with my thoughts uninterrupted.

Of course, we can't assume we are always alone out here; we can't ignore safety or other practical considerations. We scan the horizon every 12 minutes looking for traffic or obstructions. One of the two of us is always awake and on watch. The on-watch person makes any sail changes, navigation changes or calculations. We check in with our radio net once a day, sometimes twice depending on propagation. Every two hours, one of us checks everything and makes a log entry. What we have as modern voyagers may well be the best of all possible worlds – complete isolation whenever we want it, tempered by minimizing the actual risk involved.

All is well.

Day 7: Sat 22 Nov
Ship's time: 1645 (10:45 a.m. CST)
Position: 20°22.17' N, 0°04.49' W
Course & speed: 269° M @ 5.2 knots through the water and over ground
Wind: E @ 7 knots true, 2 knots apparent
Weather conditions: Sky 60% clear with many cumulus clouds; barometer 1014

Journal Entry and Notes: Winds are still extremely light – from time to time nonexistent – and predicted to be so for another day or two. This morning we implemented a new sail plan, and it's working well in the extremely light air. The asymmetrical gennaker is flying to leeward (port) with a poled-out 130% Genoa to windward.(starboard) in a classic double-headsail "butterfly." In seven knots of true wind, which is only two knots of apparent wind over the boat, we are maintaining a speed of more than five knots. If we're not careful, we'll pass ourselves.

I have seen no wildlife today with the exception of Alan, who tells me he saw seven whales, six ducks, a pony, and Elvis in a ski boat. I think he may have spent the day cloud-watching. At least I hope so.

All is well.

Day 8: Sun 23 Nov
Ship's time: 1900 (2100 UTC; 3 p.m. CST)
Position: 19°44.4' N, 2°27.5' W
Course & speed: 257° M @ 8 knots through the water, 7.5 knots over ground
Wind: E @ 12-14 knots true
Weather conditions: Sky 80% overcast (cumulus); barometer 1015

Journal Entry and Notes: We have now traversed two time zones, at fifteen degrees of longitude each, since leaving Gibraltar. It finally occurred to me to change the ship's clock when I noticed that at the end of my watch this morning at 9:00 a.m., the sun still hadn't risen.

Two other quick notes:

#1) When flying a spinnaker, always tape the spinnaker halyard snap-shackle closed to prevent it from accidentally opening, which will cause the spinnaker to plunge dramatically into the sea; and

#2) If you forget to do #1, always marry a man who with a smile on his face will haul a soaking-wet spinnaker aboard and then will climb to the masthead seven stories above a rolling Atlantic Ocean swell to retrieve the spinnaker halyard.

We are now zipping along on a good downwind course in what might be (fingers crossed, knock wood) the tradewinds.

All is well.

Day 9: Mon 24 Nov
Ship's time: 1715 (1915 UTC; 1:15 p.m. CST)
Position: 19°21.5' N, 5°10.3' W
Course & speed: Due west @ 9 knots
Wind: E @ 17-20 knots
Weather conditions: Sky 70% clear with isolated cumulus;
barometer 1015

Journal Entry and Notes: We have definitely found the tradewinds (yay!) and are moving at a good course and speed, wing and wing. The wind is full in the sails, and the sun is warm on my face. The seas are a bit sloppy. Although the waves are moderate in size (four to maybe about 12 feet), they are choppy and coming from two or three directions at once – astern and both quarters. Our sails propel us over and past many of them. Still, the overall sensation is a bit like a tilt-a-whirl.

Today I saw many hundreds, possibly thousands, of flying fish moving in schools (flocks?) across the wave tops. They skim for a while, then fly, moving in unison in constantly changing patterns just like those curtains of tiny silver fish one sees underwater, the ones that shift as a single entity in response to the smallest stimulus near any one individual. The flying fish will surface with a whirr in formation, hundreds at once, then will undulate up and down the wavetops or perhaps take a shortcut through the base of a whitecap, then might elevate to a foot above the waves entirely for a while before executing the world's most impressive synchronized diving display. If their flights were my screensaver, I would never re-wake the screen.

All is well.

Day 10: Tue 25 Nov
Ship's clock: 1900 (2100 UTC; 3 p.m. CST)
Position: 19°12.14' N, 38°08.93' W
Course & speed: 269° M, 254° T @ 6-8.5 knots
Wind: ENE @ 10-16
Weather conditions: Sky 90% clear; barometer 1017

Journal Entry and Notes: The sun has set, but the sky is still discernibly blue. Off the port bow the moon is a perfect mother-of-pearl crescent, with the full black sphere visible in relief. Venus is hanging nearby like some accessory, like Cindy Crawford's beauty mark. To the south, Castor and Pollux and Betelgeuse look like airline heavies on final approach. Already the constellations are thick with stars. I will probably spend my watch tonight exactly like I spent it last night: staring into the Milky Way towards Sagittarius to the star-stuffed center of our galaxy. And I love this feeling in the middle of the ocean of being part of everything that there is and also being a speck on a nit on a flea on a tick on a hair of an ear of the smallest field mouse in the jungle. May it never end.

All is well.

Day 11: Wed 26 Nov
Ship's clock: 1515 (1815 UTC; 12:15 p.m. CST)
Position: 18°52.87' N, 040°10.77' W
Course & speed: 270° T @ 6-8 knots
Wind: E @ 4-6 knots
Weather conditions: Sky 80% overcast (cumulus and cirrus); barometer 1016 and steady

Journal Entry and Notes: Everyone always wonders how Columbus managed to navigate his way to the New World with the primitive resources available to him. I wonder how he managed to do his laundry.

Our little washer-dryer combo, though a godsend at anchor, does not drain or spin on the typical heel or roll we experience underway. So we can't use it while we're at sea. It can actually be fun doing laundry on the aft deck with a big bucket of fresh heated water, but the problem is drying. If I hang the clothes and towels on the lifelines, they will be stiff with sea spray in an hour. If I hang them in the cockpit, they are very much in the way if we have to make a sail change. If I hang them belowdecks, they will still be wet when we arrive in Florida in December.

I guess the only answer is to wear fewer clothes. Maybe Columbus was a nudist like Alan. Or more likely, he smelled really, really bad.

The wind has died (the forecast says temporarily), and we are still under a butterfly rig making slow but steady progress on course. ETA Florida, knock wood, is sometime between December 10th and 14th.

All is well.

Day 12: Thu 27 Nov
Ship's time: 1830
Position: 17°41.14' N, 042°54.47' W
Course & speed: 260° T @ 7-9 knots
Wind: ESE @ 15-20 knots T
Weather conditions: Sky 100% overcast, barometer 1013 and falling

Journal Entry and Notes: Happy Thanksgiving! We had the last of our apples with toasted cheese sandwiches, made with the last of the fresh bread. We'll look forward to a proper turkey dinner at Christmas. Today we are thankful that the adverse current that has annoyed us for several hundred miles has disappeared, and the wind has filled in from the east-southeast. Seas are getting lumpy again, but we're happy to pay that price for better wind.

At dusk just now, the wind is increasing, and there are dark clouds on all horizons. The barometer shows a slightly downward trend. In preparation for a potentially stormy night, therefore, we socked the gennaker and put up the main to go back to our very flexible wing and wing configuration. Now if we need to shorten sail, we can do it without delay.

All is well.

Day 13: Fri 28 Nov
Ship's time: 1800 (2100 UTC, 3:00 p.m. CST)
Position: 17°22' N, 045°17.17' W
Course & speed: Due west @ 6.5 knots
Weather conditions: Sky 70% clear, barometer 1011 and falling

Journal Entry and Notes: Hoo boy I could sleep for a week. As expected when we saw storm clouds on the horizon at dusk yesterday, we were visited by a parade of squalls during the night. Coming at you, they look like rampaging monster jellyfish, with a round black cloud head atop streaming dark grey tentacles of rain. You can almost hear the ominous music as they race toward you, head a little out in front of the tentacles, with what looks like pure malice. They move so fast there's no chance of evasion. At least these squalls carried no lightning. They did, however, carry blustery winds. I'm glad we doused the gennaker, so that we could reduce and increase sail and change course as needed – which was constantly, all night – to counteract the wind speed and swirling changes of direction. No problem; just had to pay attention.

Today was a rest day, though, after a very active night; and we did no tasks unless strictly necessary. Right now I'm looking forward to a full six hours of uninterrupted off-watch sleep. What a glorious thought. All is well.

Day 14: Sat 29 Nov
Ship's time: 1800 (2100 UTC, 3:00 p.m. CST)
Position: 17°50' N, 47°38.57' W
Course & speed: 310° M (292° T) @ 6 knots (motoring)
Weather conditions: Heavy rain, barometer 1010

Journal Entry and Notes: It has poured rain most of the day today. After several hours of an exhilarating sail on the thirty-knot winds at the leading edge of the showers, we have lost the wind entirely to the downpour. I feel like I've gone through a carwash with the windows down. I look like it, too. Although our clear vinyl enclosure keeps the elements out when zipped shut, we have to open it up to trim and change the sails. Moreover, we have had to go out on deck several times to set the preventer, un-foul the furling line, check the whisker pole, keep an eye out for traffic. And it is pouring, pelting, sheeting, dumping cat-and-dog rain.

After an entire day of these conditions, the rain, the sea, and the sky have sort of blended together. The world is grayscale, with no boundary lines at all. We could be in a Truman Show holosphere for all we know. Rain has pounded the waves flat as a flitter. The ocean looks like a sheet of brushed metal coated with baby oil.

The overall effect has a dreamlike quality to it. There is no horizon. There is no visibility to speak of, and often the mast and bow disappear into the rain and fog entirely. There is no sound but water – a muted swishing of the boat through the water, and the constant patter, sometimes the pounding, of rain.

On the bright side, there's hot beef stew and cornbread for dinner.

All is well.

Day 15: Sun 30 Nov
Ship's time: 1945 (2245 UTC; 4:45 p.m. CST)
Position: 18°45.47' N, 50°07.52' W
Course & speed: 310° M @ 7 knots over ground
Wind: NE @ 11 knots
Weather conditions: Rain, barometer 1013

Journal Entry and Notes: It continued to rain all last night and most of today. Now I know why the ocean seems to be so full of water all the time.

A tiny bit of blue sky is peeping through dead ahead, though.

All is well — a little soggy at this point, but well.

Day 16: 1 Dec
Ship's time: 1800 (2200 UTC, 4 p.m. CST)
Position: 17°21.4' N, 052°16.4' W
Course & speed: 254° M @ 7.5 knots
Wind: NE @ 10-15 knots true
Weather conditions: Seas 1-6 feet; sky 60% clear; barometer 1012

Journal Entry and Notes: For the past seventy-two hours we have been monitoring a potentially dangerous weather situation via weatherfax and GRIB files, which we download via the single sideband radio. The ten-day weather forecast models show a cyclonic low-pressure area forming south of Puerto Rico and spinning northeast along our route to Florida. If the models are correct, and American weather forecasting is usually superb, a sailboat won't be the most intelligent place to be in that general area. Two things we have learned the past six years are (a) nothing is more dangerous than Mother Nature, (b) unless it's a sailor who ignores the weather to keep a schedule.

Two days ago we looked at the charts and plotted all the various options. Based on the wind and the storm track and courses to appropriate alternate landfalls, we realized that our decision point would have to be around noon today. The weather update this morning confirmed the storm.

So to make a long story short, today we activated Plan B, made a hard left, and will make landfall in – oh darn – the southern Caribbean instead of Florida. I was seriously disappointed at first. We had planned to be back home in the States for Christmas. Depending on where we can make a good landfall, we may not even cross our track to complete the circumnavigation before then. The absolute closure of ending the Atlantic crossing at our starting point of Fort Lauderdale was something I had been daydreaming about for a week.

Then I spent my watch this afternoon thinking about warm bright turquoise water, white beaches, an astonishing variety of rum drinks, callaloo, parrot-fish, steel drums, a foredeck hammock, and sentences that end with "mon." We can always fly home for Christmas, then fly back to the boat and sail her home afterwards. If we don't cross our track this year, so be it. I have always felt that I didn't fully appreciate the phenomenal beauty of the Caribbean when we were here. For gunkholing, you can't really beat it anywhere in the world.

Even if it's only for a little bit of extra island time (perhaps "reprise" is the right word), I'm now very excited about Plan B. I swear I didn't doctor those weather forecasts before I showed them to Alan. Really.

If we do happen to cross the Caribbean track we crossed six years before, our circumnavigation will be officially complete, even though we won't have returned to our actual starting point of Fort Lauderdale. It's thrilling to think we are so close. If the wind continues to serve for Trinidad, we will cross our track northwest of Tobago and make landfall as circumnavigators.

All is well.

Day 17: Tue 2 December
Ship's time: 1800 (2200 UTC, 4:00 p.m. CST)
Position: 15°48' N, 054°34.2' W
Course & speed: 252° M @ 7 knots over ground
Wind: E @ 8-12 knots
Weather conditions: Seas slight; sky 60% clear; barometer 1011

Journal Entry and Notes: It would be easy to believe in UFOs if I didn't know that the big red and white light hanging low in the southwestern night sky is Mars, flashing as it appears and disappears behind filmy clouds. It would be easy to believe in sea monsters and mermen if I didn't know that what I often catch out of the corner of my eye is a wave splashing away, just being a wave. It would be easy to believe in omens if I didn't know that the calm seas, good wind, and fair weather we've had since the very hour we changed course yesterday were mere coincidence.

Today was pleasant and peaceful and darn near perfect here on the Atlantic.

All is well.

Day 18: Wed 3 Dec
Ship's time: 1800 (2200 UTC, 4:00 p.m. CST)
Position: 14°12' N, 056°52' W
Course & speed: 251° M @ 7-10 knots over ground
Wind: E @ 13-23 knots true
Weather conditions: Seas 6-12 feet; sky 95% clear; barometer 1012

Journal Entry and Notes: Great wind, outstanding sunny day of sailing. Lumpy seas, though, bumpy and choppy. When we move around the boat, it's back to the Tarzan handhold-to-handhold mode – with the occasional lunge and miss, bam, whomp, stub, and bruise. How Alan manages to shave every day (well almost every day) in these conditions I have no idea. Today I had a go at my legs and stopped just short of requiring a tourniquet. And while we're on a topic that is almost certainly more than anybody wants to hear, why on earth don't marine toilets automatically come with seat belts? We never got around to inventing that harness.

The beauty of lumpy seas, however, is the weightless sleeping. Our pilot berth is enclosed on one side by a bulkhead and on the other by a lee cloth; and both sides are well-padded with pillows. When the boat glides down a swell or bumps along a choppy crest, one's body actually rises above the berth and seems to float for a bit before re-settling. About half the time, one is either rising up or floating. It may not quite be the weightlessness of outer space, but it's phenomenally restful.

I wonder if there's a market on land for a mechanized, padded, enclosed trampoline bed. Hmm.

Every night the moon gets a little fuller, and every day the air gets a little more tropical.

All is well.

Day 19: Thu 4 Dec
Ship's time: 1630 (2030 UTC, 2:30 p.m. CST)
Position: 12°25' N, 59°23' W
Course & speed: 250° M @ 9-11 knots
Wind: E @ 22-30 knots true
Weather conditions: Seas 6-15 feet; sky 60% clear; barometer 1010
Sails: Wing and wing, single-reefed

Journal Entry and Notes: Yee-haw! Now this is sailing! We've had excellent wind for thirty-six hours. A record 24-hour run is within reach. Our best day so far has been 225 nautical miles, which we did on the passage from Tongatapu to New Zealand. Midnight to noon today we made well over 100 miles over ground, and the wind has only gotten better. ETA Trinidad (knock wood) is tomorrow afternoon.

Speaking of landfall, our decision to change course for the Caribbean has turned out to be a good one. Not that it would have mattered, since we can only make our best decision at the time from the data available. But the low pressure area we decided to avoid has matured into Tropical Storm Odette. If we had continued northwest to Florida, our route would have joined Odette's path, and we would have had a very, very bad week. Oh how I appreciate 21st Century electronics. Even a decade ago we would not have had sufficient access to the communications technology and long-range ocean weather models that warned us in plenty of time to divert to a good alternate landfall.

We are getting very close to crossing our from six years ago. The circumnavigation is almost complete. Can't believe it. Incredibly excited. Can barely sit still. I think back to our first crossing and am bloody amazed that I made it. Am bloody amazed that I tried.

All is well.

Day 20: Fri 5 Dec
Ship's time: 1800 (2200 UTC, 4:00 p.m. CST)
Position: CrewsInn Marina, Chaguaramas Bay, Trinidad

Journal Entry and Notes: We made it! At dawn this morning the island of Tobago was fine on the port bow. At around noon in a forty-knot rainy squall we crossed our prior track to make our circumnavigation officially complete. A couple of hours ago we pulled up to the customs dock in Chaguaramas Bay, Trinidad. And about ten seconds ago, Alan handed me a glass of champagne.

I feel – how do I feel – I feel totally exhausted, sore, a little stiff, with various body parts telling me they are not amused at being banged and crunched; and I could definitely use a shower and some clean clothes. I feel grateful for getting across the Atlantic safely and around the world safely. I feel humble that I have crossed three oceans; and in awe that such a dream could come true.

But mainly I feel, mainly I feel . . . OK, think James Brown here, add an R&B band and a horn section, and . . . WHOA, I feel good (nuh, nuh, nuh, nuh, nuh, nuh, nuh). Like I knew that I would now (nuh, nuh, nuh, nuh, nuh, nuh, nuh). I FEEL good (nuh, nuh, nuh, nuh, nuh, nuh, nuh). Like I knew I would now (nuh, nuh, nuh, nuh, nuh, nuh, nuh – bump bump).

SO GOOD (bump, bump). SO GOOD (bump). I got you (unh unh unh unh unnnnnnh).

WHOA . . . (repeat ad lib until champagne runs out or one falls asleep standing up.)

Cheers! Here's hoping that your dream, whatever it may be, comes true.

All is well. And good night.

EPILOG
DALLAS, TEXAS

After a leisurely, gunkholing trip through the Caribbean to return *Heartsong III* to Florida whence her idyll began, we pulled into Fort Lauderdale and began preparing the boat for sale. There were tears, and many of them. This magnificent sailboat saved our lives over and over again. She also was the site and vehicle for love, for adventure, for fun, introspection, and peace.

We are often asked why we didn't keep her. Well we were returning to Dallas, and Dallas – though beautiful and diverse and vibrant – is regrettably land-locked. There are nearby lakes, some quite large and deep. But keeping an ocean-going vessel like *Heartsong III* on a lake is like keeping a large dog in a small apartment. It's just not fair to the dog.

Upon return to land life, much to our surprise, we slotted back in to our old careers without much drama. Oh the angst upon leaving that we would never work again! That our resumes would have giant holes in them! That we would have to spend the second half of our careers flipping burgers – not that there's anything wrong with that.

Having devoted so many years to professional training, we hoped that we would be able to work in our fields upon return to civilization. However – and this a crucial point – we had to assume that we threw all that away when we cast off the lines in Florida and set sail. Indeed, we spent significant time coming to terms with that choice before we left. We had to be good with never working again. Otherwise, the stress of wondering and worrying would have – for me, anyway – colored the entire trip. When we departed, we jettisoned all hope and thought of what might await our return.

So it is with humility, gratitude, and almost shock that I report that upon our return to land life we both found gainful employment in our fields, doing work we particularly love. Our work is indeed the most satisfying and rewarding work either one of us has ever known. The only downside is having to wear actual shoes.

I don't know whether the joy we get from our careers now is related to the relief of pressure from having taken time off in the middle, or to the changes in our outlook that the trip's challenges forced both of us to make. If we had continued to slog to weather on our previous career paths, without a break, would we have achieved the same degree of fulfillment? I don't know.

What I do know is that we tacked. And it worked. And presumably, it would work for anyone who has a dream and the motivation to make it happen while he or she is still young enough to do it.

Our land friends sometimes ask whether we have developed any wisdom about the world and our place in it, about the nature of the universe, about religion and spirituality, about human rights, liberty, and those random geographical demarcations we call countries.

Those topics are often on my mind, and yes I would say it would be impossible to experience a transformative physical journey of any kind without experiencing a mental and spiritual journey as well.

But that is a different book.

In the meantime if you want to have a chat about the universe, feel free to come by and see us.

Bring a nice shiraz.

POST-EPILOG
DALLAS, TEXAS
2018

As I sit here rereading these words more than a decade after the conclusion of our sailing circumnavigation, I am processing some ugly news from my doctors. I have been diagnosed with Stage 4 ovarian cancer.

By definition, Stage 4 cancer is metastatic. At Stage 4, there is no cure. After months of dense-dose chemotherapy and major surgery, there is the possibility of remission for a few years, and possibly more than a few, for which the redhead and I fervently hope.

But there is no cure.

The moment I received the diagnosis, I had two immediate, full-blown crystalline thoughts, and I'm guessing you already know what they were.

The first was: Please dear Lord take care of my sweet redheaded husband.

The second was: Thank God we went sailing.

Glossary and Map

GLOSSARY

These definitions are not intended to be complete or exhaustive, but rather are specific to usage in this book or, in some cases, specific to Alan's sense of humor.

Aft	Towards the back of the boat.
Avast Ye	Desist from your current activity; or "I say there good sailing person, could I have your attention please?"
Abaft	Behind, as in direction, not anatomy.
Anchor	A metal, hook-like or plough-like object attached to a boat and designed to grip the ground beneath a body of water to prevent the boat from drifting.
Anchor chain	The metal chain connecting the anchor to the anchor rode.
Anchor rode	Rope connecting the anchor chain to the vessel.
Backstay	Long cables, reaching from the top of the mast to the stern, to support the mast; or what you say to a seagoing puppy named "Back."
Beam	A boat's width at the widest point. Often preceded by the word "Jim" to initiate celebration.

Beam reach	Sailing with the wind coming across the vessel's beam. This is normally the fastest point of sail for a modern sailboat.
Beam seas	A sea in which waves are moving perpendicular to the direction a ship is moving and thus hit the boat from the side. A beam sea can cause the boat to make an uncomfortable side-to-side or wallowing motion.
Beating	Sailing as directly as possible towards the direction from which the wind is blowing. Typically, a sailboat in ocean conditions can beat at no smaller angle than a 50-60° angle on the wind. See Tacking.
Belowdecks	The interior of a boat.
Binnacle	The stand on which the ship's compass is mounted, often at the same location as the wheel.
Boom	A horizontal spar attached to the foot of a sail to hold it out from the mast.
Bow	Pointy (front) end of a boat, pronounced like "tree bough," as opposed to a ribbon decoration.
Broach	The loss of control of a sailboat's motion into a sudden sharp turn, often causing the boat to heel heavily and sometimes leading to a

capsize. Broaching can occur when too much sail is set for a strong gust of wind, or when waves from behind the boat push the stern to one side.

Broach to   See Broach.

Chandlery   A store that sells marine equipment.

Channel 16   A marine VHF radio frequency designated as an international distress frequency; monitored and used for hailing another boat before switching to a specified working channel for extended conversations.

Clew   The lower aft-most end of a triangular sail where the sheet line attaches the sail to the boat. For example, on a sloop, the mainsail clew is usually attached to the boom.

Close hauled   Beating into the wind.

Coaming   The raised surround of the cockpit, used for seating and as a barrier to keep water out.

Cockpit   The outdoor command center and main outdoor seating area of a boat, usually aft of the mast, where steering and navigational controls are located.

Companionway	The entrance to a boat's interior by way of a vertical ladder or steps down from the cockpit or deck.
Deck	A boat's top outside surface, not including the cockpit, that the crew can walk on.
Dodger	A frame-supported canvas or fiberglass structure (usually with clear vinyl windows) that protects a boat's cockpit and companionway from the elements at sea.
Double reef	See Reef.
Following sea	Wave or tidal movement going in the same direction as the boat. Usually a more comfortable ride than a head sea or beam sea.
Forestay	Long cables, reaching from to top of the mast to the bow of the vessel, to support the mast.
Forward	Towards the pointy end (front) of the boat.
Gennaker	A large, triangular sail similar to a spinnaker, used when sailing downwind, and not attached to the forestay like a jib.
Genoa	A large, triangular foresail, larger than a traditional jib, attached to the forestay with the foot extending aft of the mast.

Gunkholing	A type of cruising for pure enjoyment, meandering short distances from place to place and spending nights in protected anchorages. The term originally referred to the gunk, or mud, typical of creeks, coves, and marshes.
Hard	See "On the hard."
Head	The %*##$+*! boat toilet that always breaks down at the most embarrassing moment, leaving you stranded and wishing you were in a Marriot in Wisconsin.
Headseas	Waves that come at the boat from in front of it, directly opposing the forward motion of the boat.
Heel	The lean of a boat to the side, caused by the wind's force on the sails.
Hook	Anchor.
Jib	A medium-sized triangular foresail attached to the forestay.
Jibe	To change from one tack to the other with the wind coming from aft of the sailboat. The sails and boom move from one side of the boat to the other side as the stern passes through the wind. Occasionally a dangerous maneuver.

Keelhauling	A severe punishment, often resulting in death, by dragging a sailor along the bottom (keel) of a boat, either from side to side or from bow to stern.
Knot	A unit of speed in the water equal to one nautical mile per hour, equivalent to 1.15 miles per hour on land.
Lazarette	A storage area beneath the deck, accessed through a hatch on the deck.
Leeward	In the direction that the wind is blowing towards.
Lifelines	Cables, usually covered with white rubber, attached to stanchions around the deck, to prevent people from going overboard. Also, they are handy for hanging laundry to dry.
Line	A rope when it is aboard a boat.
Mainsail	A large triangular sail aft of the mast, with the vertical side attached to the mast and the horizontal side attached to the boom.
"Man overboard"	Gendered terminology left over from pre-deodorant, non-bathing manly days of sailing when women refused to go to sea until men smelled better.

Mast	A vertical pole on a ship that supports sails and rigging. A sloop has one large mast near the center of the boat.
Mayday	An emergency word used internationally as a vocal radio communications distress signal.
Net	See Radio Net.
On the hard	On land, usually referring to a boat on a cradle for repairs or painting.
Outhaul	A line used to control the shape of a sail, often to pull the sail out tightly.
Painter	A rope attached to the bow of a dinghy and used for tying up or towing.
Pitch-pole	To capsize a boat stern over bow, rather than by rolling over sideways. Often refers to a violent capsize from large following seas.
Port	Left hand side of boat as one faces the bow; or. To the left as one faces forward; or, alcoholic beverage often consumed before falling overboard from the left hand side of the boat.
Quartering seas	Waves striking the side of the boat at about a 45° angle aft of (or forward of) the beam.

Quartering wind	Wind striking the boat at about a 45 degree angle or more aft of the beam.
Quay	Large dock, often made of concrete.
Reef	To reduce the area of a sail exposed to the wind, usually to guard against adverse effects of strong wind or to slow the vessel. Single reef, double reef, or triple reef refers to an incrementally greater reduction in sail.
Radio net	A specified radio frequency or group of boats that communicate by radio at a certain time daily to report position, conditions, information, and gossip.
Rode	See Anchor Rode.
Sheet	A line, attached to the clew of a sail, used to control the setting of a sail in relation to the direction of the wind. This word does not refer to the sail itself.
Sheet line	See Sheet.
Shrouds	Thick cables running from the top of the mast to the side decks and attached to chain plates that are attached to the hull. The shrouds support the mast. They are often covered with protecting metal sleeves.

Single reef	See Reef.
Single-sideband	A short wave radio system, abbreviated "SSB," that can broadcast hundreds to thousands of miles. Ham radio operates on SSB.
Sole	Floor of the interior and cockpit of a boat.
Spinnaker	A very large, light sail flown from the front of a boat for downwind sailing.
Squall	A fast-moving weather front with sudden, heavy winds and rain showers.
Stanchions	Vertical waist-level posts, often stainless steel, mounted along the edge of the deck to which cables ("lifelines") are attached as a safety measure.
Starboard	Right hand side of boat as one faces the bow; or, to the right as one faces forward.
Stern	The back end of a boat; or, serious demeanor not often seen afloat.
Slog to weather	Usually refers to sailing into the wind and waves; a very uncomfortable ride.
Tack	(1) A zig-zag path a boat must take to get to a destination when the wind is blowing directly from that

destination. (2) The act of turning the boat through the wind to change direction; sails and boom will move from one side of the boat to the other; also called "coming about." (3) The forward bottom corner of a sail.

Through-hull — A metal or plastic fitting that goes through the hull from the bilge to the water and allows water or fluid into or out of the boat; usually has a valve to close the fitting if needed.

Triple reef — See Reef.

VHF radio — Very high frequency radio; a short-range, line-of-sight radio system for communications on land or at sea.

Whisker Pole — A pole attached to the mast whose outboard end is used to control and hold out the aft end of a gennaker or spinnaker.

Windward — In the direction that the wind is blowing from.

Wing and wing — A sail set used when sailing almost directly downwind; composed of two sails flown all the way across the boat from side to side; usually the mainsail to one side and the jib or Genoa to the other, sometimes (often called a "butterfly") the jib or Genoa to one side and the gennaker or spinnaker to the other.

The Circumnavigation Route

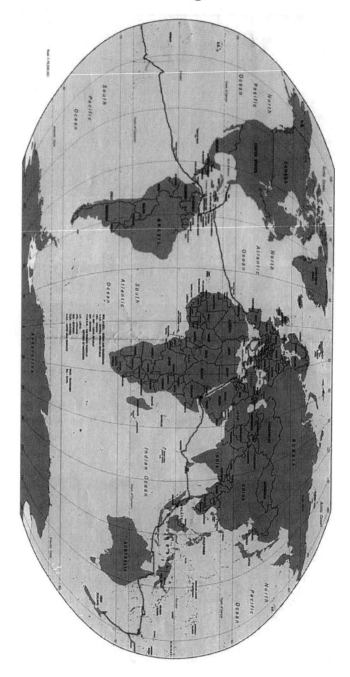